CULTURAL POLITICS

# Shakespeare, cinema and society

# CULTURAL POLITICS

**Writing Ireland:** colonialism, nationalism and culture
David Cairns and Shaun Richards

**Poetry, language and politics**   John Barrell

**The Shakespeare myth**   Graham Holderness

**Garden – nature – language**   Simon Pugh

**Teaching women:** feminism and English studies
Ann Thompson and Helen Wilcox (editors)

**Race, gender, Renaissance drama**   Ania Loomba

**Pre-Raphaelites reviewed**   Marcia Pointon (editor)

**Comics:** ideology, power and the critics   Martin Barker

**Shakespeare, cinema and society**   John Collick

Further titles in preparation

# Shakespeare, cinema and society

John Collick

MANCHESTER UNIVERSITY PRESS
MANCHESTER and NEW YORK

distributed in the USA and Canada by ST. MARTIN'S PRESS, New York

Published by Manchester University Press
Oxford Road, Manchester M13 9PL, UK
and Room 400, 175 Fifth Avenue,
New York, NY 10100, USA

Distributed exclusively in the USA and Canada
by St. Martin's Press Inc.,
175 Fifth Avenue, New York, NY 10010, USA

British Library cataloguing in publication data
Collick, John
    Shakespeare, cinema and society. — (Cultural politics).
    I. Drama in English. Shakespeare, William. Adaptations: Cinema films
    I. Title II. Series
    791.43'75

Library of Congress cataloging in publication data
Collick, John
    Shakespeare, cinema and society / John Collick.
        p.        cm. — (Cultural politics)
    Bibliography: p.
    Includes index.
    ISBN 0-7190-2447-1 — ISBN 0-7190 2448-X (pbk.)
    1. Shakespeare, William, 1564-1616—Film and video adaptations.
2. Film adaptations—History and criticism. I. Title. II. Series.
PR3093.C64        1989
822.3'3—dc19        89-2830

ISBN 0 7190 2447 1 hardback
      0 7190 2448 X paperback


Typeset in Joanna
by Koinonia Limited, Manchester
Printed in Great Britain
by Hartnolls Limited, Bodmin, Cornwall

# Contents

103, 153.

| | |
|---|---|
| Acknowledgements | *page* vi |
| Introduction | 1 |
| | |
| **PART ONE** | |
| 1 **Victorian bardolatry** | 12 |
| 2 **Silent Shakespeare and British cinema** | 33 |
| | |
| **PART TWO** | |
| 3 **The theatre of light** | 60 |
| 4 **Symbolism in Shakespeare film** | 80 |
| | |
| **PART THREE** | |
| 5 **Shakespeare and the Russian intellectual** | 108 |
| 6 **Kozintsev's *Hamlet* and *Korol Ler*** | 128 |
| | |
| **PART FOUR** | |
| 7 **Hamlet on a bicycle: Shakespeare in Japan** | 150 |
| 8 **Kurosawa's *Kumonosu jo* and *Ran*** | 166 |
| **Conclusion: Shadows in the mirror** | 188 |
| | |
| Notes | 196 |
| Further reading | 200 |
| Index | 203 |

# Acknowledgements

Stills from the National Film archive, London, by kind permission.

The still from *Henry V* is reproduced by courtesy of The Rank Organisation PLC and from *A midsummer night's dream* by courtesy of Celestino Coronado.

For Judith

# INTRODUCTION

# Shakespeare and film: the critical heritage

The critical works written so far on Shakespearean cinema are interesting for a number of reasons. They form a small body of analysis that, at first, seems rife with controversy. These arguments are largely concerned with textual purity. How should a Shakespeare play be filmed? What film techniques settings and methods of editing will ensure that the movie stays faithful to the original text? Should Shakespeare's works be made into movies at all? Many of the studies that try to address this question are prescriptive. When they criticise an extant film their approach implies the existence of an ideal; a correct way to film *Hamlet* or *Othello*, against which all films can be compared. Jonathan Miller once remarked that television is a good medium for capturing the intimacy of the dialogue between Iago and Othello, the implication being that video can be effective as long as it brings out certain innate qualities in the text. The transformation of daughters into sons has been seen as a basis for criticising Akira Kurosawa's film of *King Lear*, *Ran*. The fact that this was a necessary act of appropriation, so that the film would be comprehensible in Japanese culture (where, historically, women would never inherit a fief from their father) excuses the transformation up to a point, but the final product is still not regarded as an entirely acceptable version of *King Lear*.

Many of the producers and directors of the films have contributed to the critical heritage, justifying their various approaches or trying to draw a coherent theoretical framework which will encompass Shakespearean cinema and their contributions to it. Their attitudes have shaped the discussion and, in turn, have been influenced by the conclusions and positions that have emerged in literary and theatre criticism over the past ninety years. Yet what is remarkable is that, despite the controversy, the area focused on by these critical works is very narrow. Not only is it limited but it is also unrepresentative of Shakespeare film production as a whole. Furthermore many of the conclusions or theories that are voiced are repetitions of debates formulated as far back as the early nineteenth century.

To see this we need only look at the number of movies produced
since the end of the last century. If we compare it with the area covered
by critical works written to date (in English) then the difference is stag-
gering. Since 1897 the works of Shakespeare have been the subject of
well over two hundred films, and countless television programmes.
More than half of these productions are either foreign, silent, or both.
Yet with one exception the major studies of Shakespearean cinema
confine themselves to a handful of sound films. Furthermore, although
the works of famous international directors like Roman Polanski or
Akira Kurosawa are acknowledged, most of the works discussed in
book, magazine or journal surveys of the genre come from English or
American studios. The rest are consigned to critical oblivion.

There are specific reasons for this exclusiveness which can be traced
back to the way Shakespeare is perceived in literary criticism and the
orthodox traditions of film history. Using the assumptions and beliefs
enshrined in these two fields a small group of films have been foregrounded as those closest to the 'spirit' of Shakespearean drama. This
exclusiveness exists for political reasons, chiefly because these films are
seen to represent, and reinforce the promotion of, a certain reading of
Shakespeare as correct, natural and universal.

The historical development of this perception of Shakespeare during
the early nineteenth century will be covered in Part I. In this introduction
I want to discuss its terms of reference and their implications. To date
there are only a handful of major critical works that tackle Shakespearean
cinema. In 1972 Charles Eckert edited *Focus on Shakespearean films*, Jack
Jorgens wrote *Shakespeare on film in 1977* and Roger Manvell produced
*Shakespeare and the film in 1979*. In 1987 Volume 39 of *Shakespeare survey* was
devoted to Shakespeare in the media. As well as these general studies
there are several more specialised works, concentrating on certain films
(as in Grigori Kozintev's two books, *Shakespeare: time and conscience* and
*King Lear: the space of tragedy*) or on specific areas of Shakespeare film
production; Robert Hamilton Ball's *Shakespeare on silent film* covers the
period from 1897 to 1928.

The extent to which many writers elide whole areas of Shakespeare
production can be gauged by the introduction of Jorgens's book. He
talks of Shakespeare films made before the invention of sound as 'one
and two reelers struggling to render great poetic drama in dumbshow'.[1]
The implication is that the genre of Shakespeare cinema began in the
1930s and consists of a handful of well known films; among them Laurence Olivier's *Henry V*, Roman Polanski's *Macbeth* and Peter Brook's *King
Lear*. Jorgens's main argument is that a Shakespeare film must have a

sound track so that the spoken text can be reproduced faithfully. In other words, for Jorgens the meaning of a Shakespeare play is concentrated in the poetry. This thesis is supported by Manvell and, remarkably enough, Ball in his book on silent Shakespeare film.

Yet the concentration of production of Shakespeare film in England and America before World War I was greater than at any time in the history of cinema. It was the only time when Shakespearean film was consciously awarded the status of a genre by the movie industry in both countries. During this period a Shakespeare movie was a specific kind of film, created with its own set of production values and geared towards a recognised audience. Why, then, is such a major and important area of Shakespeare film production given such an insignificant status?

Once again the reasons are due to the critical heritage that surrounds Shakespeare; a tradition that has developed within English and American culture since the beginning of the last century and which became enshrined in Britain's educational and literary establishment through the work of the New Critics. The economic upheavals of the industrial revolution prompted the search for an understanding of culture, and literature, which endorsed the ethics of industrial capitalism. This project was caught up with the hunt for a niche for the writer and reader within a society whose ideology was concerned with the mystification of economic relationships. As Catherine Belsey points out in *Critical practice*, the perception of literature which developed from the Romantic response to industrialism cast the writer and reader in the roles of producer and consumer, and then proceeded to invest the relationship with a spiritual significance. Within the framework of New Criticism, people like I. A. Richards and F. R. Leavis developed the work of Romantic writers such as Charles Lamb; reiterating the idea that a literary text was the product of a single, creative mind. The sensitive reader, one who consumed the text in the correct way, acknowledged and condoned the beliefs and values expressed by the writer: 'the right kind of reader is the one who manages to recreate in himself more or less completely the collection of impulses which the poet expressed in the poem'.[2]

This process of critical understanding divorces both the reader and the writer from their historical circumstances. It implies that a personal response to literature, and to the truths that it embodies, can only be achieved if the text is read in isolation. In other words the 'meaning' of a Shakespeare play can be understood entirely from the text by the sensitive critic. By implication this meaning transcends history: a critic reading the play in the correct manner will experience the same feelings and beliefs that Shakespeare attempted to express four hundred years ago.

In fact this response to literature is not just a case of careful reading. Alan Sinfield has pointed out that as far as English secondary school examination boards are concerned, understanding a Shakespeare play is indeed a case of the sensitive reader apprehending the meaning of the isolated play. Nevertheless the pupil's response is carefully engineered and very definite distinctions are created between correct and incorrect interpretations. Not surprisingly the 'correct' response tends to endorse the ideology of a capitalist economy.[3] An understanding of Shakespeare is achieved through the apprehension of the truths embodied in the text, yet, as Belsey points out, the apprehension of those truths is nothing more that the confirmation of the reader's beliefs (which Belsey refers to as 'common sense'), beliefs which are ideologically constructed. The specific political nature of these ideas, as far as England is concerned, will be examined in closer detail in Part I.

The need to ensure that readings of Shakespeare conform to the understanding of the plays formulated in Britain during the industrial revolution, and at the height of the Empire, has determined the nature of Shakespeare film criticism so far. The demand for a personal consensus between the reader and the writer, and the demarcation of correct and incorrect responses to the text, conditions the way in which Shakespeare films are created and understood. A film of a Shakespeare play is regarded in the same way as a reading, in other words the task of the director is to understand and articulate the values and truths that are supposedly embodied in the poetry. This has two effects. Firstly it means that the central issue in many of the discussions about Shakespeare film is concerned with the ability of cinema to articulate the truths of the text. Eckert sees the argument as being polarised between those who think that the cinema can never recreate Shakespeare's poetry and 'those who, for a variety of reasons, but principally because they have a great love for the cinema, are tolerant of even gross liberties if they feel that the spirit of Shakespeare is retained or his poetry and ideas metamorphosed into cinematic equivalents'.[4]

Secondly films which don't appear to reinforce the supremacy of the poetry or the values it supposedly embodies are ignored, suppressed or re-appropriated. Silent cinema is dismissed because the text isn't the most significant source of meaning. Foreign films tend to be accepted as long as their treatment of the plays appears consonant with the approach encouraged in British culture.

It is with foreign films that the contradictions in the traditional approach to Shakespeare and Shakespeare film are most apparent. There are unavoidable problems in trying to make a movie produced in Japan or Russia appear to endorse the values and meaning identified in Shakespeare's work by British literary criticism. There is a very real ideological need to confirm the universalism of Shakespeare's poetry, otherwise the claims that the text is relevant to any sensitive reader at any point in history become problematic. Yet there are obvious cultural differences which, in a post-imperial world, cannot simply be dismissed as irrelevant or wrong.

The critical responses to Akira Kurosawa's Kumonosu jo represent various attempts to come to terms with foreign Shakespeare films that appear to contradict traditional readings of the plays. We will look at these in greater detail in Part IV but, broadly, few of the Shakespearean film critics have reconciled Kumonosu jo's position in Japanese culture with traditional perceptions of Macbeth. Jack Jorgens marginalise's the film's Japanese 'elements', interpreting it as a study of the opposition between society and nature. The chapter on Kumonosu jo in Manvell's work does examine its relationship to Japanese culture, but only in an anecdotal form, Manvell draws no theoretical conclusions. What is most surprising is that analyses of the film in cinema criticism, by writers like Donald Richie and Ana Laura Zambrano, often come to conclusions that are wildly different to those in reviews by Shakespeare scholars. Because neither Richie nor Zambrano feel the need to endorse orthodox readings of Macbeth (their work is concerned with supporting the auteur theory of film, which they do by discussing Kumonosu jo as a Kurosawa movie) they don't try to marginalise or re-appropriate the film's Japanese origins. It is worth pointing out that the re-appropriation of foreign films doesn't just manifest itself in criticism but is an important part of the process of release and distribution outside the country of origin. Kumonosu jo ('The castle of the spider's web') was retitled Throne of blood in England. This name has little relevance in Japanese culture but fits in with orthodox readings of Macbeth as a tale of violent treachery. Grigori Kozintsev used Boris Pasternak's translation of Hamlet for his film yet, when it was released in England, the subtitles were taken from the English version of Shakespeare's play. The elimination of the Russian text enabled those critics who believe in the supremacy of the English original to sidestep the theoretical challenge posed by a Shakespeare film made in a foreign language.

Shakespeare film criticism uses and endorses the method of literary analysis developed by the New Critics and promoted as the correct response to a literary text in the British educational establishment. In summary the tenets of this approach are as follows. The understanding of a text is an act of personal consumption. Secondly the correct response to a play will allow the sensitive individual to understand the experiences and truths communicated by the writer. Thirdly these values, when embodied in good literature, transcend historical and cultural difference. Finally the purpose of a good Shakespeare film is to reproduce, like a sensitive critic, the meaning of the essential text.

In the third part of this introduction we will examine the various radical approaches that have been developed to challenge the ideological hegemony of this kind of analysis. Before that it is important to identify the connections between the position of Shakespeare film analysis and the methodology of film history.

## Film history

The Shakespeare film history that reproduces the assumptions of Romantic and New Criticism tends to echo the theories of orthodox cinema history. The artistic and cultural characteristics of cinema in both Britain and America are the direct result of the industry's economic development, yet this relationship is rarely acknowledged in the standard histories of film. As Gramsci and Althusser have pointed out, ideology conceals the real economic relationships within a society, making the dominant code of beliefs appear natural and coherent. In the case of cinema the transformations in film technique and production, as manufacturers responded to shifts in market forces, or attempted to explore potential new areas of expansion, are represented as inevitable historical developments. Because the inception of cinema involved the identification and exploitation of a new, unexplored market, orthodox histories of the medium have tended to invest it with its own specific characteristics. This uniqueness is seen as primarily technological, hence the development of film is constructed retrospectively, as a progression through very definite stages. Broadly speaking most film histories begin with the arrival of moving pictures in the late nineteenth century. They then discuss the rise of the industry during the 'primitive' and 'non-filmic' days before World War I. Finally it is accepted by most orthodox historians that cinema emerged as a fully fledged medium with the invention of sound in North America during the late 1920s.

Bound up with this evolutionary vision of history is the concept of a film language, a code of editing and representation which is unique to the medium, and which has been formulated through a laborious process of trial and error, to express the essence of cinema's presentational capabilities. Considerable radical work has now been done to deconstruct the accepted language of film, relocating it as an important part of the economic expansion of Hollywood during and after World War I. Writers like Noel Burch have identified the way in which a specific method of film making (the so-called 'Hollywood code of editing') has been divorced from its immediate social and historical context and advocated as the ideal universal standard.

Part of this process involves the construction of an idealised hierarchy of works from the filmic down to the non-filmic. This scale of values effectively suppresses any connection cinema may have with other areas of cultural practice. Charles Monaco begins his introductory study of cinema (How to read a film, 1981) by comparing film in turn to photography, painting, theatre, the novel, music and architecture, a method that reinforces the supposed differences between each. Susan Sontag, André Bazin and Hugo Munsterburg have all sought to formulate a theoretical distinction between theatre and film. This has a special significance for this study because many writers see Shakespeare film as partly a 'translation' from the stage to the screen.

One persistent criticism that is levelled at early films is their 'theatricality'. The directors of the first Shakespeare movies are especially liable to attack for their 'unfortunate misunderstanding of their medium which led to unoriginal reproduction without proper transformation, of stage action and stage business'.[5] This approach dehistoricises the relationship between film and other areas of cultural production. In Part I we will see how historical evidence reveals that at this early stage, cinema and theatre existed in a close economic and aesthetic relationship. For the time being it is worth pointing out that by mystifying the real relationships between cinema and other art forms Shakespeare film criticism has become locked in highly abstract debates about the transmission of meaning from one idealised and ahistorical field to another. This argument has been raging since Charles Lamb claimed that the theatre was unable to recreate Shakespeare's sublime poetry, and it is still unresolved. Most of the orthodox histories which treat Shakespearean cinema as a genre construct unresolved competitions between 'good film', 'good theatre' and 'good Shakespeare'. Jorgens, in outlining his approach to Shakespeare film, claims that 'in order to fully understand and appreciate good Shakespeare films, we need the vocabularies of all three disciplines – literature, theatre and film'.[6] Indeed this separation of areas of cultural practice is so persuasive that it has coloured radical debates about the nature of Shakespeare film. Graham Holderness, in a materialist essay on Shakespearean cinema, echoes the belief that theatre and cinema are, by their very nature, fundamentally distinct genres.[7]

## Towards a revaluation of Shakespearean cinema

Radical developments in literary and cultural analysis over the last ten years have now provided us with a means of breaking out of the closed loop of formalist and prescriptive Shakespeare analysis, and a way of contextualising both it and the films themselves in their social and historical moments. Writers such as Catherine Belsey, Graham Holderness, Noel Burch and Michael Chanan have already begun to do this. The strategies that have been adopted seek to identify the cultural and historical source of a text or a film's meaning. Instead of suggesting that the meaning of a text is the product of a single artistic consciousness this approach recognises that its form, content and cultural position is determined by the economic and political forces that condition its production. At the same time the economic and social contradictions inherent in a capitalist economy manifest themselves in a text or film as a plurality of images and discourses.

In the case of Shakespearean film this process is compounded by the mythological status that Shakespeare and Shakespeare's works have been awarded in contemporary society. Lévi-Strauss stressed that myth, as a cultural artefact, developed as a conglomeration of beliefs, images, structures and motifs. A myth is the sum of its versions, even though many of those versions may contradict each other. Historically the reproduction of Shakespeare in society operates in a similar way. Although specific readings of the texts are idealised as correct and universal the position of Shakespeare is, in fact pluralistic. Shakespeare is not merely a specific body of texts, the name denotes a broad area of cultural practice and meaning which encompasses film, art, theatre, literature, education and history. Therefore a Shakespeare film is not a hermetically enclosed work with a set of specific and coherent meanings, it is the sum of a number of discourses culled from these various areas of production.

To acknowledge the specific location of a Shakespeare film within the economic and political structures of a society necessitates the recognition of the mechanism of ideology and its political sources. Orthodox Shakespeare film criticism operates within a very narrow area; it concentrates on those movies that support traditional assumptions about the nature of literature and, in doing so, it selectively edits out those elements that appear disruptive or challenging. Because of this its conclusions are frequently incorrect or contradictory. It invests a Japanese film with meanings that a Japanese audience would find baffling or ridiculous. It suggests that Shakespeare's works are universal, transcending historical and cultural differences, yet it often cannot analyse non-English films without rigorously suppressing or re-appropriating them.

Orthodox analysis creates a hierarchy of Shakespeare films; it is able to do this by marginalising the material conditions of society as unimportant factors in a movie's production. The best way to challenge the assumptions of this approach, and to analyse the ideology that it reinforces, is to reincorporate each film into its historical moment. This entails breaking each movie down into its cultural components and contextualising them within a specific ideology. Thus instead of thinking of Kurosawa's films of *Macbeth* or *King Lear* as isolated interpretations of Shakespeare's texts we can place them within a host of social and aesthetic traditions; Japanese drama, Japanese Shakespeare, Kurosawa's position in society, his work, and so on. Within the field of cinema analysis considerable work has already been done on silent film, Japanese film and other areas of production by critics like Burch and Chanan. Similarly there is a growing body of radical criticism concerning Shakespeare and the political nature of his reproduction in culture; *Political Shakespeare* (eds. Sinfield and Dollimore) and *Alternative Shakespeares* (ed. Drakakis) are two instances of this. This book represents an attempt to apply a similar approach to Shakespeare film.

The book is divided into four sections. Each part deals with a film or group of films produced within a specific aesthetic and cultural tradition. Because Shakespeare film and orthodox Shakespeare analysis are inextricably connected the book reproduces, to a certain extent, the established canon of movies. There are specific reasons for this. Firstly many of the Shakespeare films are intertextual in that they recreate and develop the approaches of earlier movies. Secondly it is only possible to expose the structure of the ideology that has created this canon by contextualising both it and the films within their social and historical moment. Thirdly the connections between certain movies that are stressed in orthodox criticism stem from real, historical relationships between certain groups of films and the people who create and review them. This is partly because of similarities in the social and cultural position of the directors, producers and critics and partly because, in Anglo-American culture, making a Shakespeare film is treated as an identical process to a perceptive act of textual criticism. Therefore anyone in England or

America who creates a Shakespeare movie tends to endorse the established attitude to literature and the hierarchy it has constructed, even if the film is intended to be radical. Finally film companies rarely make a movie out of a Shakespeare play simply because they're short of material. There are very definite reasons for reproducing the plays and the tradition to which they belong.

To discover these reasons I intend to take each film, or group of films, and identify the various discourses, images or structures that were used in their creation. Because this involves the consideration of a large amount of historical material the book will concentrate on specific examples, rather than trying to present a comprehensive study of the whole area of Shakespeare film production. What I also intend to do is to explore the reason for the appropriation and canonisation of Shakespeare's work by critics and film makers. Thus Part I, in dealing with British silent films, will examine the development of Shakespeare production in British theatre, art and literature, within a historical framework. Part II will concentrate on the economic and cultural forces behind Warner Brothers' 1935 production of *A midsummer night's dream* and will examine how these have shaped the style, content and cultural location of later films. The second half of the book is intended as a challenge to the re-appropriation of foreign Shakespeare films by English and American critics. Part III will concentrate on Grigori Kozintsev's *Hamlet* and *Korol Ler* and, finally, Part IV consists of a discussion of Akira Kurosawa's *Kumonosu jo* and *Ran*.

# PART ONE

# Victorian bardolatry

In this first chapter I want to look at the prehistory of British Shakespeare film. This isn't to say that an unbroken line of development exists between Victorian Shakespeare on the stage and the early silent films, or that the position of Shakespeare in nineteenth-century culture is readily apparent and unambiguous. The idea that the Victorians' 'discovery' of Shakespeare somehow re-established a genuine and authoritative understanding of the plays is a myth that has persisted into this century. A hundred years ago it helped to give a fragmented and diverse culture a sense of unity by foregrounding a particular perception of Shakespeare as true, natural and eternal. It is an easy matter to take this argument into film history and suggest that the early Shakespeare movies continued this tradition in a new, revolutionary medium.

While it's true that early British Shakespeare film existed in a symbiotic relationship with the theatre, it's also misleading to assume that by studying these genres we can make authoritative statements on the position of Shakespeare in Victorian society. On the contrary, both areas of production were the site of a complex struggle between contradictory political and economic interests. Furthermore this conflict was absorbed into Shakespearean cinema via several routes, not just the theatre. We can't fully understand Victorian Shakespeare, or British Shakespeare movies, without looking at the roles of Shakespeare in the Romantic movement and in narrative art. The position of the plays in these areas of social practice reflects the attempts made to create a role for literature, culture and the intellectual during the industrial revolution. Their combination in the early Shakespeare films marks one resolution of the tensions between these three often radically opposed interests and the demands of a new industrial society.

In this chapter I have avoided treating Victorian Shakespeare as a single, unbroken tradition. Instead I've separated out the main areas in which ̱ ̱ ̱ ̱ ̱peare was used to work out those cultural responses to ̱ ̱ ̱ ̱ ̱hich determined the form and content of British Shakes-̱ ̱ ̱ ̱. These are the melodramatic theatre, Romanticism, the spectacular Shakespeare productions of the late

## British theatre and the Patent Laws

The early Victorian stage was the site of a struggle between burgeoning, urban middle-class drama and the legacy of the fossilised and unworkable theatre acts of the previous century. The role of Shakespeare in this battle was, at first, relatively minor. It wasn't until after the 1840s that the most popular theatre genre, melodrama, shed its radical working-class associations and became a vehicle for bourgeois culture. Then Shakespeare came into his own through the spectacular productions of actor-managers like Herbert Beerbohm Tree and Henry Irving. To understand the melodramatic Shakespeare that became cinema we need to establish the history of this kind of theatre, and the images, acting methods and literary models which it generated.

The oldest and most powerful influence on Victorian Shakespeare production came from the imposition of the theatre laws of the previous century. The Restoration ban on the spoken word in drama forced the majority of theatres to abandon the use of speech to communicate meaning. In fact only three London houses were legally entitled to have actors speaking on stage, Covent Garden, Drury Lane and (with a restricted licence) the 'Little Theatre in the Haymarket'. The theatre world was split between the three Major houses and the rest (the Minors). People who attended the latter (i.e. the vast majority of theatre-goers) had to make do with a diet of politically 'safe' musical entertainment. Pantomime, circus, opera and singing were all acceptable as long as none of the performers spoke.

The theatre acts of 1737, 1751 and 1755 expanded the power of the original royal patents by introducing state censorship and giving local magistrates the right to ban (by denying licences) all forms of theatrical entertainment. These moves were political: theatres, often renowned as disorderly houses, were thought of as breeding grounds for unrest. Under the terms of the 1737 act the Lord Chamberlain had the power to censor any politically or morally suspect plays. He could also inflict the Poor Laws on players who stepped outside the boundary of legitimate drama. If any of them dared to utter prose on a stage that hadn't been granted a licence they could be prosecuted as vagabonds. The ban on speech was effective, few performers dared to defy it openly. Instead they began to explore a variety of ways of circumventing the law, using other types of entertainment to push drama beyond the narrow boundaries decreed by Parliament.

It wasn't a very difficult challenge. Superficially the law was simple and straightforward, no talking on stage, but the actual definition of what did, or did not, constitute speech was far less obvious. There were many vague areas; for example at what point would blank verse, which would be illegal if spoken, become permissable when delivered rhythmically with an orchestra playing in the background? The illegitimate theatre stumbled across the legal divide with increasing regularity. In 1809 *Macbeth* was turned into an opera at the Royal Circus; on another occasion *Othello* was performed with a pianist playing an inaudible chord every few minutes. Faced with the ingenuity of the acting profession the task of distinguishing between illegal and legal drama was virtually impossible.

Thus the Patent Laws gave added impetus to a series of revolutionary changes in British drama. The main aim of most companies was to get around the ban on actors speaking on stage. At first theatres tended to retain familiar styles of presentation while finding some other method of signifying speech and dialogue. One way of achieving this was to transfer the text to scrolls which were then held up in front of the audience. The effect was not dissimilar to the speech balloons of the eighteenth-century political cartoonists. As in silent film the audience was shown short written texts representing dialogue, interpreting the visual image and furthering the narrative; 'all that could not be rendered clear by action, was told by means of what were called 'scrolls': pieces of linen, on which whatever the Dramatis Personae wished to communicate with each other, for better understanding of the audience, was expressed in writing, painted on the cloth, and which the Performers alternately fetched from the different sides of the stage and presented to the full view of the audience'.[1]

While ingenious, these Gothic spectacles were too inflexible to allow them to develop into a fully fledged theatrical movement. Music and song were popular alternatives to the spoken word. Sentimentalism; the mythology of intense, wordless feelings developed by contemporary novelists and the Romantic movement, was rapidly growing in popularity. In this context music had the added advantage of claiming to express what was inexpressible in words. As early as the 1750s a host of non-patented theatres had begun to undermine the monopoly of Covent Garden and Drury Lane with popular musical entertainment. The major post-act dramatic movements sprang directly from the use of music as a subversive antidote to the law. In the 1730s a type of Italian comic opera became very popular in the illegitimate theatres. Soon these romantic and unashamedly sentimental plays were being parodied by

British companies. After 1737 a new genre that was a part pastiche, part imitation of the Italian style, emerged. It was popularly known as burletta.

Burletta marks the evolution of a form of theatre that is predominately silent. The assumption that eighteenth-century and nineteenth-century drama used the text as the ultimate source of meaning is incorrect. From the start of the industrial revolution right through until the beginning of this century the spoken word was a minor element in English theatre. Instead the audiences followed and understood most of the performance by watching and interpreting mime, images and spectacle.

Burletta quickly became a general term used to describe any performance in which verse was recited to a musical accompaniment. Given that the legal definition of legitimate drama was open to question many theatres were quick to tread the fine line between song and speech. This gave the authorities the onerous task of distinguishing between plays which were permissable and those that went too far. George Coleman the Younger, who read plays for the Lord Chamberlain, was quick to realise that burletta and comic opera could easily cross the boundary between legitimate and illegal drama. Writing in 1830 he pointed out that many theatres 'made their Recitative appear like Prose by the actor running one line into another, and slurring over the rhyme; – soon after, a harpsichord was touch'd now and then, as an accompaniment to the actor'.[2]

In using burletta to experiment with the boundaries of legitimate drama and the possible combinations of music and speech, the illegitimate theatres of the early nineteenth-century gave birth to melodrama. First called melo-drame (music-drama) it drew its overall style of production from the comic operas of the previous century. Like its dramatic ancestor it evaded the Patent Laws by using music to accompany the action. However, instead of basing its appeal on the sentimentalism and humour of the Italian opera it evolved in tandem with the pseudo-Jacobean narratives of the Gothic novels and penny dreadfuls.

Melodrama drew on a vast body of literature, folklore and history. Plays were based on the legends of Sweeney Todd and Dick Turpin and, as the genre became more respectable, such grand events as the Battle of Waterloo. Shakespeare's plays were occasionally used, with the most violent and spectacular plays presented as dramatic narratives. Half-hour versions of Macbeth and Hamlet were shown in which most of the text was excised, leaving the ghosts, battles and murders. Melodramatic theatre combined all those stylistic features that had developed in the eighteenth-century to undermine the licensing acts: stereotyped characterisation; gesture instead of speech as the prime signifier of emotion and intent; tableaux vivants; violent spectacle and relentless narrative.

Realism and psychological complexity were virtually unknown on the early melodramatic stage. Although many Gothic authors (several of them wrote for the theatre) used both narrative and the mechanism of suspense to interrogate the horrors of industrial society, melodrama remained firmly rooted in a world populated by stereotypical characters and situations. It transformed the problems of social injustice into a conflict between good and evil personified as easily recognisable class types. There were strong financial reasons for this. The use of pre-determined figures to represent moral absolutes was closely linked to the mechanism of theatrical repertory. With a rapid turnover of plays that could be acted by a cast assigned to fixed roles a theatre stood a better chance of keeping financially solvent in the face of stiff competition. The economics were simple; successful plays could be repeated for as long as they drew the public while failures were quickly forgotten after one or two bad nights. An entertainment that provided continual variation on a number of popular themes or styles was assured of a reasonably steady, if not phenomenal, audience.

Typecasting enabled a company to cover most of the characters in any one play. This division of labour ensured that non-melodramatic works, like the tragedies of Shakespeare, also became encoded within a system of stereotypes. The standard set of characters from melodrama provided a template that could be adapted quite readily to Shakespeare's plays. In melodramas there was usually a hardy but slightly stupid hero, a villain (often aristocratic) who was destined for a spectacular end, a heroine, a venerable and saintly elderly parent, a comic servant and various crowds of bandits, hearty sailors and rustics. As Joseph Donohue points out, plays like Hamlet slot neatly into this scheme: Hamlet and Ophelia for the hero and heroine; Claudius the villain; Polonius the aged parent and the humorous working-classes represented by the gravediggers.

Melodramatic plays were, above all, visual. Each character was immediately recognisable, not only by their dress but also by the code of stances and gestures they adopted. Before the repeal of the 1737 Licensing Act in 1843, the players were faced with the difficult task of communicating to their audiences with as little speech as possible. The problem was compounded by the increasing size of theatre auditoriums, a factor that influenced Major as well as Minor theatres. The new Drury Lane, rebuilt after the old building burnt down in 1809, seated nearly four thousand people. From the gods the stage appeared miniscule, 'not a feature of the face can be distinguished,' grumbled one theatre-goer, 'far less the variations and flexibility of the muscles, the turn of the eye and graceful action'.[3] The acting profession developed a complex language of gesture which enabled the audience to read the emotions of their characters through signs. At the beginning of the twentieth-century stage gesture had become an art in itself. Turner Morton described the syntax of this, by now very sophisticated, language in an article for *Pearson's magazine*. As far as he could see, with the 'Art of gesture', 'every action of the true actor or actress tells a story as eloquent – often more eloquent – than words'.[4] When silent film replaced melodramatic theatre as the chief source of entertainment for the working-class the silent language of gesture transferred quite readily from stage to screen.

In the space of a few years melodrama came to dominate the repertories of Victorian theatres, both legitimate and illegitimate. Alongside pantomime and circus this new genre enticed the public away from the staid diet of plays performed at the Royal Houses. To reverse their declining popularity they, in turn, were forced to adopt the more commercially viable forms of theatre used by their vulgar counterparts. James Smith, in *Melodrama* (1973), claims that when Macready first appeared in *Othello* in 1816 at Covent Garden it was alongside the pantomime *Aladdin*, and that at 'Covent Garden and Drury Lane performing monkeys playing banjos were more popular than Kemble and Kean playing the classics'.[5]

During the beginning of the industrial revolution the association of the patent theatres with aristocratic patronage contributed to a growing discontent amongst radical businessmen about the injustices of British society. Evidence of the social origins of this rebellion is implicit in the locations of the provincial theatres that were eventually granted patents in 1820. Many were situated in growing industrial centres such as Manchester, Newcastle, Birmingham and Hull. The righteous indignation of the rebellious middle-class audience, when it felt itself to be financially and socially discriminated against, can be witnessed in the events surrounding the famous riots at Covent Garden in 1809. At the time both patent houses were increasingly forced to show burletta and melodrama to prevent the audiences flocking elsewhere. The fires that gutted both theatres in 1809 left their managers helpless in the face of the growing competition from a host of illegitimate Minors. Evidently, in the case of Covent Garden, the management were anxious to move up-market, dissociate themselves from the seedier aspects of the non-patented theatres, and regain ground lost during the period the house was out of action. When Kemble's theatre was rebuilt he raised the admission prices by a shilling. The new auditorium also had more private boxes (now totalling three tiers) with a proportional loss of gallery space. The response to the changes was dramatic. Every night for three months performances were brought to a halt by the audience. Amidst constant booing and heckling there was a continual cry for a return to the old prices. The rationale behind the introduction of more private boxes (i.e. that they would save the upper-classes from having to mingle with their inferiors) carries the unmistakable stamp of a class struggle. Fired by radical enthusiasm the new entrepeneurs felt they had a greater right to the dramatic classics of their country than the supposedly enervated and decadent aristocracy. Kemble's misguided attempts to captivate a flagging aristocratic elite merely perpetuated the sense of injustice felt by the rest of the audience.

The enormous popular success of melodrama contributed to the abolition of the Patent Laws. By 1832 the overall quality of British drama was thought to be so bad that a parliamentary committee was created to inquire into its decline. Their deliberations led to the theatre act of 1843 which lifted the centuries-old ban on speech. With the repeal of the 1737 Licensing Act melodrama lost its subversive role. Actors and managers in the Minor theatres no longer had to tread the fine line between legitimate and illegitimate theatre. Even so, although the act of 1843 removed the need for melodrama the majority of theatres that sprang up in its wake specialised almost exclusively in this type of play. The careers of Kean and Irving show plainly that melodrama, in all its myriad forms and sub-genres, had become the established mainstay of nineteenth-century theatre. Between 1850 and 1859 Kean compiled a 'repertory combining Shakespeare with gentlemanly melodrama'.[6] John Stokes believes that Irving's success was due to a 'calculated mixture of pure melodrama, historical melodrama and Shakespeare'.[7]

Overtly the abolition of the Licensing Act in 1843 was intended to make plays freely and legally available to all instead of confining them 'to the only places ... where they can least intelligently be heard'.[8] In fact it signalled the successful appropriation of theatrical entertainment by urban middle-class society. The politicians, dissenters and liberals who had felt themselves alienated from the control of culture during the early nineteenth-century were sufficiently confident of their power by 1878 to clamp down on working-class entertainment with the Theatre Suitability Act. Under this new law all theatres were granted an annual licence, providing they met certain safety requirements and didn't sell alcohol in the auditorium. Many small theatres were finished simply because their building's foundations couldn't carry the weight of the now-compulsory iron safety curtain.

The Theatre Suitability Act ensured that only the respectable theatres survived. Companies that did show works of dubious taste or sentiment to the wrong people were refused their yearly licence and subsequently forced out of business. High-class sentimental and patriotic melodrama dominated the late nineteenth-century stage. By now this genre relied heavily on lavish and expensive spectacles. Directors used complicated mechanics and painstaking research to create a believable reality on stage. Shakespeare's works were increasingly popular because his supposed educational and historic qualities allowed the producers to incorporate a whole range of visual effects and details without being accused of irrelevance. At this point the disparate trends that constituted the Victorian Shakespeare tradition (painting, history and narrative) were finally combined on the stage under the guiding hand of actor-managers like Irving and Tree.

## Shakespeare as Romantic narrative

The history of theatre legislation goes some way to explain the form and content of Victorian Shakespeare production on stage and, eventually, in film. What has yet to be addressed is the position that the plays themselves held in British culture from the 1750s to the 1890s, when the first Shakespeare films were made. His growing popularity during the eighteenth century was closely linked to the effect of industrialisation on intellectual perceptions of British society, history and culture. Initially his works were adopted by disaffected radicals like Fuseli and Coleridge. Yet by the late 1800s they formed the backbone of a new national patriotic literature. For the early Romantics the plays seemed to champion those ethics that would defend humanity against the destabilising effects of capitalism on art. Yet, at the same time, it was Shakespeare's works that were transformed into commodities using the latest mass-production techniques. They were distributed to a new class of consumers as illustrated texts, transformed into spectacles using the latest state-of-the-art theatre mechanics and edited into improving narratives to educate the next generation of empire-builders. This duality in cultural perceptions of Shakespeare is not contradictory, rather it illuminates the uneasy relationship between the intellectual and society during periods of extreme economic and social change. The use of Shakespeare as a sounding board for cultural values by these disaffected individuals represents an inevitable compromise between them and the developing capitalist state.

After the Civil War the Puritan ban on drama encouraged the growth of play reading as an alternative to attending the theatre. From the Restoration onwards the Patent Laws ensured that, for the majority of educated people, the only direct access they had to the works of Shakespeare was through the printed word. With the growth of a literate middle-class public there evolved a ready market for published editions and a collection of the complete works, bearing Shakespeare's name, was printed as early as 1709. The transformation of Shakespeare into a saleable commodity was accompanied by a change in critical attitudes to his plays. His texts ceased to be part of publicly received dramatic performances. Instead they were thought of as works produced by a single artistic consciousness to be experienced in the privacy of the home.

The term Romanticism has been used as a description for a number of similar developments in art, literature, drama and politics between 1750 and the late 1840s. The concept was formulated in the late nineteenth-century, almost fifty years after it had supposedly died out. It was this Victorian definition that remoulded radical and directly interventionist beliefs into a singularly unworldly code of aesthetics. It's hardly surprising that the central role in this emasculated canon was given to the Romantic poet. Many of the artists working at this time were acutely aware of the effect of capitalism on artistic production. Without the economic security of the patron-artist contract they had to redefine the relationship between those who created art and those who consumed it. Much of their writing involved the evocation of an elaborate mythology surrounding the figure of the isolated genius. The poet created her or his art from some mysterious source of personal inspiration and communicated it to a common humanity. The reification of early socialist, feminist and anarchist philosophy into the realms of high art was inevitable because this wide range of movements evolved from various attempts to define a cultural identity for a nascent bourgeois class.

As Raymond Williams (Culture and society 1780-1950 (1958)) points out, many of the debates that attempted to define culture in this period focused on the role of the intellectual in an industrial economy. The ethics mentioned above are similar to those of an idealised commercial society. Time and time again writers advocated the importance of innovation, the destruction of corrupt and aristocratic hierarchies and the shattering of the walls that surrounded Britain's elitist political institutions (but only so far as to admit the middle-classes). Simultaneously there was an attempt to canonise values that would act as an antidote to the evils of a new machine age. Against the dehumanising working methods and increasing oppression of the 'hands' it offered the sentimentalist's creed of feeling and suggested inexpressible bonds between members of a common humanity. While industry encroached on the countryside and the structures of agrarian society broke down, it suggested that true beauty lay in untamed nature and rustic simplicity. It also created an idealised national history of which Shakespeare was a significant part.

The tension between the need for artists to assimilate themselves into society and their resistance to its disruptive and horrific elements was reflected in the changing role of Shakespeare in literature between 1750 and the early nineteenth-century. Initially the use of history as a sounding board for Romantic idealism was problematic. No matter how much the writers of the period tried to reinvent history or create a new concept of culture, they were still divorced from the mechanisms of social change. In the early days of commercialism they, in their more lucid moments, saw themselves as part of a monstrous and threatening world. They tried to come to terms with this through Gothic fiction, a genre that had a direct and explicit link with Elizabethan drama. Here history was altogether more complex and fragmented; the past became the haunt of brutal and supernatural forces beyond the control of the individual. When viewed together many of these works operate as an extended metaphor for the enlightened Romantic sensibility dwarfed beneath the Juggernaut of industry. One only has to look at the etchings of Piranesi, which fascinated many Gothic writers, to see the extent to which the imagery of the machine age was tangled up with the symbolism of ancient oppression.

Stylistically there is a strong link between Elizabethan tragedy and certain motifs and structures that emerged in the novel in the early nineteenth-century. The use of a strong plot or narrative stemmed from the tendency of early writers to structure their Gothic tales using theatrical and melodramatic conventions. Horace Walpole's The castle of Otranto (1765) was indebted to the traditions of Renaissance drama, echoing its excesses of emotion and emphatic dialogue. The author deliberately imitated the five-act drama, dividing his book into an equivalent number of chapters. It was partly intended as a work of criticism. It advocated a new 'natural' and original art created by individual effort and based on folklore in opposition to what Walpole felt to be the cynical and dry artifice of authors such as Voltaire; 'that great master of nature, Shakespeare, was the model I copied ... The result of all I have said, is to shelter my own daring under the cannon of the brightest genius this country, at least, has produced.'⁹

By using Shakespearean tragedy as a template Walpole was able to transfer his perception of dynastic oppression and extreme violence into the past, giving them an intensity of expression that would be untenable in contemporary fiction. It also allowed him to introduce the supernatural, which he used to evoke an uncertain, dreamlike world in which the individual struggled against implacable fate (what Jan Kott was later to refer to as the 'grand mechanism'). The passage in which Manfred confronts the ghost of his grandfather not only illustrates this but also shows Walpole directly parodying *Hamlet*: ' . . . if thou art my grand-sire, why dost thou too conspire against thy wretched descendant, who too dearly pays for – Ere he could finish the sentence the vision sighed again, and made a sign to Manfred to follow him. Lead on! cried Manfred; I will follow thee to the gulph of perdition.'¹⁰

Using Shakespeare the Gothic writers created a new form of literature through which they tried to address the overwhelming and, at times, terrifying social changes of the era. However, this re-interpretation of the plays contributed to the establishment of the cultural hegemony that middle-class industrial society was searching for. While Gothic writers like Charles Maturin and James Hogg took their fragmented narratives further towards the introspective and existential realms of psychological horror, other writers and critics began to use Shakespeare as an emblem of British nationalism. 'All things and modes of action shape themselves anew in the being of Milton; while Shakespeare becomes all things, yet for ever remaining himself. O what great men has thou not produced, England! my country!'¹¹ wrote Coleridge in his *Biographia literaria*, marshalling the two writers whose work represented the creation of a new cultural identity during the Napoleonic wars. Nevertheless, although Shakespeare's genius was regarded as an antidote to the plagiaristic classicism of the Enlightenment, his writings contained much that was confusing, obscure or indelicate. They often refused to lend themselves to the Sentimental and Romantic idiom. In the end Shakespeare's plays could only really pass into the artistic milieu of nationalistic Romanticism after considerable transformation. In effect this meant their removal from the stage, and from the clutches of the Gothic novelists, and their re-incorporation into Romantic culture as narrative literature.

The Romantic concept of artistic individuality, of the ability of the writer to address experiences and visions beyond the mundane, was used as justification for the move towards isolating Shakespeare's text from the theatre and reading it as verse. One of the most emphatic advocates of this was Charles Lamb who believed strongly in the superiority of reading a text over watching it being performed, 'to know the internal workings of a great mind, of an Othello or a Hamlet for instance . . . seems to demand a reach of intellect of a vastly different extent from that which is employed upon the bare imitation of the signs of these passions in the countenance or gesture'.[12]

It is true that the acting styles developed to cope with the Patent Laws hardly lent themselves to the expression of subtle and precise nuances of feeling. A growing awareness of the psychological and sentimental complexities of the human personality was manifesting itself in Sentimental literature. Therefore it is understandable that critics like Lamb should reject the standardisation of expression in the theatre. In a literary and economic climate that place a premium on thematic originality the production-line approach of repertory drama to Shakespeare was an anathema. Consequently Shakespeare the dramatist became Shakespeare the poet, a Romantic idealisation of his verse that persists to the present day and forms much of the reasoning behind the dissemination of the plays in the British educational system. By advocating the private consumption and contemplation of the text Lamb and others integrated the plays into the mainstream of early nineteenth-century narrative fiction.

In 1807 Charles and Mary Lamb published their *Tales from Shakespear*, in which they rewrote the plays as expurgated stories for young readers. They concentrated on the emotional condition and motivation of the central characters and their personal development. Their intention was to present 'the histories of men and women'.[13] Whereas the originals were written in the present tense all their tales were narrated in the past, for example: 'When Duncan the Meek reigned King of Scotland'.[14] By treating the plays in this way the Lambs implicitly transformed them into factual newspaper accounts, reports and histories, all of which had varying pretensions to impartial truth.

This superimposition of a linear framework upon a Shakespeare play ordered it into a single, coherent structure. It suggested that the events in the text were linked through a temporal sequence of cause and effect and it eliminated the artificial element that would be obvious on stage (with the references to stagecraft, the continuous present tense of the performance, the elaborate conceits involving audience and players etc.). It also ensured that substantial, if not equal, authority was given to incidents that were important to the 'plot' but which occurred off-stage. In the case of the history plays this narrative closure absorbed into the scenario characters and events that were not mentioned by

Shakespeare at all, but which were considered historically relevant to the incidents in the play. As we shall see, this manipulation of narrative had a profound effect in the theatre and on film.

## Victorian narrative art

The transition from a radical to a conservative Shakespeare was echoed by developments in the visual arts. This time the situation was more intricate; the individual artist was automatically caught up in the world of commercial business because the boom in illustrated Shakespeare was the result of technological improvements in the printing industry. These made possible the combination of art and literature in volumes that were reasonably priced and therefore accessible to a wide market. Previously publishers had been limited to crude trade-manufactured woodcuts to supplement their texts. Now they were not only able to reproduce detailed pictures at a relatively low cost but they could also market engravings of the work of renowned artists. The potential for illustrated editions of Shakespeare's plays was considerable, especially at a time when so many of the literate population were denied access to spoken drama. Few middle-class consumers would have shared Coleridge's patience with the obscurities of the bare text, and editions liberally sprinkled with illustrations proved enormously popular. Such books provided people with permanent visual records of the plays which they could enjoy at home. These complimented, or were substitutes for, the theatre. Innumerable editions of the plays appeared during the Victorian period. Several, like Heath's *The Shakespeare gallery* (1836) became standard household works. Their success was emblematic of a general movement towards narrative painting in British art.

In 1768 Joshua Reynolds founded the Royal Academy. This institution was intended to encourage the growth of a native art movement by arranging regular exhibitions. Eighteen years later, with Reynolds's help, the businessman Josiah Boydell opened an art gallery devoted to illustrations of the works of Shakespeare. The venture was jointly organised with several renowned artists including Henry Fuseli and Joseph Wright of Derby. The aim was to further the nationalistic ideals of the Academy by providing a stimulus for a unified movement in English painting. At the same time Boydell hoped to make a profit by selling, to a list of subscribers, prints of the pictures along with newly illustrated editions of the plays.

The execution of the paintings in the gallery was still strongly in the

Romantic tradition; the artists echoed much of the quasi-revolutionary classicism of Jacques David or William Blake. Yet because their subject matter was Shakespeare, a secular writer free of the symbolic associations of Greek or Roman mythology, they created a more introspective and poetic treatment of the individual characters from the plays. The artists appropriated the Shakespeare tradition, encoded it into a series of visual images, and used it to address problems pertinent to their own existence as producers. Instead of placing tiny figures in the ordered scenery of a landscaped garden or making moral statements based on classic symbols, Fuseli and Wright made the human form the centre of their paintings. They moved away from ideal, universal images and concentrated on representing the individual at a specific moment in time. These 'characters' (for they increasingly came to symbolise the protagonists in a visual narrative), picked out by a few lights in a darkened world, were shown in the grip of various sentiments: Wright's *Experiment on a bird in an air pump* is one example. Works like this reflected both the high value awarded to sentiment and the encroachment of the specific details of an everyday secular world into art.

In his Shakespeare paintings Fuseli's human figures are similar in appearance to actors on a theatre stage. In those instances where a background can be seen it is usually flat, nondescript, highly stylised like a set or backdrop, and plunged deep in shadow. It is important to remember that at this period the theatre lights were kept burning during a performance. Poor lighting at the back of the stage, combined with the row of limelights at the front, could make the stage appear gloomy in comparison to the rest of the house.

Fuseli never used fixed-point perspective to give a sense of depth, indeed he often deliberately disrupted it. He arranged groups and single figures in two-dimensional clusters that appear especially theatrical: one striking example of this is a picture called *Titania awakes* (1793-4). Similarly, in *The witches appear to Macbeth and Banquo* (1800-10) the use of chiaroscuro conceals any background details in darkness. We see the witches as a single image in triplicate on the left-hand side of the painting while on the right stand Macbeth and Banquo. The attitudes of the five protagonists are consciously theatrical. Paintings like these and the book illustrations of the period provide a dictionary of the gestures and compositions used in the early Victorian theatre. At the time they created a visual iconography of characters and scenes from the plays which the audiences used to understand and judge the performances they saw.

Like many of the radical intellectuals of the period Fuseli became more and more alienated from British culture. He was unable, as an individual, to reconcile the utopianism of his political hero Rousseau with his own experiences and so he retreated into a highly personal and mystical defeatism as his career progressed. Meanwhile, from the mid-nineteenth century onwards, the majority of Shakespeare paintings were conservative in tone, sentiment and execution. British art was divorced from the main developments in European painting for most of the Victorian period. Artists in England, with a few notable exceptions, produced works that relied on narrative content for effect. Paintings were judged by moral standards rather than aesthetic ones. Works that offended middle-class taste were heavily censured no matter how technically brilliant or innnovative their execution.

In the case of Shakespeare the pertinence of the visual moral was not as important as in other examples of painted or staged melodrama. More pathos and sensibility could be wrought from a scene showing a dog and a coffin and calling it The old shepherd's faithful mourner than from a painting of Ophelia drowning. On the whole Shakespearean subjects in narrative art divided roughly into two camps. Scenes from A midsummer night's dream and The tempest appeared amid the relatively esoteric 'fairy paintings' of Richard Dadd, Robert Huskisson and other precursors of the Pre-Raphaelite movement. Most of the other plays were absorbed into the mainstream of historical narrative art.

In the late Victorian period painting became an integral part of the construction of a new nationally symbolic and historical mythology. The narrative method was used to display the legendary sources of a new British consciousness. In these paintings the dividing line between history and fiction became blurred. Shakespeare's plays came to represent not only great national literature but also the patriotic past. Artists executed literary and historical subjects using the same theatrical construction as Fuseli. They dressed their models in authentic clothes of the period and inserted them, as allegorical symbols, into narratives. They were used to represent the standard virtues and vices of melodrama, as well as those racial characteristics that supposedly set the British people apart from everyone else.

The chief consumers of the arts, the educated middle-classes, were particularly concerned with what they felt to be their own history. Their indignation at the fossilised elitism and aristocratic patronage of late eighteenth-century society had prompted a number of reform campaigns, including the one that led to the abolition of the 1737 Licensing Act in 1843. In historical genre art they were interested in those past events that apparently mirrored the revolutionary changes that they themselves had instigated. The trials of the Anglo-Saxons against the Norman French, the Magna Carta and the Wars of the Roses were all seen as mythical struggles of the British people against tyranny and corruption.

Within this framework we can separate the Shakespeare paintings from the history plays into three types. The first covered scenes taken from the text, the second showed incidents relevant to the 'story', but not actually part of the performance (as in John Everett Millais's painting of the drowning Ophelia). The final category consisted of historical paintings which could be associated with certain Shakespearean themes and whose composition relied heavily on theatre imagery. In their treatment of the subject matter the last two areas echoed the narrative closure imposed on the plays by Lamb in his *Tales from Shakespear*. By showing the subject of their paintings in a quasi-stage setting, many artists implied that 'real history' and the history described by Shakespeare had the same authority. Millais's *The two princes in the tower* (1878) is a typical example. This painting shows, face on to the 'audience', two androgynous youths. Their position, in relation to the walls of their prison, echoes the relative siting of actors and a backdrop. The children's helplessness is signified through their anxious, dreamy expressions and their huddled postures. A combination of sentimentality and ambiguous sexuality is used to evoke a common Victorian obsession; the plight of innocent children or women in menacing circumstances. These historical paintings foregrounded the notion that Shakespeare's plays were narratives of a past age (an effect compounded by the increasing concern, both in art and drama, with historical accuracy). Furthermore the pictures and prints widened the gap between text, performance and visualisation (for paintings, after all, are silent).

Yet as the century progressed the close relationship between narrative art and the theatre grew stronger. Apart from historical subjects, and scenes taken from Shakespeare, the commonest form of theatrical genre painting used meticulously detailed Victorian interiors as settings for various tales and moral anecdotes. The paintings of Emily Osborn and Sir William Orchardson showed box-shaped rooms in which the canvas (like a theatre audience) became the fourth wall. To evoke emotion in this silent medium artists continued to use the theatrical gestures practised by actors. Some artists went so far as to abandon the traditional proportions of a painting when dealing with allegorical or symbolic subjects and introduced a system of composition based entirely on the structure of a stage. One particularly interesting work by Robert Huskisson, *Titania asleep* (1847), shows the fairy queen surrounded by what appears to be a proscenium arch. This painting is prophetic: by the end of the century actor-managers like Tree were excising substantial portions of the text and presenting Shakespeare plays that were, so they claimed, historically accurate and composed like a series of painted narratives.

## Spectacular Shakespeare

On stage the marriage of art and theatre was at its most blatant with the tableaux vivants, a standard feature of melodrama. At certain key points in a play the entire cast would freeze, assuming the stance and composition of a living picture. Occurring at the end of scenes, or the play itself, these tableaux provided the dénoument to a crisis or moral episode. With Shakespeare production the aim was picturesque rather than moral. Directors were content with achieving a powerful spectacle, often in imitation of famous 'grand masters' like Hans Holbein. When Arthur Bouchier appeared as Henry VIII in Tree's triumphant 1910 production he was wearing an identical costume to the one shown in Holbein's famous portrait of the king. He walked to the centre of the stage, planted his feet wide apart and put his fists on his hips. The audience greeted this living painting with a spontaneous burst of applause. 'The picture was being applauded, not the actor – or rather the coup de théâtre of 'realising' the picture.'[15] This kind of visual reference was undeniably elitist, for only an educated middle-class audience would be likely to recognise the source of the image. Tree was pandering to their cultural pretensions.

A common pattern manifests itself in the theories put forward by Victorian directors to justify the inclusion of grandiose pageants and images in Shakespeare's works. Their reasoning was characteristic of many middle-class Victorians's vision of progress. It was assumed that a transcendent and ahistorical genius like Shakespeare's had been severely hampered by the primitive stage of the Renaissance and that he'd yearned for the 'complete realisation' of his poetic visions. Now the technological and intellectual advances of the nineteenth-century could transform his long passages of description into what they truly were; breathtaking spectacles. Henry Arthur Jones claimed that 'surely no-one reading the vision of Catherine of Aragon can come to any other conclusion than that Shakespeare intended to leave as little to the imagination as possible and to put upon the stage as gorgeous and complete a picture as the resources of the theatre could supply'.[16]

Following this reasoning every Shakespeare play had a passage or speech that demanded spectacle or pageantry. As additional proof Tree pointed out, in a majestic stroke of narrative closure, that Shakespeare could hardly have wished to slow up the action with long, undramatic passages of description. Obviously, Tree claimed, he'd been forced to supply these to make up for the deficiencies of the Renaissance theatre. In educational terms alone, opulent and impressive pageants were essential. They allowed history to be accurately depicted in an enjoyable and accessible way. For the middle-class audiences of the Victorian era Shakespeare brought their past to life.

By the end of the century the use of archaeological research in painting, stagecraft and set design was a vital element in any production. The measure of a play's success became dependent on the accuracy and conviction with which it was seen to capture the feel of a particular period. Certainly, by this time, a Shakespeare performance was unthinkable without the costumes from the era in which the play was set. The artist and designers embarked upon a quest for realism that involved precise research into the ephemera of everyday life in ancient times. Many directors, in flourishes of publicity, hired antiquarians to ensure that the details were correct. For the 1877 The merchant of Venice at the Prince of Wales Theatre, the producers dispatched the stage designer to Venice to study and draw the locations mentioned in the play.

Expeditions like these were expensive, so much of the research used to depict the past was taken from paintings. Works created during the period in question were an obvious source as well as those painted by contemporary genre artists who specialised in historically accurate pictures. Eventually famous narrative painters began to design sets for the theatre. The most renowned was Sir Lawrence Alma-Tadema who specialised in historically authentic scenes of 'everyday life' in classical times. He worked on Irving's Cymbeline (1896-7) and Coriolanus (1901) and with Tree for Julius Caesar (1898). Tree was perhaps the most vocal advocate of spectacular Shakespeare. In 'Henry VIII and his court' he declared that 'not the least important mission of the modern theatre is to give to the public representations of history which shall be at once an education and a delight. To do this the manager shall avail himself of the best archaeological and artistic help his generation can afford him, while endeavoring to preserve what he believes to be the spirit and intention of the author.'[17]

Henry VIII had been treated as an excuse for sumptuous and lavish productions since the time of Kean. Tree astutely preceded his version with a press conference in which it was claimed he was setting out 'to

give an absolute reproduction of the Renaissance'.[18] Certainly the cast
and production team spared no expense in creating an unparalleled
display of pageantry. Cardinal Wolsey's entrance in the first scene was
accompanied by a procession of twenty-nine attendants and hardly a
scene passed without a similar display of authentic costumes and
artifacts.

Tree's remarks on Shakespeare's 'intention' throw light on the role
of Shakespeare in popular British culture after the Theatre Suitability
Act. As far as theatre or painting were concerned all links with the radical
and alienated intellectuals of the early nineteenth-century had been
severed. Instead it was the establishment that had the greatest investment in the performances of this era. To begin with, the notion of
spectacle was seen as an affirmation of the brilliance of British technology
(stage designers and builders often needed considerable mechanical
and engineering knowledge). Tree's pageants existed on the relatively
unambitious edge of an industry capable of using gas, electricity and
mechanics to simulate volcanoes, floods, shipwrecks and mining dis-
asters. Furthermore, when Shakespeare was encoded within the value
system of Victorian culture, and then appropriated by directors like
Tree, the supposedly eternal and timeless visions of the Bard were
remarkably in step with British imperial ideology. As with narrative
paintings and Lamb's *Tales*, historically authoritative performances were
used to emphasise and endorse the ethics of nineteenth-century
capitalism. At the same time directors and critics could point out that
associated values like progress, endeavour, civilisation etc. were expressions of an ahistorical wisdom because they appeared in great literature
written three centuries before. Spectacles and tableaux vivants lent
themselves particularly well to this form of propaganda. The final tableau
from Tree's *The tempest* not only demonstrates the use of dumb spectacle
to convey the basic 'meaning' of the text, but it also shows how selective
editing of the play, combined with carefully structured imagery,
mobilised the play in support of the political and colonial status quo:
'we see the ship sailing away, carrying Prospero and the lovers, and all
their train. Caliban creeps from his cave, and watches the departing ship
bearing away the freight of humanity which for a brief spell has saddened
and gladdened his island home, and taught him to 'seek for grace' . . .
The play is ended. As the curtain rises again, the ship is seen on the
horizon, Caliban stretching his arms towards it in mute despair. The
night falls, and Caliban is left on the lonely rock. He is a king once
more.'[19]

Tree's stage interpretations of Shakespeare at the Haymarket and Her

Majesty's Theatre were famous for their pageantry, historical accuracy and educational value. They were the culmination of a century of spectacular Victorian theatre and they marked the successful commercialisation of the plays in the theatre and their subordination to the ethics of the British empire. There were occasional complaints from critics grown weary of interminable costume processions, and a few experimental performances given on bare or abstract stages. Nevertheless Tree's work summed up the quintessential nineteenth-century understanding of the plays as unmediated visions of history. He enjoyed enormous popular success and his audiences were considerable.

Although *Henry VIII* was Tree's greatest commercial triumph, his version of the problematic *King John* is also very important for the study of Shakespeare film. Records are scanty and there is no original print left in existence, but the first Shakespearean film ever made was of a fragment of Tree's production of this play.

When British Shakespearean cinema started, in 1898, the plays were very firmly situated in industrial middle-class culture. Despite radical appropriations a hundred years before, Shakespeare had apparently lost all associations with the disaffected intellectualism of the Romantic movement. The conglomeration of narratives, texts, episodes and images that constituted Victorian Shakespeare had been swiftly absorbed into a new consumer society and recreated as commodities for a literate theatre-going public.

This picture is deceptively simple because it ignores two important factors. Firstly the reconstruction of Shakespeare as a national poet on the stage, in art and in edited narratives was only possible after substantial reworking of the text to remove any ambiguous and potentially dangerous material. Yet all the establishment could do was to marginalise this along with any 'radical' interpretations. This part of Shakespeare still existed, ready to be appropriated by the British and European Symbolists when they attempted to defy the vulgar materialism of the orthodox stage. Secondly the supposed transformation of the Romantic consciousness into a mere poetic motif had not led to the reconciliation of the intellectual with industrial society. This was yet to be fully addressed. In England Shakespeare's role in this debate would be fitful. Unlike in Japan or Russia he was too much a part of the educational and artistic establishment to offer a truly revolutionary art. Nevertheless in British film versions of Shakespeare made this century there exists an uneasy and problematic undercurrent of Romantic rebelliousness which resists any attempt to establish the spectacular, historically accurate production as the standard for Shakespearean film. Here, possibly, lies part of the explanation for the controversies surrounding the movies produced in England since the beginning of this century, and the notorious BBC Shakespeare series.

# Silent Shakespeare and British cinema

## The birth of early British cinema: theoretical perspectives

As far as individual genius goes, it soon becomes evident that individual achievement is basically a forcing ground of certain historical developments and that it is always itself forced by certain historical conditions' Michael Chanan.[1]

Considerable work has been done on the early history of British cinema. Much of this has followed the pattern of orthodox film criticism by isolating the genre from its cultural and political context and treating the appearance of cinema as the spontaneous invention of a handful of men. The camera came first, so the argument goes, then the discovery of how to use it to create films and, ultimately, how to make those films in the 'correct' way. If we accept this notion, that film in the 1890s was a radical, new and unexplored medium, then the relationship between the first Shakespeare films and the position of Shakespeare in the culture of the period is hard to determine. We can assume that the first movies, so often condemned for their 'theatricality', were merely experiments in high art made by film producers searching for new material. There is a degree of truth in this. But what this approach fails to address is the remarkable persistence of this style of film production. It was used long after the static, theatrical methods of editing had been replaced by the more dynamic and narrative-based methods of the North American producers. It reappears in the Shakespeare films of Laurence Olivier in the 1940s and 1950s. Even more significantly it surfaces in the BBC/Time Life series of Shakespeare videos that were made in the late 1970s.

We have seen how the apparent coherence of late Victorian Shakespeare production belies a history composed of a wide range of political and economic struggles. These occurred in a variety of media: the theatre; the novel; painting and radical philosophy. The spectacular productions of actor-managers like Tree not only marked a synthesis of these various fields but also the attempted dissociation of the plays from the more complex and alienated perceptions of the earlier Romantic movement. This process of amalgamation; the linking of disparate areas of cultural, political and economic development, is not only central to a radical understanding of Shakespeare and Shakespeare film, but also to film history in general. Both these subjects can only be explored fully once we move beyond the apparent history; the events, dates and names, to look at the social relationships that throw these factors into relief. Raymond Williams, in calling for a new critical methodology in his essay 'British film history: new perspectives', states this quite categorically, concluding that 'in any full assessment of history it is necessary to be aware that . . . temporary and provisional indications of attention and emphasis – of "subjects" – can never be mistaken for independent and isolated processes and products.'[2]

Michael Chanan has used this approach to try and create a materialist history of the inception of British film. In his book *The dream that kicks: the prehistory and early years of cinema in Britain* (1980) he points out that despite the glorification of late Victorian inventors as amateur scientists their activities were symptomatic of the overall development of Britain's industrial economy. As the production method of each of the components of early cinema was perfected (the camera, celluloid, precision machine-manufactured shutter mechanisms etc.) those involved became embroiled in various rivalries concerning the filing of patents. The establishing of sole rights to an idea or invention is, quite simply, an attempt to monopolise a market. British manufacturers, at this time, were still basing their working practices on such out-dated competitive principles. Businesses in America were already implementing co-operative and scientific management practices. In Britain, now in the grip of an industrial decline, entrepreneurs continued to use practices established in the early half of the century. They were reluctant to invest in new methods once a steady flow of capital had been established. The arrival of cinema in England occurred at that moment when the material, economic and political forces of commercial capitalism had reached the stage that 'fragments and divides and . . . leaves the business of co-operation virtually to chance, that is, to the influence of the market'.[3] Thus the process that brought together photography, celluloid manufacture, precision lenses, the magic lantern and dioramas appeared to occur on an individual level, rather than through the joint creation of a new market by different industries.

Because he regards the creators of film as, in reality, synthesisers, Chanan uses Lévi-Strauss's term *bricolage* He adapts it to refer to the experimental bringing together of technologies and skills to create the first film equipment. This is also applicable to the process of compilation at a cultural level; the gathering together and adapting of already established aesthetic concepts or structures to create something new. We have already seen how this worked with Victorian Shakespeare production. Chanan also uses it to locate the cultural origins of film. The ability of cinema to project moving figures and to create a fictitious, enclosed world wasn't revolutionary. Since the 1820s audiences had been visiting diorama shows in which light was manipulated to give the illusion of passing time. Similarly, at magic lantern shows, intricate levers and quick slide changes were used to give the illusion of movement. There is little difference between the cultural position of these and the very first films, merely an increase in the sophistication of the production techniques. Chanan also locates the production and consumption of the first movies alongside the development of the music hall, the popular magazines of the period and the scientific and educational lectures in the Mechanics Institutes and Broad-Church-funded workers colleges. He suggests that the films that encapsulated and sanitised the world for bourgeois audiences, or warned the working classes against the evils of drink, functioned at the same level as the illustrated articles of the newspapers and magazines. Similarly photographic sequences which echoed the music hall skits gave way to comic films, which were then shown as part of an evening's entertainment at the halls.

The first Shakespeare films weren't part of the mainstream of British cinema: the plays belonged to the more sophisticated world of the theatre rather than the music hall. Even so they sprang from the same synthesising process as the rest of the movies made during the last few years of the nineteenth century. The first two, King John and the shipwreck scene from The tempest, are classic cases of bricolage; experiments in creating a new commodity through the combination of various pre-established forms.

## The first films

In the last few months of the nineteenth century Tree presented his version of Shakespeare's King John at Her Majesty's Theatre. Tree's version was one in a line of triumphant Shakespeare productions and it ran intermittently until January of the following year, drawing an audience of over one hundred and seventy thousand people. In keeping with the tradition of Victorian theatre this production combined all that was to be expected in a play directed by one of the leading British actor-managers. It was a vivid and impressive mixture of finely realised historical detail, pageantry and silent, 'painterly' composition. Tree took Shakespeare's play and inserted it into his own version of medieval history. Where the text was found wanting he fleshed out the chronological gaps with processions and additional scenes. The final product was less of a play than a sequence of set tableaux and events used to mark out historical episodes in the forging of British imperial democracy.

According to one theatre critic who went to see King John such visions marked the triumph of antiquarian research and historical accuracy. He pointed out that the problematic text, for all its structural incoherence, was of minor significance because 'Mr Beerbohm Tree has done the best thing possible in the circumstances by cutting away the superfluous matter, arranging the piece in three acts, and by a succession of splendid tableaux, giving us a grand idea of the pomp and circumstance of war and politics in the thirteenth century.'[4]

The tableaux vivants created for King John show how the relationship between narrative art and drama echoed the development of the diorama and the scenic photograph. For the battle sequences the settings were built out of flats that incorporated painted figures. When the players posed amid the scenery the illusion of a vast and chaotic crowd was created. This technique implies a drift towards the removal of the visual separation between the players and the scenery; and the concomitant distancing of the audience. The effect aimed for was the generation of a field of signs that imitated a painted surface, framed by the theatre's proscenium arch. When successful this type of set design eliminated the distinction between the moving actors and the static background.

The most magnificent part of the evening was a meticulously researched tableau which showed King John signing the Magna Carta. Following the argument that Shakespeare was, above all, educational, Tree has inserted this to cover an important historical omission in the text. The signing of the Magna Carta was a favourite subject for genre artists and a powerfully symbolic event in British liberal mythology. The victory of the feudal lords over their cruel leader King John was seen as a mirror of the social reforms instigated during the early nineteenth century. It represented a corrupt and despotic government vanquished by the 'people'.

Through the recreation of this event Tree's play transformed history into a series of images in which the imitation of external, visual reality was the prime goal. A static tableau vivant eliminated any sense of conflict or dialogue from history. It also, with its concentration on scientific accuracy, suggested that the image seen was the total and final truth. Film, because it supposedly captured such images without mediation, enforced this idea.

Despite the success of Tree's stage production of King John, the first Shakespeare film made in Britain wasn't a commercial venture. Tree, interested in the new invention, experimented with cinema for his own personal entertainment. The film of King John hasn't survived and there are no official records to show whether it was ever showed to a paying audience. Even so, using our knowledge of the play and the descriptions of the filming, it is possible to piece together a reasonably accurate impression of what Tree's first Shakespeare movie consisted of.

He supervised the filming on the north bank of the Thames, near Adelphi Terrace. At this time film manufacturers were still having difficulties making stock of consistent quality. Therefore movies, at the most, consisted of a single reel that lasted only a few minutes. Although we have no definite idea as to which part of the play Tree chose to film, Ball in *Shakespeare on silent film* makes a significant guess: 'the site on the Embankment gives the clue. There was greenery and the Thames, an approximation to Runnymede. The tableau of the granting of the Magna Carta needed no words, only pantomime for its effects.'[5] If we consider the film in the context of Victorian Shakespeare production then Ball's assumptions are quite reasonable. Tree's film of *King John* marked the final synthesis of genre painting and the active spectacles and tableaux of the stage. It combined a realistic evocation of British history with wordless, composed imagery, presenting Shakespeare drama in the form of a moving 'picture'. In this way Tree's movie marks the start of a style of cinema that developed directly from the Victorian theatre; from an essentially visual art in which the action was framed by a proscenium arch, to one composed according to the proportions of the camera's field of vision.

Tree's next film provides further evidence that Shakespeare film, at the moment of its inception, combined the drama, art and narrative of the melodramatic theatre with early film. In 1903 Charles Urban collaborated with Tree to record the shipwreck scene from his production of *The tempest*. One of the original intentions was to use the brief vignette to project a spectacular set piece on stage during the actual performance of the play. Throughout the previous century theatre mechanics and designers devoted more and more time to creating floods, train crashes and horse races on stage. Nautical melodrama continually demanded impressive battles and shipwrecks. As early as 1804 the Sadler's Wells Theatre was presenting sea engagements using models in a large tank of water. Like the painted figures in *King John* these models were used to break down the spatial boundaries of the theatre. They were symptomatic of a quest for greater 'realism' which demanded the illusion of an infinite fictitious world of which the stage was merely a part. Gas-powered volcanoes, treadmills and carefully engineered explosions provided the audiences with believable images of events that couldn't logically exist in a small auditorium.

Cinema provided a feasible alternative to this awkward and cumbersome technology, especially when the company took their production on tour. The rationale behind the film was that it would act as a convenient substitute for the original spectacle. However this is not to say that the camera was viewed as a superior vehicle for impressive effects. Orthodox Shakespeare film criticism tends to assume that the camera, by its very nature, is capable of a depth of realism unknown in the theatre. Consequently, so the argument goes, the overt artificiality of 'theatrical' cinema is bad. This argument is often used to attack the silent movies of Shakespeare performances that were popular in England before World War I. Examples like The tempest challenge this idea. Far from reading the movie as a wonderfully realistic portrayal of a shipwreck, audiences understood it as a film of a theatrical spectacle. The trade journal description even implies that the effect of the apparatus used on stage was better than that of the film. Above all the writer was anxious to stress the ability of cinema to capture the power of the original scenery, the journal points out that the tinted version 'greatly heightens the wonderful effect of what is unquestionably one of the greatest triumphs of stage production ever attempted'.[6] As well as providing special effects for Tree's company when it was on tour, the finished film was shown separately, as a work in its own right. Later, when producers in England were adopting theatrical styles in an attempt to capture a more respectable audience, several combined cinematography with live drama. In 1907 Covent Garden showed the Graphic Cinematographic Company's The ride of the Valkyrie as part of a stage presentation.

## A too artistic craze

While Tree's King John and Urban's The tempest can certainly be classed as experiments; the sensing out of possible new markets, in the short term neither of these productions led to the establishment of a Shakespeare film genre. For this to happen there would need to be a definitive and enclosed cultural perception of film as a medium distinct from any other. Without this there was a danger that the creation of genres would dissolve the components of the cultural synthesis responsible for the early film idiom back into their respective origins. A film of a scene, like Urban's movie of the shipwreck from The tempest, was hovering on an uneasy dividing line between the cinema market and the theatre; it had no specific audience. Once cinema was regarded, (however inaccurately) as a unique medium, then it was possible to apply it to different subjects or situations without any undue fear of it losing its institutional coherence. At this point genre films became economically viable because they were understood as a diversification of a specific kind of popular entertainment, with a pre-established market.

In the 1900s film making was largely a magpie industry that used images, structures and concepts from a whole host of different areas. It reproduced these in the form of a single brief image, illusion or situation; narrative-based editing didn't appear until much later. Tree's *King John* was an image from history, Urban's film; a single special effect from the play. Both of these worked on the same level as the 'magical' films of R. W. Paul; showing the audiences what Chanan refers to as the visual equivalent to a music hall gag. Films of a few minutes were not an adequate medium for storytelling. As Victorian Shakespeare was narrative-based there was no scope for reproducing recognisable versions of the plays until the first years of the twentieth century. Then a new process of film making enabled manufacturers to achieve consistent quality of stock for greater lengths. No longer limited to the single reel, film makers turned to fiction to provide them with ideas.

This move was combined with the economic consolidation of the film market after a spate of particularly vicious price wars. Board of Trade figures show that between 1908 and 1912 the number of film companies in Britain increased from three to nearly five hundred. These producers, and their distributors, not only found themselves in keen competition with each other, but they, and more morally righteous sectors of middle-class society, began to perceive a threat emerging in the 1900s from across the Atlantic. Suspicion of things American; rumours of a flood of mass-produced culture invading Britain's movie theatres, were symptomatic of a fear of an American monopoly in the European cinema industry. Economic nostalgia for a never-never land of gentlemanly business manifested itself in a deliberate drive up-market, away from the music halls and penny gaffs, towards the establishment of more respectable middle-class cinemas. In 1907 the first picture house opened in Balham. Although it still retained the piecemeal programmes of the music halls it had the atmosphere and decor of a small theatre.

Subsequently, for many years, both in Britain and throughout the Empire, American cinema was branded as a spiritually pernicious type of entertainment. Many English officials felt that the movie industry of the United States, seemingly obsessed with criminal life, violence and unholy passions, undermined the influence of traditional English values throughout the colonies. Some high-minded people even suggested that children would debase their mother tongue by using American slang they had read in the subtitles. After a fire at a film show in Barnsley, in which sixteen children died, the Cinematographic Act was passed. Chanan points out that, like the Theatre Suitability Act, this allowed councils to refuse licences under the guise of enforcing stringent safety standards. Any cinemas that showed unsuitable films were closed down. Film producers like Hepworth & Company escaped official disapproval by turning out a series of movies that symbolically displayed pro-imperial propaganda. They produced many short films that were the cinematic equivalents of political cartoons. In one (a rather ironic example given the circumstances) John Bull argued for fair trade agreements with other nations. They were also responsible for various vignettes from the Boer War.

The boom in Shakespeare film was sparked off by the American company Vitagraph, which made Macbeth in 1908. Now that longer films could be made, North American film producers (also searching for respectability) experimented with adaptations of famous stories. However, copyright posed difficulties, as the Kalem film company found out in 1905 when they were sued by the heirs of Lew Wallace for making a film of Ben Hur. As Shakespeare wasn't copyrighted his plays provided a pool of material for narrative films. As an attempt to associate cinema with art Macbeth was a limited success. Nevertheless, with impressive speed and efficiency, Vitagraph made a further six Shakespeare movies in the space of twelve months, Romeo and Juliet, Othello, King Richard III, Antony and Cleopatra, Julius Caesar and The merchant of Venice. Running lengths were between ten and twenty minutes. Towards the end of the series the productions became noticeably more theatrical. The acting and sets were increasingly used to evoke the illusion of a staged performance. Ball, in Shakespeare and silent film, claims this represents a decline in quality because Shakespeare movies that were theatrical were not exploiting the medium of cinema. Yet the historical evidence suggests that, for a film to be successfully associated with the reproduction of Shakespeare in respectable middle-class culture, it had to imitate the theatre experience.

Of the Vitagraph films the most interesting is Romeo and Juliet. As it was only the second in the series the American film turned the play into a narrative set in a generalised landscape that was intended to represent (rather than faithfully duplicate) Verona. It was shot outdoors in parts of New York and relied on the use of sequential editing to establish a coherent and linear plot. In the same year the British firm Gaumont recorded Godfrey Tearle's production of the play that was currently running at the Lyceum. Whether this was in direct response to the American movie is uncertain, but the differences between the films underline the nature of the economic struggle between the two industries. Unlike its American counterpart, the Gaumont movie specifically set out to capitalise on the respectability of a stage 'classic', providing an accurate simulation of the theatre experience for those people who presumably had little access to it. As with Urban's film of the shipwreck scene from *The tempest*, the audiences who saw the Gaumont *Romeo and Juliet* were not concerned with the recreation of reality or the use of editing to create an atmosphere. As one critic exclaimed, 'the production of *Romeo and Juliet* is so finely accurate in its leading details, and the scenery, costumes and acting so realistic that we sit and forget for the time that we are looking at the kinematographic art, *but fancy ourselves seated in a theatre* [my emphasis].[7]

Because of its association with a renowned stage production, *Romeo and Juliet* could bask in the elitism of a highly developed aesthetic tradition. It could also claim to be instructive and improving to those unfamiliar with such culture. In England it became part of a trend towards educational films. In an attempt to confound the moralists, film companies were stressing the cultural benefits of their work more and more. The same year that the Gaumont *Romeo and Juliet* appeared the Urban company included the banner 'Urbanora the world's educator' in their catalogue. Their historical section included biblical scenes and theatre pageants. By 1911 Bioscope was running regular editorials in their journal on the educational value of film. Education authorities responded eagerly to their ideas but nothing came of it in the end.

Other producers were quick to imitate the success of the Gaumont movie. The man who took the relationship between cinema and the theatre one step further to create one of the first true 'quality' films was William Barker who, in 1910, filmed Tree's stage production of *Henry VIII*. His plans for this magnificent performance were as grandiose as Tree's lavish pageantry. He paid the director a phenomenal amount of money, £1000, to appear in a film that was shot in a single day. He granted one distributor the sole right of rental, insisted on a higher admission price than normal, and withdrew the film after a specified length of time. Tragically all the reels were called in and ceremoniously burnt in front of a small crowd on 13 April 1911. Barker was setting out to award his film the same seal of cultured respectability as the stage version. In a publicity brochure for the movie Barker stated that it was a 'faithful, silent and permanent record of the wonderful, life-like portrayal and representation of some of the most important personages and incidents in the eventful history of England'.[8] Despite the claims that the production would be a permanent record of *Henry VIII* the film even aped the run of a play through Barker's bizarre insistence that all the copies be destroyed after a specified period.

It was largely due to Barker's *Henry VIII* that cost, exclusiveness and high dramatic art became associated with cinematic quality. The very notion of an expensive film with a limited run challenged the mass-production techniques used by the American cinema industry to churn out large numbers of cheaply-produced movies. However, despite the educational benefits that such a film supposedly provided, the high admission fees discriminated against the very class at which such instructive works were supposedly aimed. The primary appeal of Barker's film (and indeed of most of the early 'quality' films) was its elitism. Only those who knew of Shakespeare, who felt themselves to be the consumers of a culture in which he was a significant commodity, and who could socially and intellectually identify with an audience capable of recognising Hans Holbein's portrait of the King, would fully appreciate the experience of watching Barker's version. The film production of *Henry VIII* belonged to a tradition of silent, visual and melodramatic Shakespeare productions that began in England in the eighteenth century. It was a wholly national idiom which had little relation to the type of films being made in the United States.

Between 1907 and 1912 there was an international boom in Shakespeare film production. In England the manufacturers, following Barker's lead, concentrated on making movies based on famous stage productions. In 1911 the Co-op Cinematographic Company began a series of movies with the help of F. R. Benson's theatre company. In April of that year they released three films taken from his theatre's productions of *Julius Caesar*, *Macbeth* and *The taming of the shrew*. Their fourth film together, *King Richard III*, has long been regarded as a *bête noir* by cinema criticism. It has acquired a certain notoriety, chiefly through the work of writers like Rachel Low who attacked the film in her BFI-sponsored history of early British cinema: 'It would probably not be unfair to say that *Richard III* represents the pre-1914 stage adaptations at their worst . . . It shows not the slightest appreciation of the possibilities of film making, ignoring not only the obvious advantage of performing outdoor scenes out of doors, but even those elements of continuity and editing known at the time and employed all over the world in the most humdrum little films.'[9]

Low's reasoning behind her attack on *King Richard III*, and her concept of 'good' cinema, show how retrospective histories of Shakespearean cinema seek to give authority to one type of production by excluding, marginalising or simply ignoring variant forms. Low was working in a historical tradition that was narrative-based, that viewed the growth of film as a process of natural development. In this scheme *King Richard III*, and films like it, were immature because they didn't use the correct editing methods. Yet if we locate the two kinds of film making, North American and English, in their historical context then what we see is two specific cultural perceptions of cinema vying for dominance in an as-yet unexplored market.

The standards by which Low judges *King Richard III* are the methods of editing and spatial organisation developed in North America in the first two decades of the twentieth century. These became enshrined as the 'Hollywood codes of editing'. Burch characterises these as a narrative-based manipulation of filmic space which is intended to give the impression that the area of the diegesis is spatially coherent. To give an example; a character exiting one room will appear in the adjacent one wearing the same clothes, just as in real life. Furthermore the action follows a definite temporal sequence. Using this standard, an ideal film would make the screen as 'transparent' as possible to an audience educated to regard the depiction of reality as the ultimate artistic triumph.

The 'language of film' that was developed from this method of production demands a mobile camera, one which penetrates the dramatic space and is capable of following the protagonists in a narrative through their world. *King Richard III* uses a static camera. The film is set entirely on a stage and the audience's viewpoint never moves from its position at right angles to the backcloth. There seems to have been a deliberate attempt to make the theatrical methodology explicit. The film is notable for the predominantly empty foregrounds and, in several cases, the footlights and stage boards are clearly visible. The crowds cluster together in theatrical groupings and almost always face the camera. The acting styles are extravagant, F. R. Benson and the other players draw on the full repertoire of melodramatic expressions and gestures. The sets are two-dimensional, in many instances the bottom of the backcloth can be seen. There are no close-ups in the Co-op movie, or any other recognisable filmic devices that could be used to focus on the emotions of the characters. The film isn't cut to accomodate the pace of the story and, most significantly, outdoor scenes are shot on the same stage as the indoor ones. Instead of trying to make the images as visually persuasive as possible the cardboard sets and stylised acting techniques continually draw attention to the means of the film's production and the fact that what the audience are watching is a play; a wholly artificial construct.

The movie is thirty minutes long and each of the seventeen scenes is preceded by a title showing a brief description of what is about to happen and one or two lines of dialogue from the relevant part of the text: 'Title 17: Lord Mayor of London offers crown to Richard, which he reluctantly accepts. Title 18: "Then I salute you with this royal title, long live King Richard, England's worthy King." '[10] In films made according to the stan-

Richard III (1911)

dards set by D. W. Griffiths and the Hollywood studios title cards were supposed to be part of an internal diegetic narrative. They offered an anticipation of continuity by linking scenes or summarising dialogue. The cards quoted above, in the context of the film, don't really do this. The first one, in effect, describes a whole incident which the film then re-enacts visually, the second merely emphasises what the audience know already. They are offering indications of an anecdote which the viewer then constructs while watching the images. Yet even with the descriptions and excerpts from the text the movie follows no immediately obvious sequence; many times the actors deliver their lines without any explanation being offered via the title cards. The long scene in which Clarence is murdered and then dragged off-screen is particularly obscure and must have appeared incomprehensible to an audience unfamiliar with the play.

King Richard III has an unusually high number of cards which would suggest that the directors are struggling to maintain the central position of the text in a hostile environment. This impression endorses the argument that silent film is an inadequate medium for Shakespeare because no one can be heard speaking the lines. This is an argument that Low, Jorgens and others use to imply that the main problem for King Richard III, and indeed for any film made before 1927, is the lack of sound. The most the actors could do in these early years was to mouth the text while title cards supplied the occasional quotation. At the same time the players were forced to fall back on the language of gesture. Subtlety of expression gave way to grandiose and stylised arm-waving and face-pulling.

Why did this style of film making, which many critics have castigated as regressive and non-cinematic, persist in England? America was forging ahead with its consolidation of narrative-based editing techniques, pioneered by movies like Edwin Porter's The great train robbery (1903). British film makers were certainly not unfamiliar with narrative film making or outdoor shooting, as Rescued by Rover (Hepworth, 1905) demonstrates. As far as Shakespeare was concerned the reasons for the persistence of this kind of movie production and editing were economic. A cut-throat battle for the film market was being waged between the chief industrial countries of Europe and North American during the 1900s. At home British manufacturers were frantically searching for some defence against the gradual encroachment of American melodramatic narratives into the country's cinemas. The answer appeared to lie in the creation of a unique and distinctive national film idiom. Shakespeare, or, more specifically, Victorian Shakespeare production, was an ideal expression of a uniquely English, high-class culture. Thus it provided an eminently suitable subject for British cameras. In this context *King Richard III* isn't a primitive film at all. The descriptive title cards provide the clue, what we are seeing when we watch this film is a series of tableaux vivants or 'living pictures'; a gallery of illustrations drawn from a famous Shakespeare play.

The boom in theatrical and 'painterly' English Shakespearean cinema fizzled out between 1912 and World War I. In the wake of threats of state censorship, leading producers within the film industry set up the British Board of Film Censors. To stave off any direct government interference this dedicated itself to monitoring all films for any hint of moral danger. With the appearance of this committee many of the reasons for making quality Shakespeare films disappeared. They no longer had any real market. The cinema in England had consciously awarded itself the social respectability that producers like Barker and the Co-op company had striven to adopt through the production of high-class films adapted from stage classics. On a more unhappy note the quality film genre itself was overwhelmed by the stylistic and economic influence of the North American film industry. In the *Kinematograph and lantern weekly* for 9 April 1914 a reviewer voiced dissatisfaction with the intellectual pretensions of the quality films. In castigating Shakespeare films as an esoteric artistic craze he indicated a popular trend towards imported movies.

Certainly in Britain by 1913 Shakespearean subjects were being transformed into films using narrative-based, realistic production codes. On the surface the intention behind the movie of John Forbes-Robertson's version of *Hamlet* (which was filmed that year for Gaumont) reiterated the aims of Barker and the Co-op series. Yet, although it was based on the renowned actor's final performance at Drury Lane, it avoided any conscious acknowledgement of the methodology of spectacular Shakespearean theatre. There were no tableaux vivants and the outdoor scenes of the play were filmed on location at such picturesque places as Lulworth Cove and Hartsbourne Manor. In the final movie the landscapes are as vague as the stylised Verona of the Vitagraph *Romeo and Juliet*. The movie is constructed as a narrative with scenes interpolated to fill the supposed 'gaps' in Shakespeare's text. The accent is on naturalism, as opposed to the historical realism of *King Richard III*. Ultimately *Hamlet* owes more to the tradition of the Vitagraph and Kalem films than to the Victorian theatre.

In 1915 D. W. Griffiths brought out a film that, with its huge budget, grandiose imagery and moral didacticism, underscored cinema's pretension towards high-class culture. More significantly, films like *Birth of* a nation and, later, Intolerance (1916) marked the consolidation of the 'Hollywood codes of editing' as the basic 'language' of international film. World War I effectively destroyed movie production in Europe, leaving the North American firms with a clear market to exploit after peace was declared in 1918. It wasn't until the 1930s that British cinema was sufficiently confident to try once more to establish itself as a medium for national identity. Not surprisingly Laurence Olivier's film of Henry V, made during a period when the British nation was at its most isolated, consciously recreated the structure and atmosphere of the Shakespeare films of the silent era and, through them, the glorious patriotic spectacles of the Victorian stage.

## A tradition fragmented: Laurence Olivier's Henry V

During the early twentieth century the influence of recent radical changes in stagecraft in Europe, and the growing popularity of Modernism in the theatre, eclipsed the pageantry of directors like Tree. Nevertheless, the association of Shakespeare with an idealised representation of history still persisted. In the 1930s, when an attempt was made to revitalise the nation's cinema, many of the films made were uncannily similar in tone and treatment to that of the silent 'quality' films, especially Barker's 1911 recording of Tree's Henry VIII. The success of Alexander Korda's The private life of Henry VIII (1933) was due largely to its very Victorian evocation of a mythical 'merrie England'. The film was one in an intended series of historical biographies but when Korda followed it with a film about the foreign painter Rembrandt he suffered badly at the box office.

Despite the use of Renaissance England as a source of material Shakespeare did not eventually resurface in British film until 1944 with Laurence Olivier's Henry V. Even so, many of the painterly, spectacular codes of representation used in the silent cinema made before World War I were recreated in this movie intact. For example; the scene where King Henry rallies his troops before Harfleur, with its cramped set, massed crowds and picturesque naturalism, could have come straight from the spectacular stage. Certainly the situation in besieged England during the early 1940s was ideally suited to a revival of the patriotic style of presentation used in the movies of Barker and Benson. Like Barker's Henry VIII Olivier's film pandered to the cultural pretensions of its audience. It supported the mythical idea of a wholly integrated British literary culture in which Shakespeare was as meaningful to the masses as the songs of

Henry V (1942)

TC18·126

Vera Lynn. During the early days of the war Olivier began a series of radio broadcasts in which he read excerpts from Shakespeare. The idea for a film of Henry V developed from his transmission of a number of patriotic passages from the play. The movie began production in 1942 as a Two Cities film, produced by Fillipo Del Guidice.

Like the Victorian actor-managers, Olivier and the other script writers (Alan Dent and Dallas Bower) omitted a number of scenes. Their intention was to simplify the character of King Henry by removing any speeches that cast doubt on either his character or his motives. They edited out the threats to sack Harfleur, Bardolph's death, the murder of the French prisoners, and the English traitors, along with other ambiguous passages. Finally, having whitewashed Henry's character, the makers of the film dedicated it to the armed forces. Nevertheless the ideological stance adopted in the film is significantly different to that in Tree's productions. Henry V has a more liberal ethos than the silent Shakespeare films: one of its key themes is that history belongs to an idealised 'common people'. The film starts in Elizabethan times, at the Globe Theatre where the cast is preparing to show Shakespeare's play. From there it moves into a semi-fantastic world modelled after the style of medieval paintings. The designers of the sets for Henry V based them of the pictures of the medieval artist Pol de Limbourg. The non-naturalistic scale and absence of post-Renaissance fixed-point perspective were faithfully recreated. The overall impression is of an idealised and symbolic beauty, especially during the scenes set in Agincourt village and at the palace at Rouen. From this lyrical world Henry V moves into the central set piece, the night before the battle and the actual fighting at Agincourt. The structural development is then reversed, the camera moves back through the composed beauties of de Limbourg's Book of hours and ends back at the Globe Theatre where the players bring their performance to a close.

Yet into this complex re-assertion of the British spectacular tradition there intrudes a number of disruptive elements which contradict and undermine its heavily determined and somewhat anachronistic characteristics. In several sections in the film stylistic inconsistencies undercut the unity of the film, transforming it into a jumble of different structures. The two most significant are; the influence of the nascent theories of Expressionist stagecraft and cinematic montage, and the fact that Henry V is a sound film.

The Expressionist techniques of directors like Eisenstein shared many of the aesthetic and cultural roots of the British codes of representation used in melodrama, especially the desire to transcend the boundaries of fixed stage space. Yet they had developed as a reaction to the rigid naturalism of the spectacular theatre and its overwhelming reliance on the compositional techniques of genre painting. Thus the conflict between the theatrical *Book of hours* scenes, the formalised montage used to film the battle and the dream-like atmosphere of the night before Agincourt, seriously undermines the strong mythic cohesiveness of Olivier's film. Orson Welles summed up the conflict of styles by claiming that in *Henry V*, as far as he could see, one minute the characters conversed on a stage, the next they rode out in full armour on to a golf course.

The fact that Olivier's film has a soundtrack separates it from the movies produced in the first two decades of the twentieth century. Of course speech was nothing new to the audiences of *Henry V*: since 1927 they had been able to hear movie actors speak. yet the relationship between the film and the spoken text is an uneasy one. The reliance of the British spectacular tradition on visual codes of meaning made protracted dialogue and speech unnecessary. Indeed the Two Cities film of *Henry V*, like virtually all of the Shakespeare films produced before 1950, was made using a style of film production that hadn't yet adequately reconciled itself to the introduction of sound. As a result the production team are left championing two different causes. On the one hand the intricate visuals of the film need little of the text to complement their implicit reiteration of the spectacular tradition and the mythology of British wartime culture. On the other hand Oliver, and the producers of the movie, definitely perceive the text as the idealised source of meaning and so the speeches are delivered with the precise and measured enunciation of a BBC radio broadcast.

Ultimately the spoken word sits awkwardly with the images and, in many cases, illustrates, rather than integrates with, the film. Overall the effect is not clumsy; the oscillation between the fantasy world of the play and the Globe stage draws our attention away from the problematic content of some of the poetry, while rationalising the fact that all the characters speak in highly stylised and often incomprehensible verse. Elsewhere the text is regularly used in the same way as the title cards of the silent films; as indications of, or accompaniments to, a visual narrative or episode.

Olivier's *Henry V* contains all those qualities that characterised British Shakespeare production in the Victorian and Edwardian plays and films. Produced at a time when England was physically isolated from the rest of the world it reinforced the notion that Shakespeare's works represented, on a historical and allegorical level, the continual re-assertion of national, middle-class identity. In an enclosed piece of 'merrie England', signified by the reconstruction of the interior of the Globe Theatre, a group of common men acted out the trials and triumphs of a 'band of brothers' faced with a belligerent enemy.

After World War II the codes of representation drawn from the Victorian spectacular theatre no longer possessed powerful ideological and patriotic associations. Although Henry V and Hamlet were constructed from multiple sources; genre art, radio, melodrama and silent film, each field still had close connections with British literary and cinematic tradition. In the late 1940s and 1950s the disappearance of the sense of a homogeneous wartime culture meant that the style of film making used in Henry V no longer had the same emotional and ideological authority that it did in 1944. Although King Richard III, made in 1955, has much of the visual apparatus of a silent quality film it exists in a very diluted form. We only need to compare Olivier's portrayal of the hunchback king with F. R. Benson's, or see images from the Book of hours in the pastel fairy-tale costumes, to be aware of the connection. Yet gone is the pageantry, spectacle and the piling up of historical ephemera that characterises the earlier films. Instead the world of King Richard is made up of wide, flat sets punctuated by a few, heavily determined theatrical symbols; the throne, a suspended crown, a headsman's block. Olivier's evocation of a generalised stage space marks the transition point between patriotic films like Henry V and the more stylised productions of the BBC's very 'British' Shakespeare.

Laurence Olivier's films of Henry V, Hamlet and King Richard III represent the decline of the Victorian spectacular Shakespeare tradition in England. But this tradition was only one part of the overall development of Shakespeare film presentation before 1950. In Europe and, eventually, North America, an alternative style of drama and stagecraft was evolving. In the wake of Wagner's operas the revolutionary theories of people like Adolphe Appia and Gordon Craig created a new code of theatre aesthetics, different to the spectacles and tableaux of the Edwardian British performances. This was still a silent medium, one in which the unification of the human form and a plastic stage was attempted through the use of evocative and Expressionist lighting. Via the experiments of the Film D'Art the 'theatre of light' became translated into a highly symbolic form of cinema. In movies like Olivier's Hamlet certain elements of this new dramatic aesthetic appeared amid the more staid, melodramatic imagery, but this type of production was explored to a far more radical extent outside England.

## The BBC series

In a strictly formalist sense a comparison between the BBC TV Shakespeare series and film versions of the plays is coloured by perceived
differences between the medium of television and that of cinema. This
was stressed time and time again in the flood of critical articles and
discussions that the BBC series produced during the late 1970s. These
differences are not inate characteristics of the two media but of the
institutions that have brought them into existence and continue to determine their economic and ideological positions. Television and cinema
are wholly dissimilar and it is risky to gloss this over by including television representations in any analysis of cinema because it implies some
form of ahistorical unity. On the other hand neither are these two forms
of art hermetically sealed and as Shakespeare film compiles social and
cultural representations of the plays in theatre, literature and art so these
representations often re-appear on TV. The BBC series is an example of
this process: the videos displayed a perception of Shakespeare that
synthesised a wide range of cultural tropes.What is remarkable is that
this representation was extremely close to one manufactured in film
seventy years before. The aims behind the series, and the form and
content of the final product, bore remarkable resemblance to the British
silent films.

In the 1970s the BBC, with the backing of several American-based
multinationals, set out to record the entire dramatic works of Shakespeare on video. The productions were shown on British television
between 1978 and 1985. During this time the programmes excited a
considerable amount of controversy, fostering debates about the
relationship between Shakespeare and the screen. On the whole the
reaction to the series was unfavourable. Martin Banham, one year after
the series began, condemned the programmes as boring. Some years
later Graham Holderness, in a radical analysis of Shakespearean cinema,
saw the programmes as symptomatic of the suppression of the radical
potential of filmed Shakespeare by conservative education and broadcasting institutions.

Apart from the occasional radical article, one of the remarkable
features of the discussions surrounding the BBC series was the way in
which the arguments of the critics echoed Victorian debates about the
need for textual purity versus the economic and cultural desirability of
a plurality of representations. This conflict had resurfaced at regular

intervals since the appearance of the first Shakespeare films in Anglo-American culture. Anthony Davies has pointed out that a debate similar to this occurred between Harley Granville-Barker and Alfred Hitchcock and that their positions echoed identical opposing views voiced by Charles Lamb and Herbert Beerbohm Tree (who despite his claim to be an Edwardian Lamb, continually sacrificed the text to the image). Granville-Barker argued, like his predecessor, that any pictorial representation detracted from the poetry. Hitchcock suggested that such an approach was unrealistic and purist; that films of Shakespeare would be produced and would be made, first and foremost, as films and not as essays in textual criticism. Superficially this debate; between the need to retain textual purity, and the need to create good, marketable television, was seen as the main problem facing the producers of the BBC series. In the critical works that tackled the programmes the problems of the series were relocated as a tension between 'ideal' Shakespeare production and stolid 'worthy' BBC costume drama.

In the end the BBC versions were nowhere near the 'ideal' Shakespeare film. They were, on the whole, pedestrian and dull. Nevertheless they represented an attempt to encapsulate those qualities that are, by common consent in orthodox criticism, the ingredients of Shakespeare film at its best; reverence to the text, good acting in the classical tradition, a genuine feel for the 'spirit' of the play and an atmosphere that is quintessentially British.

This conflict between formula-based ideals; between the perceived 'good' Shakespeare production and the 'ideal' TV programme, concealed an economic struggle between conflicting notions of the relationship between the media (specifically television) and the mass market. There were three main structures that generated these perceptions of the social roles of Shakespeare, TV and the audience: the BBC and its associated position as a state-regulated educational broadcasting body; the four American-based multinationals who funded the series; and the artists and intellectuals called in to support the aesthetic and educational aims of the series and to direct the programmes themselves (Cedric Messina, Jonathan Miller, Jane Howell and others). What emerged from the synthesis (and conflict) generated by the combination of these three was a series of programmes remarkably similar in form, spirit and function of the silent Shakespeare films of the Edwardian era. One of the main goals behind the BBC project was the creation of a permanent library of tapes, copies of which would be sold to educational establishments all over the world. This emphasis on universalism manifested itself in rigid demands for a standardised product from the American backers, who drew up a set of guidelines for the producers. From even a cursory glance at these it's obvious that what is being recreated is the Victorian ideal of a high-class, historically 'accurate', character-centred (and by implication, narrative-based) Shakespeare. Each video was to have a famous actress or actor in a leading role and the action was to be set in the period and location of the play; ancient Rome for *Julius Caesar*, Renaissance Verona for *Romeo and Juliet*. The costumes had to be authentic, modern dress was out of the question. There were to be no provincial or strange accents (an essential requirement, it was felt, if the videos were going to be intelligible abroad). Finally any other potential deviation from these rules, radical or otherwise, was firmly discouraged by the catch-all ban on 'monkey tricks'.

The equation of period costume, historical authenticity, the 'BBC accent' and a famous name with a 'standard' Shakespeare suitable for international export is an interesting and revealing reflection on the position of the American-based multinational corporations involved. Armand Mattelart has examined at length the promotion of a specific culture by such economic giants in an attempt to unify a global market. The Shakespeare videos had to possess a coherent appearance because such uniformity implied a consistent quality and a specific product image which could be associated directly with mythical perceptions of British culture. The videos could only be bought as part of a complete set, putting them well out of the affordable price range of most individuals. A collection of varied and separately available interpretations would have thrown into question the supposedly coherent universalism of the orthodox understanding of Shakespeare's works and, by implication, undermined the hegemony of the economies involved in their marketing.

The processing of Shakespeare's plays into universal commodities caused no end of problems for the producers. Cedric Messina cited the problem of making the obscure Elizabethan jokes at the start of *Romeo and Juliet* intelligible to, for example, Mexican viewers. He argued the need for simplicity and straightforwardness. Yet in the end, because the 'straightforward' result imitated a specific Anglocentric, nineteenth-century perception of the play (as a romantic tale of two doomed lovers in Renaissance Verona) it would have been far less comprehensible and relevant to any community in South America than an adaptation produced there (or even the musical *West side story*). Because of the daunting task of meeting the sponsor's demands while creating intelligent and comprehensible versions of the plays, many of the directors who were invited to take part refused. In the end the series, far from being uniform, displayed many of the same tensions that can be seen in Shakespearean theatre and film production at the beginning of the twentieth century. In turn each of the directors involved strained to achieve a compromise between the dictates of the backers, the nature of the medium as they saw it, and their perception of the plays themselves.

The videos were conceived of as a product; great emphasis was placed on the fact that they were to be a uniform and enduring record of the plays. Yet they were made within the institutional framework of television. This is a state-controlled medium geared to the almost continual dissemination of information and culture in a journalistic format: 'broadcast TV offers relatively discrete segments: small sequential unities of image and sound organised into groups which are either simply cumulative, like news broadcast items or advertisements, or have some kind of repetitive or sequential connection, like the groups or segments that make up the serial or series.[11] Television is a continuous medium that is broadcast into the home. Culturally its frames of reference are based on the idealised, white middle-class family unit, which it uses as the focus for most of its drama. The early limitations of the technology, and the role of television as a commodity within the home, has meant that it has tended to work on a more intimate dramatic level, within small, enclosed sets, focusing on the day to day interactions of individuals.

This helps to explain the re-appearance of the silent film idiom in the BBC series. The episodic presentation of material is similar to that in the popular Victorian magazines and the sketches of the music hall, a method of representation that formed the basis for early cinema production. The pluralism of British television, (i.e. its continual output of variety, news, light entertainment, educational programmes, films etc.) imitates the context in which the early Shakespeare movies were produced and shown. Individual programmes or series 'compete' in a varied schedule that can embrace Shakespeare at one end of the scale of dramatic 'seriousness' and Tom and Jerry cartoons at the other. In other words, despite the transformation of TV programmes into isolated commodities in the form of videos, people's perception of them is still within the television context. On top of this the use of TV to disseminate government information, news and education makes it seem a far more 'naturalistic' medium than film. Structurally, any Shakespeare production on the small screen will be competing, as far as 'realism' is concerned, with news bulletins and wildlife programmes.

Some directors of the BBC Shakespeare programmes circumvented this problem by trying to make the plays naturalistic and, in doing so imitated the archaeological accuracy of the Victorian theatre. This caused inherent problems as the technical accomplishment that Tree and others strived for can now be achieved with relative ease. Consequently it has far less impact or significance. Others stylised the plays to the extent that they became obviously and directly separated from the realistic dictates of the medium. In the theatre this move led to the alienation that Brecht felt was vital to revolutionary theatre. On television the fact that what was being watched was a video of a Shakespeare play (i.e. a theatrical performance) automatically generated the disjunction between the viewer and the internal world of the drama, and simultaneously stripped it of any radical associations. The Expressionist, minimal sets of Jonathan Miller's King Lear were not dissimilar in intention from the mud flats Kozintsev used for Korol Ler. However, the straightforward camera work made it obvious what they really were; box TV sets. Even the stylised Shakespeare programmes were wholly realistic videos of a theatre experience. This is because the interpretation of Shakespeare was only permitted a broader scope of experimentation and radicalisation when it consciously adopted the apparatus of the theatre. Even then it was 'realistically' filmed as such, without the many and varied 'monkey tricks' that video is capable of, and which it has used to radical effect in other literary adaptations.

Jane Howell's production of Henry VI (broadcast during January 1983) is a case in point. The set used was an abstract, Expressionist one with forms consciously derived from modern urban landscapes (it was deliberately made to look like a boarded-up children's playground). Yet despite the radical, non-representational aspects of the performance, the handling of the camera and the structure of the programmes themselves continued to evoke an orthodox, passive evocation of 'worthy' theatre-based Shakespeare. As Neil Taylor pointed out, there was a separation between the 'theatre' set and the medium and this effectively eliminated any possibility of a wholly radical approach. Jonathan Miller's productions demonstrated the same disjunction between a stylised representation of the diegesis and the institutional orthodoxy of video. The question is how Miller and Howell were able to do this and comply with the overall aim of producing 'straightforward' Shakespeare videos. One answer is that the BBC series, like Barker's Henry VIII or Benson's King Richard III, sought aesthetic and intellectual prestige by attempting to simulate a high-class theatre. Despite the avowed egalitarian aims of the producers, stress was placed on cultivating an elitist atmosphere (for example: each programme was heralded by the words 'The British Broadcasting Corporation presents', as opposed to the usual acronym of 'BBC'.

In this way the BBC Shakespeare marked the resurgence of a tradition in British theatre and film production that was at its most popular during the late Victorian and early Edwardian periods. In the case of cinema the boom in this style of movie occurred during the silent era, between 1907 and 1912. During World War I it died out, chiefly because of the economic pressures imposed on the film industry during and after the conflict. It was revived towards the end of World War II with the films of Laurence Olivier, most notably *Henry V*. Then, between 1947 and 1980, its codes of representation became ossified in a few isolated Shakespeare movies before being finally used to create the BBC's 'standard' text-book videos. Despite the overwhelming significance attached to the text in Olivier's films and the BBC series the words and poetry were of minor importance for most of this tradition's history.

# PART II

# The theatre of light

We have made the curtain the fourth wall of realism. Are we now to see upon it more of reality than ever the stage could give? Or is it to be the theatre of imagination, of vigorous beauty, which has battled with realism for twenty years?.' Kenneth Macgowan.[1]

The combination of a powerful imperial ideology in retreat, and a culture that remained isolated from Europe during the second half of the nineteenth century, meant that the archaeologically realistic style of Shakespeare production in Britain survived well into the twentieth century. The development of the various images of the playwright and his plays, in the country's picture houses and theatres, was closely tied to the ideological and economic assaults on these British industries from North American film producers. All the paraphernalia of the Victorian stage; gesture, spectacle and tableaux vivants, were marshalled in the battle against mass-produced story films from the United States. Even after World War I, when the North American companies began to consolidate their hold on the European market, and narrative-based editing techniques and Expressionist-style photography started to intrude into the carefully preserved unity of British Shakespeare film, the movies were still largely created using the traditions of the painterly, silent tableau of the Victorian stage. Once the belief that Shakespeare was the author of historically authentic plays was firmly entrenched there was little change in the overall presentation and reception of Shakespeare as a subject for cultured, patriotic movies. Even now, although the position of British Shakespeare in the cinema industry has lost its authority or become fossilised in the medium of television, the assumption that it represents the standard and authoritative approach to the plays still persists. Most people have been brought up to equate Shakespeare with great British actresses and actors dressed in period costume and speaking in mellifluous accents.

Shakespeare's 'revival' at the start of the nineteenth century was largely the work of intellectuals, philosophers and writers seeking to define an adequate cultural response to industrialism. Their canonisation of his work was successful in so far as it provided abundant material for books, paintings, plays and ultimately, films. However, this rapid absorption of the material into orthodox culture severed the links between the plays and the intellectual radicalism of the Romantic movement. This process coincided with a growing disenchantment felt by bourgeois writers and artists across the whole of Europe, a disaffection that reached a crisis point after the failed revolutions of 1848. The subsequent angst of this group, increasingly divorced from the mechanisms of government, accelerated a trend towards mystic nihilism. In England the initial enthusiasm of those intellectuals who embraced the political idealism of Rousseau, Thomas Paine and William Godwin, gave way either to an alienated and introspective cult of ennui, or to a new rational pragmatism.

Fuseli's later work is symptomatic of this. Initially committed to radical politics he realised that the individual artist had no part to play in an economic and industrial revolution. Ultimately he saw himself as little more than another victim of incomprehensible market forces. Subsequently his paintings became less concerned with the accepted iconography of Romanticism (and that movement's perceptions of Shakespeare) and more involved with his own personal symbolism. His development reiterated many of the features of the transformation of Romantic culture into that of the Symbolist or Decadent movement, and the eventual relocation of the consciousness of the intellectual within the depths of Freudian psychoanalysis. This second, far more introspective attempt to reconcile the artist with capitalist society created the theatrical, artistic and literary structures out of which there developed an Expressionist form of Shakespeare film production. This approach to the plays was formulated in the aesthetic theories of stage designers like Adolphe Appia and Gordon Craig. They called for the elimination of crude Naturalism in art. Instead writing, painting and the stage would be filled with mystical forms that hinted at a transcendent world of meaning. Superficially this denial of vulgar realism was partly intended as a rejection of the literalism of industrial culture and its pursuit of scientifically precise and wholly utilitarian art. This polarisation is deceptive.

Although these Symbolists appeared to imitate Romanticism's rejection of commerce as mechanistic, soulless and alienating, their movement was not radical, interventionist or in any sense political. Bertolt Brecht pointed out that the Expressionist methods of stagecraft represented a classically bourgeois rejection of the material world. The self-proclaimed aesthetes transplanted the evils of society into the world of dreams and mystified the solutions as personal, abstract quests for spiritual fulfillment. The methods they formulated to do this actually utilised the ideology of advanced industrial capitalism, changing it into an ethic of positive transcendentalism. Artists evoked a psychological mysticism as being the essence of art while at the same time formulating a code of practice based on mechanistic production methods. Theatres became factories; the workers dehumanised as marionettes in the service of the final, totally enclosed work of art. The rejection of naturalism went hand in hand with a rejection of nature, which was decried in favour of the pure experience available through the application of advanced technology (light organs, projected scenes, recorded music etc.). As the Symbolist novel *A rebours* ('Against nature', 1884) declared, 'the main thing is to know how . . . to forget yourself sufficiently to bring about the desired hallucination and so substitute the vision of reality for the reality itself.[2] Films that belong to this tradition, like Warner Brothers' *A midsummer night's dream*, Orson Welles' *Othello* and Derek Jarman's *The tempest* demonstrate a palpable indifference to the vulgar realist and literal approach to Shakespeare presentation in the theatre and film. Yet it was the economic development of the methods of movie production that allowed the Expressionist 'revolution' to occur in commercial cinema.

The British spectacular films were made using an undifferentiated competitive business-inventor approach to manufacture. Movies tended to be made as the experiments of entrepreneurs seeking to discover new markets. Production was, at this stage, run along the lines of a small business with little of the division of labour that characterised large industries in North America. Aesthetically this meant that, at first, the appearance and cultural position of a film was the product of corporate activity, with the economics of the entertainment industry as the spur. Consequently there was a tendency towards standardisation and ideological stagnation. The concept of a single guiding hand behind the artistic side of a film only manifested itself in the form of the actor-manager, who often just repeated a stage performance on film. This approach persists today; a corporation like Time/Life or a film company decides to produce a Shakespeare film and uses a renowned actor or theatre director to interpret the text. There is little cultural difference between Peter Brook's *King Lear* and William Barker's film of Tree's *Henry VIII*, even if the visuals have changed: the ideological position of the final product (a film of a high-class theatre experience intended for a sensitive audience) remains.

But even though the actor-manager, in the early years of film making, had little contact with the production process, his manifestation in the films as an emblem of culture signalled the beginning of a shift towards

THE THEATRE OF LIGHT

the isolation of the creative act as the prime source of a movie's value: 'it was absolutely necessary for the division of labour in film production to develop if film was to take on the hues of art, which in turn means if the individual qualities of individual films were to become commercially important.'[3] This had a double-edged effect. The removal of the aesthetics of film from other parts of its production, and the concomitant foregrounding of the 'essential' text, also opened the way for a resurgence of the concept of the lone intellectual struggling for self-definition through his or her art. The marginalisation of Shakespeare in film production meant that the plays could again be appropriated and used to work through the problems of the individual living on the fringes of society, albeit now in a more introspective and alienated way. The differences between the spectacular tableaux of Olivier's Henry V and his brooding, Expressionist Hamlet show this perfectly. The first, a film produced very much in the corporate spirit of the Home Front, pays scant attention to mystical idealism. The second is a study of a tortured intellectual in which a great actor plays the part of a prince trapped in the labyrinth of his own mind.

The development of an Expressionist mode of Shakespeare production is complex and it poses problems due to the diversity of subject matter. The British silent Shakespeare films were part of a specific genre, produced as a commercial attempt to command a home market and protect it from American control. The film producers worked within a predetermined tradition of painting and theatre. Shakespeare films like Welles' Othello and Jarman's The tempest were made on the periphery of a movement that was fundamentally intellectual. Symbolism, Expressionist theatre and the cinemas that it was allied to, attempted to reconcile the individual with society on a much more personal level. Hence these films often appear individualist with patchy and uncertain production histories, although they are as institutionalised within the economy of commercial cinema as any other movie. Compared to the British silent films they are few and far between. To lump them all together under one blanket heading is dangerously formalist. So, in this and the next chapter I have focused on the Warner Brothers' film of A midsummer night's dream. This is for two main reasons. Firstly it represents a focal point in the relationship between Shakespeare production and the economic and historical development of the 'new stagecraft'. Secondly the tensions between its subject matter, execution, cultural status and its highly commercial production throws the discrepancy between the Symbolist intellectual perception of Shakespeare film and the actual politics of cinema production into stark relief.

## Adolphe Appia

Before I concentrate on those specific, historical instances of the 'new stagecraft' which had important implications for Shakespeare film I want to discuss briefly their theoretical heritage. Since the beginning of the nineteenth century the use of intensely detailed naturalism to create a believable reality on stage had been steadily losing its popularity among certain echelons of the European theatre-going public. As early as 1808 Schlegel suggested that the dependence of contemporary set design on a convincing portrayal of the ephemera of the everyday world had severely restricted the physical scope of drama, overwhelming it with 'superfluous and distracting objects.'⁴

Schlegel's remarks signified a general disenchantment with the limitations of stage realism; a reaction to the production values that made the precisely realised details of day to day existence the most important element in a performance. Stage naturalism, with its reliance on fussy detail and classical Renaissance perspective, was a major barrier between the theatre and symbolic 'truth'. In practical terms realism placed enormous constraints on a dramatic performance. As Schlegel pointed out, many sets relied on fixed-point perspective to give the appearance of depth. The flats would be constructed so that any real or painted surfaces that were at right angles to the front of the stage (for example, a road surface stretching into the distance, a corridor or avenue of trees) led to a single point in the centre of the backdrop. Objects at the back of the stage were reduced in size to complete the illusion (some enterprising designers even used children dressed up as soldiers for their battle scenes so that the troops in the 'distance' appeared smaller). Unfortunately fixed-point perspective was only one hundred per cent successful for an observer sitting directly opposite the vanishing point. The people on either side of the line of sight saw a stage littered with distorted scenery. For them the optical illusion was shattered. At the same time the players were confined to a narrow band across the stage: if they moved among the scenery they would dwarf the 'distant' objects and the whole spectacle would look ridiculous.

One of the landmarks in the development of nineteenth-century European theatre was the 1882 performance of Wagner's *Parsifal* at Bayreuth. Wagner's Romantic evocation of Teutonic mythology and history certainly lent itself to the spectacular treatment. Theatre directors seized upon the opportunity to render the exploits of gods, knights and heroes in as grandiose a manner as possible. This particular version of *Parsifal* was no exception; the stage design alternated between the ostentatiously lush and the mechanically impressive. In one memorable scene the journey to the castle of the grail was recreated with all the visual and technical splendour of a trip on the Flying Scotsman; 'the whole of the elaborate "set" forest moves across the stage, forming a quadruple panorama, the realistic effect being much heightened by the front portions moving much quicker than the back . . . The whole of this elaborate change is accomplished with perfect smoothness, not a creak or sound of any sort betraying the means.'[5]

Yet certain members of the audience were disturbed by the tendency of the theatre to reduce everything to a series of realistic tableau and mechanical gimmicks. In *Parsifal* the journey to the castle may have been technically brilliant, but undue emphasis on the visual effects detracted from the actual opera; the same machinery could have appeared to equal effect in any other performance. Theatrical productions were in danger of being reduced to a parade of special effects. For many the spiritual and romantic magnificence of Wagner's original vision was entirely shattered by the banality of the final staging. In fact the production was so contentious that it sparked off the beginning of a radical critique of nineteenth-century stage design.

The popularity of Wagner's theories stemmed from his search for a neo-classical unity, which was implicitly tied with the quest for a new German cultural identity in the 1880s and 1890s. In his operas he placed great emphasis on the concept of *gesamtkunstwerk* or 'total work of art'. This was an attempt to recreate the unity of ancient Greek theatre; music, drama, characterisation, mystical and religious symbolism would come together in one integrated whole. Up to a point he was successful. Yet in concentrating on the score and libretto it seemed that the 'master' had ignored one vital element; the scenery. Consequently the whole effect of the operas, *Parsifal* in particular, was undermined by conventional theatre design, the painted settings, realistic props , two-dimensional flats and fake perspective.

It was the disjunction between Wagner's concept of the unified *gesamtkunstwerk*, and the unoriginal and crude sets of the 1882 *Parsifal* that led Adolphe Appia to begin working on his revolutionary book *Music and the art of the theatre*. Like many of his contemporaries Appia believed that an opera by Wagner almost attained the status of a wholly integrated work of art but the productions were let down by the stage design. Appia's basic theory was quite simple: instead of faithfully constructing a naturalist set and then placing the singers in front of it he believed

that architecture and scenery should reflect and evoke the mystical symbolism of the performance. 'We must no longer try to create the illusion
of a forest,' he wrote, 'but instead the illusion of a man in the atmosphere
of a forest.'[6] Like Schlegel, Appia thought that the sight of three-dimensional figures acting in a landscape made from a box with painted walls
was fundamentally ridiculous and destroyed all the dramatic mood of
the production. As far as he was concerned the opening scene of the
Bayreuth Parsifal had summed up the situation perfectly. During the first
few minutes Appia had been entranced by the mysterious atmosphere
of the dimly-lit set. Then, with the entrance of the knights, the lighting
was turned up to reveal a cheap, painted backdrop and the evocative
mood was dispelled.

What was needed was a reintegration of the set into the drama and
this could only be achieved through the use of minimal, non-representational sets which would then be 'sculpted' with light. Appia recognised
that the incidental effect he saw at the beginning of Parsifal could be used
as a powerful tool, but only after the theatre had abandoned the painted
set. Once this had gone stage lighting could be liberated from its sub-
sidiary role; 'the arrangement of painted canvas to represent the setting
demands that the lighting be exclusively at its service to make the painting visible, a relationship having nothing to do with the active role
played by lighting and quite distinctly in conflict with it.'[7]

In Appia's theatre light was to be an integral part of the scenery instead
of just being used to illuminate the props. Until recently the difficulty
of managing lamps and limelights, along with the practice of keeping
the auditorium lit throughout the opera or play, had allowed only for
the crudest, most general illumination. The invention of controllable
and more sophisticated electric lamps opened up a new medium for
the expression of mood. With the correct manipulation of light and
shadow a simple three-dimensional set could become a wholly plastic
environment, reflecting a variety of feelings and atmospheres. No longer
would the inside of a castle hall and a peasant's hut be the same size
(i.e. the width of the stage). Light could expand or contract the audience's field of vision. Furthermore, with imagination, it could create a
significant relationship between actor and set. A figure could become
a landscape, a landscape the symbol of an emotional condition.

Appia's sketches for the settings of The ring cycle are far removed from
the cluttered scenery of Tree's King John. Their simple, three-dimensional
architecture, when hidden by shadow or partly illuminated by pools of
light, echo the more abstract landscapes of the German Romantic painter
Caspar Friedrich. In many ways the designer's emphasis on the evoca-

tion of mood and mystical symbolism is quite different from Wagner's neo-classical concept of the *gesamtkunstwerk* as a unification of different art forms. In fact Appia's combination of light, music, drama, art and set design into one integrated, atmospheric whole was very similar to the Symbolist's idea of synaesthesia; the saturation of all the senses by a hermetically sealed work of art. It also held within it the beginning of a cinematic movement which would use light, Expressionist architecture and symbolism to create meaning.

## Hubert von Herkomer and Gordon Craig

There is no precise break between the theories of the British Romantics and the Symbolist period. It is true that the Pre-Raphaelites, like some Romantics, often advocated socialist principles. However the actual economic position of groups like the Arts and Crafts movement did little to challenge the principles of laissez-faire capitalism in late nineteenth-century Britain. Politically the British Symbolists and Decadents reformulated some of the Romantic responses to industrialism and, in doing so, perpetuated the trend towards a more mystical perception of the individual consciousness and its relationship to society.

In the visual arts there is a strong link between William Blake and Dante Gabriel Rossetti, William Morris and Edward Burne-Jones via the work of the artists who termed themselves the 'ancients' and the esoteric fairy paintings of Richard Dadd and others. Echoing Blake's denial of an oppressive world dominated by reason, the Pre-Raphaelites tried to reject the rigid material and stylistic constraints of historical narrative art by returning to a neo-Classical symbol which they used to hint at some concealed, transcendent truth. Instead of showing specific events depicted with archaeological accuracy they focused on general scenes from literature and romance, legends and elegiac mythology. These were sometimes Greek or Roman in origin but were more often directly based on folklore or the medieval versions of early English tales (for example, Thomas Malory's *Morte d'Arthur*). Furthermore they tried to reject the constraints of narrative art in favour of allusive symbolism, a move that provoked a strong reaction from viewers used to paintings that told a direct or unequivocal story.

Despite, or rather because of, these attempts to rediscover in art the impure reflection of a divine idealism, their work casts an interesting light on their uneasy position in a changing society. One of the points at which the ambiguities of their contradictory (because it oscillated between the rejection and championing of capitalism) artistic philosophy appeared was in the relationship between the cultural aspirations of avant-garde theatre and the economics of early commercial cinema. In England this is illustrated by the careers of Hubert von Herkomer and Gordon Craig.

Hubert von Herkomer began his career as a painter. In 1883 he used his business acumen to found an art school on the same principles as the Arts and Crafts movement, although he blatantly embraced the commercialism that his contemporaries tacitly condoned. Less concerned with the rejection of industrial culture, he experimented with crude technology. Among other things he invented an 'organ' that would allow people to 'compose' in light. When became involved in amateur dramatics he explored the use of projected light for dramatic effect.

Four years later *The sorceress*, first in a series of experimental plays, was shown to an audience of well known theatrical people, including Ellen Terry and Gordon Craig. Herkomer wanted productions like these to achieve the successful synthesis of art, music and drama. By the time the second (*An idyll*) appeared he had coined the phrase 'pictorial musical play'. Herkomer was especially interested in the Wagnerian idea that drama could be unified under one guiding vision. *An idyll* was a historical drama set in an idealised fourteenth century village. What little plot there was was straightforward and Romantic. The setting, the play's evocation of the life of Saxon peasantry and the music were heavily influenced by Wagner's operas. Herkomer modelled the scenery on his own paintings. The set for the first scene of *An idyll*, 'Towards the close of day', was virtually a carbon copy of a painting he did in 1872 called *After the toil of day*. It was realistic, and visually, had little to set it apart from the scenery of any other Victorian historical drama. Yet the intention behind the production was radically different. Painters working in the narrative tradition based their execution on theatrical codes of meaning. Producers on the orthodox stage imitated art to achieve the picturesque, they pieced their plays together using images, icons and structures that were already well established in art, drama and literature. What Herkomer wanted to do was to actually create the entire drama from scratch using the compositional techniques of an artist. Painting and music would provide him with the tools to realise the *gesamtkunstwerk*, hence the name 'pictorial musical play'. 'The first word denotes the plastic picture; the second, the musical sounds that attune one to the picture; and finally, the word play, to give sufficient motive for the display of the two arts – painting and music.'[8]

Despite the radical implications of his theory, *An idyll* was very much part of the orthodox tradition of the Victorian stage. The silent gestures of the actors were as grandiose as they were simplistic and the final product was little more than a series of tableaux-vivants. Yet Herkomer took the imagery and composition of the commercial theatres and transformed them, using light, into what can only be described as a proto-cinematic theatre. His interest in the capabilities of projected light as an expressive medium bear this out. When he built his theatre in 1888 he took the revolutionary step of introducing electric lamps so that he could create expressive chiaroscuro effects during the performances. In *An idyll* he had achieved the illusion of moving clouds and the approach of twilight by throwing light on to a gauze curtain through coloured glass. One of his ambitions was to project actual figures and scenes on to material to break down the spatial limits of the stage, although he didn't develop this idea any further. Instead, with the arrival of film, Herkomer saw his chance to realise drama that would fully embody the concept of the *gesamtkunstwerk*: 'my great ideal is to present films from the artist's point of view. At present almost all suffer from the somewhat crude realism of the camera. What I want is less realism and more art. . . . It needs an artist to superintend the lighting of a film.'[9]

With this project in mind he formed the Herkomer Film Company with his son Siegfried. They began to make short dramatic films. Sadly these were uninspired melodramas that had only a passing resemblance to the 'pictorial music play'. Herkomer's artistic background forced him to think in terms of two-dimensional composition. Unaware of, or uninterested in, the plastic possibilities of three-dimensional stagecraft he ended up reworking the familiar conventions of the tableau-vivant. Ironically Herkomer's plays and films were regarded as rather staid and conventional because audiences were already used to seeing wordless tableaux, projected images and painterly composition in their plays.

The first genuinely commercial Shakespeare film was made as part of an early attempt to use cinema as a vehicle for fine art, along the same lines as Herkomer's dramatic experiments. In 1900 a French company, the Phono Cinema Théâtre of Paris (a name reminiscent of the 'pictorial musical play') made a number of experimental sound films. The technology was straightforward: while the movies were projected on to a screen an assistant turned the handle of a phonograph, varying the speed to achieve a rough synchronisation between the images and the sound. Two of the short pieces were Shakespearean; an aria from Gounod's *Romeo et Juliette* and Sarah Bernhardt in *Le duel d'Hamlet*. This film showed the fight between Laertes and Hamlet. The audiences heard the sound effects of the battle via the phonograph (when the film was shown at other theatres people stamped their feet and rattled cutlery behind the screen).

Despite the fact the Le duel d'Hamlet encapsulated the idea of a living picture the subject matter of the film was less important than its association with a famous actress. On the playbill the title was almost lost beneath Sarah Bernhardt's name. Despite its intellectual pretensions Le duel d'Hamlet belonged to a type of film that had its roots in the fairground Magic lantern shows and music halls. Short features that showed moving pictures of famous people were a popular sub-genre of early cinema: they signalled the growth of the 'star system' that later became an important component of commercial film and theatre. The roots of this fascination with the lives and personalities of actors and actresses off stage began with theatrical repertory where the dramatic roles were subordinate to the performer (simply because the plays changed every night). In Britain, when London companies toured the provinces, actors' names were used to draw the public. By the turn of the century the 'star system' was an accepted feature of the dramatic world and films like Le duel d'Hamlet were used as a kind of advance publicity, to bolster the reputation of performers in the provinces and abroad.

However it is unlikely that Le duel d'Hamlet was made specifically as advance publicity for Sarah Bernhardt. By now her own reputation was sufficient to fill most theatres. Instead the Phono Cinema Théâtre placed her name at the top of a variety bill that included the famous clown Little Tich, underlining its own commitment to a certain artistic tradition. It was associating itself with the sophisticated cabarets of Paris. Like Isadora Duncan and Gordon Craig, Bernhardt had acquired the reputation of a bohemian artist. This was perpetuated by the various myths that developed around the film. One claimed that the star, much given to swooning, passed out at seeing herself on the screen.

It was via the experiments of another aesthete, Gordon Craig, that the theories of the 'new stagecraft' were used in attempt to transform a Shakespeare play into the Symbolist dream of a total work of art. Unlike Herkomer, Craig entirely forsook the painted realism of the spectacular theatre and concentrated on designs for three-dimensional stages. In 1912 he was invited to Russia to work with Stanislavsky's Moscow Art Theatre on a production of Hamlet. Craig believed that the entire production of a play should be in the hands of a single guiding vision. In his own words, the actors were to become marionettes devoid of individuality, to be manipulated like the brushstrokes of a painter on a canvas.

Craig's collaboration on the Russian production of Hamlet shows the implications that the theories of the 'theatre of light' had for Shakespearean cinema and film production as a whole. The vast monolithic architecture of the sets and the use of light to express mood and atmosphere closely followed Appia's ideas. As far as Craig was concerned his set would be as vital a part of the play as the characters and, through the careful use of projected light, would take on a malleable, plastic quality. In his original plans for *Hamlet* there were to be no scene changes. Instead the monolithic structures were to be wheeled across the stage in a predetermined sequence of patterns, each transformation signalling a change of location. At the same time Craig continually tried to eliminate the boundaries between all the various aspects of the performance: plot, characterisation, scenery and lighting. His idea of a total work of art encapsulated many of the characteristics of cinema as envisaged by directors like Carl Dreyer and Orson Welles. The theory of the actor as marionette not only echoes the approach of Meyerhold (who believed in the theatre as machine) and the early Eisenstein, but also has strong links with the use of the landscapes of the human face and body as Expressionist icons in films like *The passion of Joan of Arc* (1928). Finally, Craig's insistence on the performance as the product of a single creative imagination anticipates the auteur theory of cinema.

In the case of *Hamlet* any belief in the supremacy of the text was entirely counter-productive to Craig's ambition. As the spirit of the 1882 *Parsifal* disappeared under a mass of trite stage technology so the intrusion of any 'original' *Hamlet* into Craig's production would (and did) cause serious disruptions. Craig thought that the theatre was choked with words and that only silent drama could achieve the artistic expressiveness he searched for. He continually attempted to replace the text of Shakespeare's play with a series of Expressionist motifs. At one stage he came up with the idea of the 'daemon death', a symbol of Hamlet's relationship with fate. This character would appear beside him during the 'To be or not to be' speech. Craig even suggested that they should be bound together with a gold thread but Stanislavksy, increasingly dismayed by Craig's ideas, dismissed it as impractical: 'It seems to me, in fact I have even dreamed about it several times, that during Hamlet's monologue a figure comes up to him, a bright golden figure. And at one time it even began to seem to me that this figure is always with Hamlet . . . And I think that this figure which appears to me near Hamlet is Death. But not dark and gloomy as she generally appears to people, but such as she appeared to Hamlet – bright, joyful, one who will free him from his tragic position.'[10] Craig's concept of the scene remains embodied in one of his many production sketches. He thought the silent tableau of the two figures signified the inner consciousness of Hamlet far better than the clichéd speech.

Unfortunately the final production was a pale imitation of the original scheme. The gigantic block sets, never before attempted on stage, could barely support their own weight. Rather than risk moving them the company changed scenes behind a curtain. This destroyed the effect of a fluid and expressive dramatic space that could be transformed according to the mood, atmosphere or setting of the play. Laced with compromises the Moscow *Hamlet* oscillated between the sublime and the risible. The fusion of landscape and player worked impressively in some scenes: a still of Hamlet (Vassily Kachalov) sitting brooding on his chair in front of dark, rectangular towers shows how powerful the imagery could be. On the other hand such eccentricities as the disembodied clusters of spears waving back and forth behind a low wall in the last scene were thought laughable (though they did anticipate the ranks of massed spears in Eisenstein's *Alexander Nevsky*). The Moscow Art Theatre *Hamlet* was a flawed masterpiece, branded as too cold and intellectual by the critics, and Craig's reputation was severely damaged.

Craig's idealism, though far removed from the final production of the play, points to a close similarity between the aesthetics of the theatre of light and that of various European film movements during the first twenty years of cinema production. It is interesting to note that Grigori Kozintsev, the Russian director responsible for *Hamlet* (1964) and *Korol Ler* (1970), also believed that Craig's concept of stage design had important implications for cinema because it 'freed the imagination in a way similar to the methods of film.'[11]

Craig's *Hamlet* represents the early twentieth-century Symbolist theatre at its most transcendent and obscure. Cinematically it is closest in form and economic position to the films of Orson Welles, another self-styled bohemian whose productions were both erratic, badly organised and extremely mystical. The demands of a market-based business make the concentration of meaning in the perception of a single, alienated vision a risky business. Welles's Shakespeare films, like the Moscow *Hamlet*, were dogged by financial and production difficulties, for no other reason than the reluctance of financiers to sink money into the projects of a reputedly difficult director. Ultimately the interpretation of such artists tends to become mixed with the institutional ideology of movie making at the historical and social moment in which the work is produced. The final result, as we shall see in the case of George Melies, Warner Brothers, Welles and Derek Jarman is often a movie that is caught between various ideological and institutional tensions. Consequently such films sometimes display a less restrained and less controllable symbolism than the mystical and anti-realistic work of Craig. It is in these fragmented and contradictory movies that the coherence and apparent consensus over what constitutes culture, Shakespeare and film, breaks down to reveal an uncertain and grotesque vision of society and social relationships.

## George Melies

The search for a transcendental symbolism was double edged. On the one hand it led to the neo-platonic idealism of Appia and Wagner, on the other it slipped into the world of determinist psychology. The paintings of many European Symbolists tried to echo the logic of dreams and were replete with Freudian and Jungian symbols. This process also occurred in film: both Chanan and Burch suggest that the process by which the very first cameras were used to construct images copies the psychological development of an infant's perception. From a fragmented concept of the world the child gains a more integrated awareness of whole objects and people. The desires that a baby transposes on to the fragments of its mother are transfered into dreams and fantasies as it grows older. Hence, throughout adult life, the repressed wishes and fears of the infant are re-enacted in the world of dreams. There the rigid categories by which the adult understands reality are fragmented, disrupted and broken down. The films of directors like George Melies, with their detached limbs, exploding bodies and giant heads, can be seen as the cinematic equivalent of early infant visions and subsequent adult dreams and nightmares.

Freud, in his *Interpretation of dreams* (1900), claimed that dreams are the expression of unconscious, infantile wishes. When the individual is awake these are suppressed by the conscious mind. But, once a person falls asleep, these desires (and fears) bypass the censorship of the ego by becoming translated into dream symbols. Because these appear nonsensical and apparently harmless the conscious mind doesn't recognise them for what they truly are. Freud cited two processes by which the forbidden desires becomes a dream 'rebus'. With condensation the dreaming mind creates composite absurd images with multiple meanings. Displacement causes the desire to be translated from its true source or object to another, inconsequential image. The result, in the dream work, is a puzzle which conceals the desire as a nonsensical image or experience. The purpose of interpretation is to locate the original fear or desire by working back from the dream to the hidden meaning.

In the 1960s a number of critics used Freudian analysis to construct a formalist critique of grotesque art. The term grotesque has a long and chequered history: originally used as an architectural term, it was adopted in the late nineteenth century by critics like Ruskin and used to encompass all aspects of culture that appeared simultaneously horrific and humorous. The writings of Dickens and Kafka and the paintings of the Symbolist movement have all been cited as 'grotesque' and the term can be applied to many of George Melies's films. In summary the Freudian analysis of the grotesque is as follows:

The grotesque derives its impact by expressing the conflict between the unconscious mind, the consciousness and the laws of bourgeois society. It transplants the mechanism of censorship, taking it from its 'safe' location in the dream world and placing it in the 'real' world. Thus the repression of the fear or desire becomes obvious and ineffective (i.e. the dream symbol, in a real context, is ridiculous or impossible and therefore has to be acknowledged as a camouflage for some genuine fear or passion). At the same time the interpolation of the dream symbol (for example, in Melies' films, giant heads and moons with faces) into reality, or a 'realistic' medium, leads to the breakdown of rational categories. Conscious understanding, which is educated to perceive objects as distinct and separate, is unable to comprehend an image that transgresses 'natural' barriers. Hence universal laws of category become meaningless. In Celestino Coronado's film of Lindsay Kemp's *A midsummer night's dream* Bottom is transformed into a monster that is part plant, part animal and which has a giant phallus projecting from its forehead. The juxtaposition of incompatible objects, and the isolation and exaggerated size of the phallus, contravenes the categories created by a rational perception of the world. The result is both funny and frightening, i.e. it is grotesque. Finally, because the appearance of a grotesque dream symbol in the 'real' world demonstrates an inability of the individual to master its unconscious desires it echoes the perspective of children. Children have difficulty controlling their desires and fears, yet they live in a world that demands this control, chiefly for incomprehensible, adult reasons.

What we are seeing here, both in grotesque art and cinema, and in the psychoanalytical theory that was later used to deconstruct it, is the internalising of the position of the intellectual in the Freudian subconscious. The perspective of the child, as constructed in the late nineteenth-century and early twentieth-century literature and in the 'magic' films of Paul and Melies, echoes the perception of an absurd, alienating universe apparently ruled by laws that are incomprehensible to the fraught individual. This pattern emerges strongly in the writings of Dickens and Kafka, mainly because their family backgrounds subjected them, on a very personal basis, to the dilemmas, fears and desires that were being experienced by all those intellectuals trying to come to terms with their position in industrial society. Both writers were, as children, the victims of unsupportive fathers (a bully in Kafka's case, a spendthrift in Dickens's) who forced them to work in businesses they hated. In a letter to his father (which he never posted) Kafka wrote 'the world was for me divided into three parts; one in which I, the slave, lived under laws that had been invented only for me and which I could, I did not know why, never completely comply with; then a second world, which was infinitely remote from mine, in which you lived, concerned with government, with the issuing of orders, and with annoyance about their not being obeyed; and finally a third world where everybody else lived happily and free from orders and from having to obey.'[12]

From the late nineteenth century psychoanalytical theory and grotesque art existed in a perpetual dialectic. Grotesque art, literature and film expressed the anguish of the individual consciousness reduced to childlike helplessness in an absurd world, and Freudian analysis supported the internalisation of this alienation. Using historical evidence we can break this loop down quite easily: Kafka's perception of the grotesque drew heavily on Jewish folklore and certain plays performed by the Yiddish troupe of actors he became involved with in 1911. The structure of Dickens's grotesque imagery, in which helpless individuals like Oliver, Nicholas Nickleby and David Copperfield wander through a threatening, mercantile society populated by grotesque characters, has strong links with early picaresque religious tracts, like Bunyan's *A pilgrim's progress*.

Similarly the makers of early grotesque and fantastic films, like George Melies, were working in a non-representational tradition of illusion and fantasy that had grown out of popular pantomime and cabaret. Melies has been credited, in orthodox cinema history, with the discovery of the illusory qualities of film. In a manifesto he wrote in 1897 he stated that his aim was to use the camera to create fantastic, artistic and theatrical scenes. As Chanan has remarked, this opposition between Melies's fantasies and the realism of Lumiere is based on ahistorical assumptions. It fails to acknowledge the illusory and magical appearance of cinema as a whole to the first audiences. Both Melies and the two English directors G. A. Smith and R. W. Paul, produced a number of magical or 'trick' films using stop-frame techniques and superimposition to generate 'impossible' images on screen. The films themselves show clearly the tradition in which they were working. The painted scenery in such works as The magic sword (Paul, 1902) and In the kingdom of the fairies (Melies, 1903) could have come from the stage of any Victorian pantomime. Melies, despite his recognition that the camera could be used to manipulate space, always positioned it in the same place so that, with its line of sight at right angles to the backcloth, it simulated the point of view of an audience in a theatre.

In this sense Melies is closer in spirit to the work of Herkomer, in whose projected clouds and magic moon we can see a precursor to the French film maker's double exposures. Even so Melies continually set out to destroy the orthodox logic of narrative-based drama, Instead he built a multitude of strictly-enclosed images that, like dreams or hallucinations, possessed their own transgressive rationale. Many of his movies have strong Freudian overtones. Melies's head is regularly seen to detach itself from his body or inflate itself to monstrous proportions; several of the monsters in films like The witch (1900) look phallic. Like grotesque dreams his movies re-constructed the elusive and subtle displacement of desire, the symbolism of the absurd and the horrors of madness. This is perhaps one of the reasons why Surrealists like Salvador Dali and Luis Buñuel admired Melies and why echoes of his imagery can be seen in the more obscure works of directors like Lang and Dreyer.

George Melies made two Shakespeare films; Hamlet (1907) and La mort de Jules César ('The dream of Shakespeare', 1907). In these he used multiple exposure and dream-like Expressionist imagery, thereby unconsciously recreating the spirit, if not the intention , of Appia's and Craig's ideas. Melies's Hamlet was far more sombre than his usual works. Limited to one reel, the director didn't try to recreate the play, or a section of the play, on film. As with Tree's King John no copy of Hamlet has survived. There is a still showing Melies as the Prince dressed in long black robes, and a précis written by his brother Gaston. The movie begins in the graveyard where Hamlet picks up Yorick's skull:

his manner strongly indicates, 'Alas, poor York [sic], I knew him well!'. The following scenes combine to show the high state of dementia of the young prince's mentality. He is seen in his room where he is continually annoyed and excited by apparitions which taunt him in their weirdness and add bitterness to his troubled brain. He attempts to grasp them but in vain, and he falls to brooding. Now is shown the scene in which he meets the ghost of his father and is told to take vengeance on the reigning monarch, his uncle; but not content with this, Hamlet's fates tantalise him further by sending into his presence the ghost of his departed sweetheart, Ophelia. He attempts to embrace her as she throws flowers to him from a garland on his brow, but his efforts are futile; and when he sees the apparition fall to the ground he, too, swoons away, and is thus found by several courtiers.[13]

There was no real attempt to create any impression of the passage of time in Melies's film of Hamlet. The film dispensed with the spatial and temporal boundaries of narrative. Instead it constructed a collage of fragmented images from the play. The result is a cinematic expression of a specific theme, that of madness, and like many of his other works it anticipates the techniques of later films. Overall, his movie attempted to tackle the sort of dramatic expressiveness pursued by the exponents of the 'new stagecraft'. The encounter between the ghost of Ophelia and Hamlet is reminiscent of Gordon Craig's concept of the 'daemon death'. The choice of Hamlet is significant: after the Victorian literary establishment had cast him iun the mould of the doomed, Byronic intellectual, many students, artists and writers used him to try and work through their own perceptions of alienation.

Melies's second film La mort de Jules César, came out in the same year. It lacked the Expressionist qualities of Hamlet and made the dream concept more explicit. Instead of mingling the illusory images with the real, La mort de Jules César strictly demarcated the former as an 'illusion', thereby bringing the whole work into line with the more conventional films of the period. The movie begins with Shakespeare musing in his study. He falls asleep and his dream; of Brutus and his conspirators stabbing Caesar, is enacted beside him. The vision ends, he wakes and begins to write. The film closes with a shot of Shakespeare's bust surrounded by flags of several nations. The effect is double edged: in Freudian terms the dream symbol, when actually articulated in a dream situation, loses most of its power to disturb. Because the vision is deliberately and obviously constructed as Shakespeare's dream it is consciously separated from the more naturalistic image of Shakespeare asleep. In this way it is closer to the rigidly defined spectacles of Tree's theatre than the theories of the 'new stagecraft'. On the other hand the projection of the dream beside the seated figure of Shakespeare operates as a symbol of the illusory qualities of film itself. It makes La mort de Jules César into one of the movies that Chanan calls 'filmic metastatements, that is, films about films.'[14] Unfortunately the orthodox ending, reminiscent of the patriotic images used by British firms, suggests that the fierce competition created by the increase in North American film production was forcing European directors to make movies that were aesthetically conservative and therefore commercially viable.

The transformation from Romanticism to Symbolism marks a shift in the relationship between the intellectual and society. The ambiguous and fragmented theories of the latter movement were reflected in the growth of a new Expressionist theory of stage design and the development of certain kinds of cinema. Appia and Craig rejected bourgeois naturalism but, at the same time, the search for neo-platonic realms of hidden truth echoed the Romantic's mystification of the means of production and the economic relationships between those who created art and those who consumed it.

Symbolism and the 'new stagecraft' adopted an other-worldly stance while investing science, technology and the act of consumption within a capitalist economy with a transcendent significance. The Symbolists and Decadents searched for pure artifice and unalloyed experience, championing the capacity of industrialism to substitute the artificial for tawdry reality, thus transcending vulgar existence. This adulation of technology fed into the work of Appia, Craig and Herkomer. For them practical science held the key to the unification of the dramatic work. Electric lights, projected images and the apparatus of early film would enable the single genius to co-ordinate a stage production in the service of her or his art. We will see how closely the theories of the 'new stagecraft' are linked with the mechanisms and products of business when we look at Warner Brothers' *A midsummer night's dream*.

The Symbolists' perception of the individual and society also had its negative side. Much of the art and literature produced within the movement was deeply involved with the theories of Freudian psychoanalysis. Here lay the popularity of the grotesque, a type of art that disrupted perceptions of the world by filling it with absurd and irrational images. By contextualising instances of this grotesque in their social and historical moments we can see how it represents an attempt to address the alienation of the intellectual in a society ruled by incomprehensible and uncontrollable market forces.

Melies's films illustrate the conflict inherent in the aesthetics of the 'new stagecraft'. On the one hand the basic ideas behind *Hamlet* and *La mort de Jules César* display an Expressionist approach to the plays; the evocation of a mood, atmosphere or emotion through the use of mystical imagery, dreams and visions. Yet Melies was a business man making entertaining short films that drew on the comic and the grotesque imagery of the pantomime to create childlike fantasies. At the same time that his movies set out to evoke a cultured and aesthetic perception of instances or images from the plays, they are economically and culturally sited within a comic medium; that of music hall entertainment. This disjunction leads to an ambiguous perception of Shakespeare that is grotesque, rather than transcendent.

Melies's films operate as a metaphor for a wider process. In Expressionist Shakespeare film an understanding of the plays that attempts to invest them with mystical and symbolic meaning is continually thwarted by the fact that the artist responsible is alienated from the means of production. Her or his perception carries no weight in a bourgeois, mercantile economy that has little time for intellectualism. Subsequently the aesthete either retreats into erratic and irresponsible bohemianism (another version of childhood) or uses the medium of cinema and Shakespeare to express an alienated perception of a grotesque world. Film makers who worked within the Expressionist tradition tried to resolve this, and their own dilemma, in a number of ways (as far as their historical and social moment would permit). In A midsummer night's dream, Welles's Othello, Jarman's The tempest and, later, Kozintsev's Korol Ler and Hamlet, we will see the extent of their success.

# Symbolism in Shakespeare film

Warner Brothers' film of *A midsummer night's dream* was released towards the end of 1935. It was ostensibly a movie of the theatre production that Max Reinhardt had presented in the United States the previous year. According to official publicity the movie was co-directed by Reinhardt and William Dieterle. In actual fact most of the on-set direction was done by Dieterle.

In film criticism the movie has often been examined via the auteur theory. There are political advantages to this strategy, which is used in the work of Jorgens and Manvell. For a critical heritage that places the author (i.e. Shakespeare) at the centre of creative meaning it is logical to approach cinema from the assumption that a film, like a play, book or poem, is really the product of one individual's efforts. Once this has been established then a film of a play can be reduced to the safe and simple level of one person's interpretation of another person's text. Secondly, in the case of Warner Brothers' film, it enables the movie, and Reinhardt's involvement in it, to be partly redeemed as serious literary work. At the same time the populist, Hollywood influences can be relegated to the background as, at best, intrusive commercialism.

For those convinced that Shakespeare is the province of high drama the interpretation of a European stage director renowned for his evocative and symbolist productions is far more palatable than that of a Warner Brothers' movie maker. At close quarters this theoretical division, between simplistic Hollywood commercialism and the more profound demonology of Reinhardt's Expressionist theatre, doesn't coincide with either the historical evidence or the evidence in the film itself. Rather it suggests that the analysis is, in fact, a re-appropriation of the film, embodying a strategy commonly applied to works that appear radical or which challenge orthodox critical belief in some way.

In the case of the Warner Brothers' film the existence of two directors is used to support the belief that *A midsummer night's dream* displays a tension between two largely exclusive methodologies, i.e. the Hollywood production values used by Dieterle and the Romantic and mystical theatre of Reinhardt. Behind this separation is a strong current of elitism, with which the North American entertainment industry is derided in favour of European theatre. When this demarcation of different elements of a Shakespeare film is used, in an attempt to re-integrate it into a standard, orthodox interpretation, the movie is dehistoricised. In other words this process of appropriation tends to obscure or exclude the real relationships between its diverse structures and their historical context. Yet in the case of the Warner Brothers' film the differentiation is illuminating simply because the actual production, and the finished product, acknowledged and played on the demarcation of its different elements (a demarcation very different to that between high and low art).

A midsummer night's dream was made as a prestige picture, a lavish production that was intended to establish Warner Brothers' reputation as an enlightened company dedicated to culture. Not only was it perceived of as a duet between a renowned movie business and a famous director but it was also used as a showcase for the studio's technical skills and acting talent. In the same way that the British silent films combined the imagery of painting, spectacular theatre and historical narrative, so A midsummer night's dream consciously acknowledged a diversity of genres: musical revues; romantic comedies; classic silent films and cartoons.

Warner Brothers' film made explicit the method of production of many other Shakespeare movies. It showed that a film of Shakespeare is not so much the reproduction of a text as a specific point in cultural production where varied concepts and methodologies are brought together within the economic framework of a country's film industry. What is interesting about this particular film is that it was produced in circumstances that led it to reveal an ambiguous tension between the self-defined needs of aesthetic intellectualism and the ideology of entertainment controlled by business. It was made using production methods culled from the 'theatre of light' designed to evoke a mystical atmosphere. This was achieved using contemporary technology, music and precise choreography; the ingredients that Appia felt were essential if Wagner's gesamtkunstwerk was ever to be realised. At the same time the film was created in a tightly scheduled studio. It was intended as a celebration of the economic and technological power of large industry and America's ability to emerge from a crippling depression. As a result the 'tension' between Reinhardt and Hollywood is a actually a demonstration of the alliance between the Expressionist stage and the economic and cultural edifice of capitalism.

## Warner Brothers

The Warner family had been involved in the film business since before World War I but their company only emerged as a fully fledged part of the North American movie industry in 1923. At the turn of the century Edison's patenting of film technology in the United States meant that production was the only area of the film industry that wasn't subject to a rigid monopoly. So many distributors, Warner included, began to make their own films in an attempt to exploit this part of the market. In 1925 Warner Brothers bought the studios and distribution chain of Vitagraph. A similar deal brought them the production facilities of another silent company, First National, and a major competitive role in the movies. From early on Warner Brothers committed themselves to the development of an effective sound system for film. Their initial period of technical and economic expansion form the mid to late 1920s was heavily geared towards this. Their experiments culminated in the release of the first 'talkie'; *The jazz singer* in 1927.

Nick Roddick suggests in *A new deal in entertainment: Warner Brothers in the 1930s,* that the company's production methods were a classic example of the Hollywood studio system. This is fundamentally an economic classification; Warner's approach to materials, personnel and products was organised along the lines of an advanced, management-based, mass production line. The film technique that Warners used for the majority of their movies stemmed from a methodology typical of the 'Hollywood codes of editing'. The key features were: a character-centred, closed narrative and a coherent and self-contained world portrayed as unmediated reality. The style and structure of the finished movies, from *The jazz singer* to *The adventures of Robin Hood* (1938), marshalled cinema in support of an apparently uncontradictory and authoritative perception of reality; a world centred on, and manipulated by, the actions, motives and fortunes of the bourgeois individual. Roddick goes on to point out that the economy of making films using the studio system was chiefly responsible for this style. In fact the aesthetic nature of the finished product was determined, in a very immediate and concrete sense, by the economic demands of a studio-based production method designed to make films quickly and efficiently.

The 1930s represented, for Warners, a decade of growth and consolidation after a drop in profits following the Wall Street Crash. The rapid turnover of the studio system allowed them to make movies covering a wide range of subjects, with the financial loss accompanying occasional prestige pictures like *A midsummer night's dream* (or the failures of bad movies) compensated for by returns from a steady flow of contemporary dramas. Warner Brothers made realistic crime films and social conscience documentaries, their repertoire included the successful musical revues of Busby Berkely, biographical films of famous historical figures, swashbuckling adventures starring Errol Flynn, romantic comedies and cartoons.

Superficially *A midsummer night's dream* seems atypical: it has no immediate relationship with any of the above. The movie was produced as a conscious exercise in prestige building, not necessarily with any cynical motives but rather as an attempt to consolidate Warner's reputation as a socially responsible company with both the public and the Hays Office. Yet when we look at the economic and cultural relations that shaped the film's production and reception we see that it, like the movies before it, was a forcing ground for many of the social tensions and contradictions that companies like Warners had already addressed and attempted to work through in other products. At the same time the nascent theories of the 'theatre of light' filtered into *A midsummer night's dream* through the work of the two directors; Reinhardt and his ex-pupil Dieterle. Thus the finished film also illuminates the uneasy alliance between the mystic, symbolist stagecraft and the commercial production of art.

One of Warner Brothers most famous films, *The jazz singer*, was a musical. Warners sank a vast amount of capital into film sound, a long-term approach to investment typical of large, advanced North American businesses. That most of the big budget films that they, and others, produced to herald the end of the silent era were revues or musicals is significant. It shows that the transition from a silent film idiom was neither easy or automatic. Because of the expense sound producers simply couldn't afford to create the epic narrative scope of films like Abel Gance's *Napoleon*. Also there was no sound equivalent to the subtle and intricate codes of representation used in silent film to transmit meaning. Yet there were ways in which the economic and technical significance of sound, as perceived by the producers, could be impressed upon the movie-going public. The most direct was by making the means of production explicit in as lavish and spectacular a way as possible. *The jazz singer* had little pretensions towards a realistic film with a coherent self-contained narrative world. It consisted of a loose story wrapped around a number of songs which, more often than not, Jolson sang directly to the camera. MGM's response to *The jazz singer, Hollywood* revue of 1927 was instrumental in starting the genre of the musical or musical revue; episodic cabarets in which a film company would demonstrate its capacity for spectacular sound production and its own particular stable of artists.

The genre of the musical waned briefly in the early 1930s before picking up again halfway through the decade, largely owing to the work that Busby Berkely did with Warners. This reflects contemporary attitudes to the Depression and subsequent recovery as well as the financial constraints imposed upon studios who were pushed to afford a continual round of spectacle. The re-appearance of the revue coincides with the beginning of the nation's slow climb out of hardship towards economic recovery. The films, deliberately encompassing the whole production capacity of the company, iterated a positive, expansionist theme. Roddick characterises it as that of a corporate group pulling together.

Berkely's Gold diggers of 1933 and 42nd street were lavish cabarets that interspersed singing and dancing with comedy and vast, spectacular dance routines. Berkely was famed for his escapist, fantastic stage shows in which chorus lines of women were marshalled into hymns to conspicuous consumerism. Reflecting a perception of an economy that is impersonal and, on occasion, dangerously soulless, these films echo the ambiguity of Craig and Appia's dictatorial theatre of marionettes: 'Berkely's attitude towards individuals is that of a silent film director, iconographic and symmetric. The community of the Berkely girls is cold and anonymous, like Lang's workers, a community created by a non-participating choreographer-director.'[1]

Yet during the mid 1930s, when Roosevelt's New Deal began to provide a way of restructuring the economy, this wish fulfillment was especially popular. It showed, to a public short of work and money, the liberating power of the capitalist dream as formulated by a company that dedicated itself to producing socially worthy films. At the same time it hinted at the darker, more alienating aspects of society in its portrayal of a perfect, almost clinical fantasy world. In A midsummer night's dream this ambiguity would be more explicitly acknowledged: in the dark, fantasy sequences in the forest and in the treatment of the rustics, and then partly redeemed through the inclusion of the liberal, apparently egalitarian structure of romantic comedy.

The main way in which the romantic comedies of the mid 1930s differed from either the Berkely musicals or the earlier comedies of the Marx Brothers or W. C. Fields was in their positive affirmation of individual equality. These films, nicknamed 'screwball' comedies, often mirrored the reduction of social issues to the personal, intimate family level in the Warner crime or social conscience movies; and similarly cast corrupt urban institutions as the villains of the piece. Andrew Bergman, in his analysis of the films directed for Columbia by Frank Capra, pinpoints the ideological purpose of such films as 'a means of unifying what had been splintered and divided. The "whackiness" cemented social classes and broken marriages; personal relations were smoothed and social discontent quieted.'[2] 'Screwball' comedy celebrated the supposed egalitarianism of liberal America. It placed class difference firmly within the personalities of individuals, thereby perpetuating the myth that America was fundamentally classless and that any social inequalites were just the result of bad attitudes.

The humour of the earlier, more socially aware silent comedies was, at Warners, separated from the realistic medium of film photography and relocated in the cartoons which the company produced after 1932. Little radical work has been done on the animated films of the 1930s: the orthodox belief that cartoons are inconsequential entertainment for children is one that movie criticism is loath to dispel. Yet, in a sense, this making 'safe' of animation, removing it from the arena of theoretical debate, reiterates the process whereby the cartoons of the 1930s produced by Warners sought to neutralise the grotesque humour of the earlier comedy films. Certainly, as far as A midsummer night's dream is concerned, animation in the 1930s needs to be examined more closely. Warners' film, with its strong fantasy elements, reincorporated into 'realistic' live action film many of the transgressive and grotesque structures which early animation had, in turn, picked up from the work of producers like Melies.

The animation produced during the late 1920s and 1930s echoes the contradiction in Symbolist aesthetics between the celebration of a transcendent Romanticism (their short cartoon The blue Danube points to a link between A midsummer night's dream and the pastoral sequence in Walt Disney's Fantasia) and frightening grotesques. In the early 1930s, animation imitated the alarming and absurd worlds of Melies; both Warner Brothers and Walt Disney used a rapid, very fluid style that often led to horrific results (some censors thought that the transformation scene in Disney's full-length feature Snow White (1937) was too frightening for children).

Alongside the more fantastic and innocent fairy tale cartoons there existed a sub-genre of nightmarish animation; of which the Betty Boop and early Popeye cartoons are good examples. In many of these, lovable, cute animals or anthropomorphic objects with childish personalities were victimised or tortured by mad scientists and monsters. These cartoons were often set in the world of dreams, nightmares, nursery rhymes or fairy tales; but the images, references and storylines were contemporary. Some even contained veiled references to underground culture: a send up of Disney's *The old water mill*, *The old mill pond*, was not only a cartoon tribute to famous jazz singers of the era, but was also liberally sprinkled with references to drugs.

The destruction, fragmentation and extreme distortions of form that occur in early animated films are similar to the displacement processes identified in the Freudian dreamwork. These cartoons operate like dreams, transferring childish fears and desires into a fantastic world. By and large the humour of later animation re-established the status quo. The situations in cartoons like the *Tom and Jerry* series are replayed time and time again without any resolution of the conflict. In the cartoons of the early 1930s this resolution is usually missing. The sense of unease is perpetuated by the frequent acknowledgement that the character's experiences were part of a vision over which it had no control.

In *The dish ran away with the spoon* (1932), a cartoon produced by Hugh Harman as part of the 'Silly symphonies' series, kitchen utensils are brought to life and sing excerpts from contemporary love songs. The cartoon becomes horrific when a lump of dough turns into a monster. The humour is far more grotesque than in later cartoons: the monster is seemingly castrated by cheesegraters as they fly between its legs, then it is flattened with a roller, minced and cooked. The film is unreal, violent, colourful and only partially successful in concealing Freudian fears of castration and dismemberment. Instead of isolating the dream-process within a real world and making it safe, the cartoon reveals its own processes as that of a dream work. Thus the mechanism of censorship becomes obvious. Warner's *A midsummer night's dream* also replays the tension between the comforting, liberal world of the screwball comedy and the far more vicious and nightmarish childhood world of the early animated film.

Before concentrating on *A midsummer night's dream* it is worth looking briefly at the other movies that made up Warner's output in the early 1930s. Roddick characterises the company's attitudes towards subject matter as, on the whole, liberal. The studio courted an image of itself as the producer of social conscience films, movies that were made as an attempt to address contemporary issues: courtroom dramas; anti-racist and anti-fascist movies and crime films. Understandably both the interpretation of the issues and the resolution were far from radical or revolutionary. 'Even the most apparently uncompromising of the socially conscious films . . . are, in the end, reassuring about the ability of America's institutions to protect its citizens.'[3] In the early 1930s, when the economy stabilised, Warner's output began with a markedly liberal interrogation of the problems of the individual in an often corrupt society. This stance became increasingly problematic as the decade progressed. The 'Dead end' cycle of films (from Dead end in 1937 to Angels with dirty faces (1938)) had its stylistic roots in earlier films about the rehabilitation of juvenile offenders, but instead of saving the criminals through the benevolent power of the state the later movies have, as their reforming heroes, anarchic wise-guys like James Cagney's Rocky. Cagney's perceived role in Warner's films and its importance for A midsummer night's dream will be examined in the next section.

## Warner Brothers' A midsummer night's dream

When Kenneth MacGowan set out to describe the development of the new Expressionist stage in his book The theatre of tomorrow (1921) he cited Reinhardt as one of the leading exponents of the wholly integrated, spatially plastic drama. For much of his career Reinhardt experimented with the use of light to create dramatic atmospheres, both on the vast sets of the Berlin theatre and amid the more intimate confines of his Kammerspiele theatre. While impressive, his ideas weren't especially revolutionary: Meyerhold thought his productions too derivative of Gordon Craig's and the acting styles excessively realistic. Between 1927 and 1928 Reinhardt used the theories of Appia and Craig in his first productions of A midsummer night's dream. His version of the play was essentially a Romantic fantasy constructed around the fairy sequences. In 1934 Reinhardt had the play staged at the Hollywood Bowl.

When Warners filmed the play the following year they were imitating the process initiated by film makers like William Barker in Britain during the silent era. They were creating a prestige movie by shooting a successful stage production directed by an internationally renowned director. However, in America in 1935 the economic and political forces that shaped movie making were vastly different. While it's true that Warners were searching for prestige, their methods of mass production meant that film making already had a rigidly controlled methodology. Unlike Barker they were not searching for any potential new markets or attempting to shore up an indigenous culture against foreign influence. Instead they were seeking to confirm the company's economic and artistic position in a long-established cinema industry. They did this by

demonstrating their capacity for ostentatious spectacle and by deliberately drawing attention to the financial and production capacity that had
been used to create it. This was the framework into which the Reinhardt
production was inserted.

Both the film and Reinhardt's original production of the play operated
within the ideological structure of advanced bourgeois capitalism.
Nevertheless there are huge historical and material differences between
Germany in 1927 and Hollywood eight years later. It's important to
realise that Warner's *A midsummer night's dream* is not just a movie interpreting a stage production which is, in turn, interpreting a text. The process
is one of appropriation made more emphatic by the fact that Reinhardt's
play is being received in the context of an American stage and film
industry that has a very rigidly coded perception of spectacle and a very
efficient production process. What is remarkable is that elements of this
visual and very positive affirmation of conspicuous consumerism
imitated many of the images and structures that Reinhardt culled from
Symbolist and Romantic stagecraft.

The film copies established Victorian perceptions of the play by setting
it in Athens during classical times. The standards for North American
portrayals of antiquity had been established in the silent films of Cecil
B. DeMille and D. W. Griffith. They drew their inspiration from the
precisely realised paintings of Alma-Tadema and tended to imitate the
fussiness of Victorian genre art in general. The vision of Babylon that
Griffith inserted into *Intolerance* was dominated by the legendary set; a
vast and spectacular piece of architecture which, on film, appeared as
an indiscriminated vista of monoliths and tiny people. Both film makers
were also influenced by the Biblical illustrator John Martin; a nineteenth-
century Romantic artist who painted apocalyptic old Testament scenes.
His huge canvases, in which minute figures struggled beneath disinte-
grating cities and mountains, transformed scripture into vast tributes to
the theories of catastrophic Victorian geology.

After the credits *A midsummer night's dream* begins with the pomp and
splendour of an epic film about ancient history. Theseus, his army and
their captives return triumphant from the wars and the population of
Athens sing a victory hymn. Yet the compositional techniques used in
*A midsummer night's dream* are very different from those of DeMille, and
can't simply be explained away by the increased costs of making an epic
sound film. After all Warner Brothers didn't skimp on the movie. In
their publicity they emphasised its expensive production and were even
prepared to accept a loss in exchange for the stamp of cultural respectability. Yet the crowds at the triumph cluster together in sets dominated

by claustrophobic verticals and blocks of architecture arranged in abstractly 'Greek' patterns. Similarly footage taken out of doors for Theseus' hunt show a minimalist approach to landscape, with a few Greek temples dotted about an otherwise empty wilderness. This chic, surrealist depiction of arcadian landscapes not only crops up in *Fantasia*, but also in contemporary advertising. There is a strong suggestion that what is being replicated is a conscious connection made between American culture in the 1930s and idealised classicism. The association was strong enough for it to be parodied in a number of films in which comedians like Eddie Cantor found themselves in an ancient Rome that had the customs and dialogue of 1930s New York.

At the beginning of Warner's film the camera switches between an establishing long shot and close-ups of the main characters in full or three-quarter profile. The overall impression is of tiers of people intermingling with a set composed of classical pillars, architraves, cloaks and plumes. Instead of an Alma-Tadema or a Martin the strongest impression is of a light and airy Craig set design; a sunnier version of his plan for the court of Elsinore in which the entire Danish court was shrouded by Claudius' gold cloak.

While the setting of Warner's film suggests the ancient splendour of the flashbacks in *Intolerance*, the smaller sets and rigidly determined choreography of the characters and the camera point to a closer and more direct link with the company's successful musical revues. Like any revue sketch the musical number is perfectly harmonised and its use shows Warner's economical approach to film narrative. In turn the camera focuses on the main human protagonists. It shows the four lovers who, through mime, indicate their relationships. The camera also picks out the group of rustics; the two most prominent members are, not surprisingly, James Cagney (Bottom) and Joe E. Brown (Flute).

At first glance the rest of the film seems like Olivier's *Henry V*; a patchwork of styles, images and motifs. In the first sequence the techniques, staging and camerawork have established that *A midsummer night's dream* is outwardly a spectacular review intended as a showcase for Warner's in-house talent. Like many musicals it uses a fantasy setting to give narrative coherence to what are, in effect, a series of turns, cameo performances and musical sequences. Thus, rather than disrupt the continuity of the film by chopping and changing from one 'turn' to another the overwhelming dream-fantasy atmosphere ensures that the different styles merge without any significant disruption. Within the dream rationale it is possible to combine the ballet sequences and the musical comedy routines with the Arabian changeling, the fairies, the goblin orchestra and the antics of the four lovers and the rustics.

Yet to categorise *A midsummer night's dream* as a product of the Hollywood dream factory is not to invest it with glib escapism. Its exposition of the mechanism of fantastic cinema, and the various images and structures it culls from its many cultural sources, are far from innocent. Warner's Shakespeare film, like many of their musical revues and cartoons, uses the ability of the camera to ape the symbolism and techniques of Surrealism to mystify the taboos of sexuality and death. In the case of *A midsummer night's dream* both these hazy and forbidden areas are drawn together, within the dream framework, using the images and motifs of childhood and childhood perception. It is here that the uneasy connection between the ideology of a big industrial economy and the self-definition of the Expressionist artist becomes apparent.

The first sequence set in the forest has visual links with the animated cartoons of the 'Silly symphony' genre. Like these it uses semi-grotesque imagery. The changeling prince romps through the gloomy wood in the company of fairies and goblins. At one point he chases after the fairies and they escape by flying over a pond. While he flaps his hands in a vain attempt to fly after them a goblin sticks its head out of the water and sprays him with a jet of water. The sequence is serenaded by a goblin orchestra (which plays with the enthusiastic mannerisms of a stereotypical Dixie band). It's dangerous to draw conclusions by identifying Freudian symbols in this scene. Flying, a spray of water and a monster lurking in a pool all had their place in popular perceptions of Freudian psychoanalysis but there is little evidence of any conscious coherence in the manipulation of these images. What the film does evoke is the structure of a generalised Freudian concept of the knowledgeable child experiencing the desires and fears of a dream. This, in turn, partially reiterates the duality of the mystical and the grotesque in Symbolist stagecraft. In this scene the disturbing elements of early animation and the uneasy mythology in Reinhardt's own understanding of the play overlap. Surreal and psychological symbols occur throughout the movie. The duel between Moonlight and Night, fought out in the form of a ballet, has strong sexual overtones. Oberon's appearance is remarkable in that it evokes a number of different associations. His pale face and black costume suggests an imitation of the references to fascism in *The cabinet of Dr Caligari*. At one point in the film he appears in the hollow stump of a tree, shrouded with cobwebs. Not only is this juxtaposition nightmarish but it also alludes to the fashionable surrealist imagery beloved of 1930s magazine illustrators.

To a certain extent *A midsummer night's dream* does try to work through the relationship between the individual and an oppressive, alien, adult world. It takes the mysticism of Reinhardt's production and translates it into positive and cathartic comedy through the characters of the lovers, the rustics and Puck. The arguments between the lovers follow the simple, knockabout pattern of the 'Screwball' comedies. The roles of Mickey Rooney and James Cagney are more significant because it is through them that the alienated childhood consciousness is articulated in the film. 'The basis of Cagney's star persona . . . was his ordinariness – better able to handle himself than many of his contemporaries perhaps, and consistently funnier, but distinctly recognisable.'[4] Cagney was, with Edward G. Robinson, most famous for his portrayal of ruthless gangsters. He appeared in a host of films during the decade including *The roaring twenties* (Warners, 1939), *Angels with dirty faces* and *White heat* (1949). These last two films showed crime and evil as being inextricably linked with the development of children and psychological instability. In *Angels with dirty faces* the gangster Cagney becomes the idol of a gang of youths. In *White heat* Cody Jarrett is a rogue 'child' who worships his mother. This obsession brings him to the brink of psychosis; his behaviour is arbitrary and laced with sadistic humour. His dying words, which he screams from the top of a blazing fuel tanker, are 'Made it ma, top of the world!'. These are extreme cases but they illustrate the equation of deviant behaviour with childhood. The resolution of a film like *Angels with dirty faces* showed how the taming of children was synonymous with the protection of society. Likewise it demonstrated the need for society to take responsibility for their 'redemption'.

If Cagney was an actor supposed to be an emblem of urban working-class man who played his characters as big, fast talking, comic kids then his appearance as Bottom is perfectly understandable. His transformation, like that in Kafka's *Metamorphosis*, is a grotesque experience that draws him into the mystical dream-like fairy realm. However his encounter with Titania is played largely as a romantic comedy with the atmosphere of a musical sketch. In a film that plays heavily on psychological imagery this passage, which should be disturbing, is leeched of any disruptive elements. Cagney's victimised child is hardly a victim, and his transformation back to normality works as a weaker, gentler version of the reconciliation between the Dead End Kids and society.

Cagney, the bluff, simple working man with the gaucheness and enthusiasm of a big kid is the opposite of Mickey Rooney's Puck. By the mid 1930s Rooney was a well-established child actor who specialised in playing infants in roles or situations that parodied adulthood. In Warner's film Puck is the knowing child who dogs the steps of the lovers

through the forest. Mickey Rooney's portrayal of the character is ener-
getic, although the continual shouting and face pulling tends to grate in
comparison to the other, subtler, performances. Nevertheless his
uncontrollability and contempt for the lovers reverses the power
relationship between child and adult. The mortals, unaware of the true
nature of the dream world, are innocent and stupid. Puck, the magic
child continually flaunts his power. The last shot of the film
demonstrates this in an unusually frank way. Theseus and Hippolyta
have retired to bed after watching the performance of the rustics. Standing outside the door of their chamber, Puck bids the audience farewell
and then slips quietly through into the room, closing the door behind
him. The connection between Puck and the bedroom is blatantly obvious and was picked up again (albeit in a much coyer, voyeuristic form)
at the end of the *Pastoral symphony* sequence in *Fantasia* when a cherub
peeps furtively through curtains at a centaur and centauress.

The fact that *A midsummer night's dream* belongs to a strong tradition of
musical fantasy in the American cinema allows the various different
styles and techniques in the film to work with little disjunction. Despite
the orthodox insistence that a distinction should be made between high
and low culture within the film, between Reinhardt and Hollywood,
between Busby Berkely and Shakespeare, there is little internal evidence
to support it. What the film does do is point out how the mystical
imagery and dream symbolism developed in the Expressionist theatre
stems from attempts to define culture, and a cultural role for the artist,
in an industrial mass-producing economy.

Reinhardt embraced the Romantic elements of the Symbolist theatre.
Because of this the links between Warner Brothers' musicals and cartoons and the ethereal world of his dream-like film are straightforward.
A large company, devoted to churning out liberal entertainment for an
American market, used structures and images that were very similar to
those of the 'new stagecraft' in its everyday production. As a result,
when it combined elements from its repertoire with Reinhardt's production to create its version of Shakespeare's play, the two styles merged
easily.

The mystical aspects of the 'theatre of light', especially the individual's
search for an ideal symbolic truth in the world of dreams, echo the
uneasy relationship between the isolated artist and a world that is apparently controlled by the arbitrary forces of production. The fact that Warners had no worries about the benefits of market forces, other than the
felt need to demonstrate their own adopted liberal position, meant that
their film was a celebration of corporate wealth. Thus the angst of the

individual's childish perspective was resolved, through the characters of Bottom and Puck, in a very gentle and humorous way. The sheer spectacle of the film also shows the importance of technology (specifically lighting) and labour control (people as marionettes in a 'factory' of the theatre) for the 'new stagecraft'. In this way it demonstrates a direct dialectical relationship between the theories of the Expressionist stage and the development of Western capitalism.

## Orson Welles's Othello

Orson Welles's Shakespeare movies, particularly *Othello*, show another aspect of the process whereby Shakespeare cinema production is used to work through the relationship between the artist and the state. In *A midsummer night's dream* the theories of the nascent 'theatre of light' were, because of their very nature, effortlessly institutionalised within the commercial apparatus of Warner Brothers. Welles's *Othello*, made by an independent and self-styled bohemian director, tried to recreate the perception of the alienated intellectual while simultaneously trying to fulfill the otherworldly idealism of Wagner's *gesamtkunstwerk*. Instead of affirming the ostentatious production values of a large movie company, *Othello* reflects the negative aspect of Symbolist Shakespeare. It portrays the relationship between the artist and the state using the imagery of the grotesque.

In his early career Welles courted the image of a politically aware artist. Productions like the 'Voodoo' *Macbeth* and the 1937 *Julius Caesar* seemed, at the time, to be direct (if somewhat tendentious) political statements about colonialism and fascism. However, Welles's aura of radicalism was due more to his deliberate courting of left-wing political groups than to the plays themselves. Despite the fact that *Macbeth* was produced through the WPA Negro Theatre Project Welles's play was full of racist undertones. One of the main themes of the production was the duality between the tenuous oasis of civilisation inside Macbeth's castle and the primitive jungle beyond. This equation of voodoo savagery with the landscape was perpetuated by the performance of a whip-cracking Hecate and the use of hidden tribal drums to signify the encroaching evil of Macbeth's treachery. Similarly, for the 'fascist' *Julius Caesar* Welles made deliberate and obvious connections between Shakespeare's play and the situation in Mussolini's Italy and Hitler's Germany, even to the point of picking a Mussolini look-alike to play Caesar. While evoking liberal fears about totalitarianism he failed to

*Othello* (1955)

acknowledge the political nature or origins of fascism, aiming instead for impressive lighting effects and choreographed references to Nuremberg.

Despite his overt association with radicalism Welles appears to have had little personal commitment to politics. His interest lay in achieving the same unified, personal expressiveness that Craig was aiming for. He directed the people on his stage movement by movement, trying to control their bodies and counting out their steps as if they were the marionettes of Craig's ideal theatre. Yet, while *A midsummer night's dream* was made following the rigid schedules of Warner Brothers, *Othello*, like many of Welles's films, was erratically produced. On many occasions shooting was suspended due to lack of money. This fragmentation is reflected both in the movie's structure and its strong atmosphere of disorientation. It also contributes to the cultural myth of the erratic, renegade artist victimised by economic circumstances.

In *Othello* the grotesque perspective manifests itself in many ways. Throughout the film coherent space is broken into a multi-faceted series of collages. The funeral at the beginning, which imitates the montage of Eisenstein's *Alexander Nevsky*, is shot in a way that prepares the viewer for a movie that interrogates and destroys any coherent and unified point of view, substituting a labyrinth of images. Tiny figures are swamped by massive architecture, a crenellated wall is dwarfed by the immense profile of the dead Desdemona as her bier is carried past the camera. After the credits (which are spoken by Welles) we are subjected to a number of fragmented pictures of Venice; figures tussling in empty courtyards, forests of ship masts, a cat watching a bird on a roof, and glimpses of Iago, the Moor and Desdemona. Iago leans against a balcony and his image is immediately dissolved in a rippling pool; when Roderigo is killed the screen is filled with an abstract combination of wooden slats, racing past in all directions. Superimposed on this, the image of Iago's sword appears and disappears like a lightning bolt. The skies are broken by a framework of ships' rigging and the characters pursue each other through a maze of canals, streets and corridors. Welles set out to create a unified world for *Othello* and he succeeded; but this world is a world of piecemeal images and absurd logic.

In the films of Welles a diluted sense of political and historical movement becomes a deeply personal study of the individual victimised by a heartless and absurd universe. There are no concrete political structures, little sense of any context other than that offered by the costumes and settings. Instead the world is suffused with the nightmarish logic of Kafka's nightmares. This translation of political necessity into psychological angst accords with Welles's self-defined status as an isolated, maverick bohemian. Certainly it comes as no surprise to learn that he was interested in the absurdist worlds of Kafka's fiction. Many of the films he directed evoked the fragmented and illogical landscapes of a war-time and post-war world. They dwelt upon the characters and psychology of villainous or victimised 'children'. 'Rosebud', the great enigma of Citizen Kane, is nothing but a boy's sledge; an emblem of the childhood memories that the millionaire clings to at the point of death. In The trial Joseph K has to stand on tiptoe like a small boy to reach the handle of the door that leads to the Law.

Welles's Othello is one of these infants, the innocent 'natural man' whose uncontrollable urges and insecurity are preyed upon by Iago. Welles came from a privileged and indulgent family of 'free thinkers'. His childish eccentricities, including the 'painting' trip to Ireland where he met Michael Macliammoir and Hilton Edwards (who played Iago and Brabantio in Othello), were freely encouraged and funded. Thus he was able to turn his own, very muted sense of artistic alienation, into extravagant bohemianism. Welles took on the lead role in most of his films. He was interested in the evocation of evil as childish aberration or adult cynicism. He was also extremely suspicious of women and his films often display a noticeable wish to return to a mythical childhood innocence. The protracted search for an actress to play Desdemona hints at an indecisiveness on Welles's part and an inability to come to terms with the sexual implications of the Othello-Desdemona relationship in the film. On the contrary sexuality is translated into commercial, political and military power in this and virtually all of Welles's movies. Welles's characters seek to overcome their oppression, both sexual and psychological, through the acquisition of money and power. Kane achieves this, ultimately hollow, control through wealth and Macbeth uses violence. Othello's nemesis is the childish impulse of sexual jealousy.

Othello like The trial and Citizen Kane is a film in which Welles evokes the sense of a chaotic, absurdist and uncontrollable world. Othello falls as much victim to circumstance as to the calculated wickedness of Iago or the uncontrollable urges of his tragic fault. The camerawork of the film is very stylised. Even in the exterior shots, which offer the greatest potential depth, the lack of strong diagonals compress space and volume into two dimensions. When Cassio and Iago await Othello at Cyprus we see soldiers and artillery arranged along the sea defenses. The firing of the cannon is punctuated by sudden and abrupt shot changes. The effect deliberately disrupts the visual and temporal continuity. In some of the more spectacular compositions the waiting soldiers are dwarfed by what appear to be the enormous waves of a raging sea. Even those settings that seem to demand an acknowledgement of perspective; the mighty battlements of Cyprus and the long collonades of Venice, are usually photographed as flat, abstract compositions of light and shadow. Most of the exterior scenes in Cyprus have the same arid inhumanity as a landscape painting by de Chirico.

Perhaps one of the most remarkable sources of *Othello's* unrealistic and dream-like atmosphere is the quality of the soundtrack. This seems to be very poor; the dubbing is obvious and often out of synchronisation with the character's lip movements. People speaking close to the camera sound far away and vice versa. In fact much of the text is delivered when the speakers have their back to the camera or are off-screen entirely. This technique makes dubbing for the international market easier and Welles repeated it in *Chimes at midnight*. Yet *Othello* is not just a film with a badly put together soundtrack. Sound is all important in the movie: Welles places great emphasis on its use as an expressive medium. The powerful score and spoken credits echo the techniques used in the radio productions of the Mercury Theatre. Why then does the use of the spoken word appear so clumsy? It is very reminiscent of the use of sound in Dreyer's *Vampyr*. In this the disembodied voices and conversations that accompany the images are used to disrupt any sense of reality and to evoke the uncertain, shifting perspectives of a nightmarish Kafka novel. *Othello* regularly achieves a similar effect; the text often sounds more like a commentary than spoken exchanges and when it is combined with ambiguously defined scenery it evokes the atmosphere of a dream.

*Othello* is possibly the most austere and intellectual of the Shakespeare films made within the tradition of the 'theatre of light'. Although it uses the imagery and codes of representation evolved in Eisenstein's Constructivist films, Welles's overall approach owes more to Craig's work. Welles sets out to achieve the *gesamtkunstwerk* as an expression of his own genius. His position in society, and privileged background, enabled him to cultivate a strong sense of alienated individualism. Thus he conceived of the role of the intellectual in terms of aesthetic expression and personal angst. The motifs of abstraction and absurdity that run through *Othello* perpetuate the director's fascination with the mechanisms of commerce and politics as channels for adolescent revenge. The film deals with power expressed in psychological terms, as the control exercised by adults over children. Iago exploits this relationship for the sake of sheer intellectual and clinical malevolence.

Othello has the texture of a nightmare and, in its treatment, structure and composition, is closest to Welles's film of Kafka's The trial. Like Joseph K, Othello is the most unsuccessful of Welles's primitive infants. Unlike Macbeth, whose method of self-expression is unrelenting butchery, Othello has no control over the characters or world around him. Ultimately Othello translates the social impotence of the intellectual and artists into an undefined sexual and psychological angst in the face of an absurd universe.

## Pop culture and Renaissance alchemy: Derek Jarman's The tempest

'Film is the wedding of light and matter – an alchemical conjunction,' Derek Jarman.[5] Derek Jarman's version of The tempest, released in 1979, is part of the same artistic tradition as the films of Welles. It was made independently of the mainstream of film production in England and America, a factor that invests it with a certain avant-garde significance. The tempest also uses many of the structures of Othello: through a grotesque, psychological reading of Shakespeare it attempts to invest the role of the isolated artist with a special mystique.

There are, however, important differences between Welles's film and Jarman's, largely because of the respective historical and social positions of the two directors and their self-defined relationship to the cultural politics of the period in which they worked. Welles adopted radical positions in order to establish his own role as an isolated intellectual within America society and culture. Jarman's perception of his own political role is crucially linked to his involvement within the gay movement. Unlike Welles, whose problematic understanding of sexuality was reflected in his adoption of a grotesque, childhood perspective, Jarman is working within a politically aware movement that provides him with a positive image of his own sexuality. Therefore, when he adopts and uses the structures and imagery of Symbolism and the Freudian dreamwork, they are immediately contextualised within a counter-culture that affirms its transgressive position by directly challenging the dominant ideological perceptions of sexual identity.

Jarman's The tempest is a celebration of transgression articulated on a very personal level. It situates the mechanism and purpose of underground art within the psychology of the individual; a further expression of the Romantic and Symbolist desire to invest the production of art with a special significance. Yet, although Jarman does internalise the process of artistic creation, he also undercuts the introspective element of this theory. By drawing on the consciously artificial techniques of the Elizabethan masque he creates in his film a vision of a mythical, Renaissance dream-world in which intellectualism and transgression appear to have important social roles (although the film never explicitly declares what these are).

Jarman's initial ideas for a film of The tempest placed the action entirely within the mind of Prospero. An early script had the insane magician imprisoned in an asylum, recreating the performances of each of the characters while they visited him. The final film was significantly different; instead of articulating the play through the visions, dreams and schizophrenia of a madman, Jarman conceived of it as a conscious tribute to the Elizabethan hermetical world picture and, through the structure of the masque, a recreation of the production styles used in films made during the silent era and Warner's A midsummer night's dream

This shift away from a psychological reading of The tempest is largely because Jarman's film career coincided with the rise of Punk Rock in the late 1970s. On the surface this was a fundamentally transgressive reaction to the escapist mysticism of late 1960s counter-culture. In fact Punk drew heavily on its forbears, especially in its music which combined the aggressive male adolescent culture of Heavy Metal with a new, more radical articulation of teenage angst. Punk was a direct challenge to the exploitation of the youth market by the music industry. It inverted the acceptable iconography of consumerism, substituting it with grotesque and violent symbols. Rejecting 'fashion' Punks wore safety pins, razor blades, dog collars , torn clothes and 'bondage trousers'. Ostensibly Punk was directly attacking commercialism by attempting to create as unmarketable a culture as possible.

Yet in many ways the iconography of Punk was similar to that of the Pop art movement. Both deliberately sought to invest everyday, disposable images and objects with the status of art in order to challenge the mystification of commodities in orthodox society. Pop art was a direct response to the growth of mass-consumer culture in post-war America, and the creation of a new market specifically aimed at teenagers. Unlike many of the earlier art movements of the twentieth century it eschewed any direct intervention in politics. Instead it developed as a reaction to the elitism of high art and the equation of aesthetic value with monetary worth. Pop artists like Roy Lichtenstein and Andy Warhol attempted to demystify high culture by investing commonplace objects with aesthetic significance. Artists working in New York and on the West Coast took

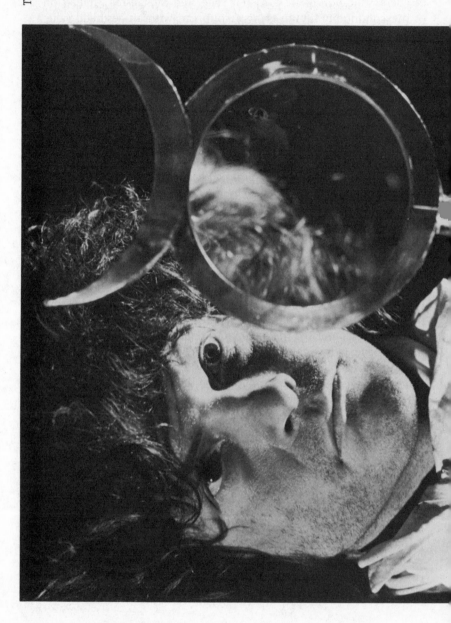

simple commodities and reproduced them as works of art. Warhol's Campbell soup cans are perhaps the most famous example of this.

Pop art's ahistorical stance meant that, although its overt project was the demystification of art, it merely reiterated capitalisms's reification of the commodity. By investing a soup can with an aesthetic value Warhol simply enforced the process whereby a product is awarded a unique significance above and beyond its use value. This bolstering of the ideology of consumer culture was compounded by Pop art's attempts to produce art using mechanical, factory-based techniques. Warhol used stencils to repeatedly stamp packing cases, Lichtenstein did the same for the half-tones in his giant comic book frames. Ultimately Pop was absorbed effortlessly into the canon of high-class culture, with Warhol's paintings swapping hands for large sums of money and Lichtenstein's cartoons marketed as posters. Given the framework within which it operated the radical significance of Pop art is negligible, the awarding of aesthetic value to the commodity was, ultimately, nothing more than the reiteration of sophisticated advertising techniques. Not only was the impact of Pop art on advertising enormous but it also contributed to the development of the paraphenalia of teenage subculture: T-shirts; posters; badges etc.

Many of the works produced by the underground film movement in the 1960s imitated the processes of Pop. Warhol's eight-hour-long Empire (1964) consisted of a single shot of the Empire State Building taken from dawn to dusk. In more general terms the Underground movement in North America imitated the techniques of Hollywood, foregrounding them in order to invest their familiar clichés with the status of art. Morissey and Warhol's Lonesome cowboys (1968) is a parody of the Western; it plays heavily on the sexual ambiguity of the myth of male bondage. Underground cinema represented an attempt to subvert the economic domination of North American film companies and to reinvest film with artistic worth. In Jarman's early underground work he sought to break away from the traditions of the Underground cinema that had developed from the Pop art movement and thereby reject Pop's adulation of the consumer item. His first experience with film production on a large scale was when he designed the set for Ken Russell's The devils. After this was finished he began to produce a number of films using amateur 8mm stock.

In consciously rejecting the imagery and techniques of directors like Warhol Jarman moved towards the avant-garde European cinema of people like Jean Cocteau and Luis Buñuel. The art of mirrors (1973) and In the shadow of the sun (1974) echo the fragmented structures and dream symbolism of movies like Cocteau's *Testament d'Orphée* (1957). By refusing to endorse the ideology of capitalism, and by returning to the psychological iconography used in these earlier films, he became allied to the alienated tradition of the bohemian intellectual. Indeed Jarman's theories of film and theatre production echoed those of the 'theatre of light'. Like Appia he felt that the unification of the various elements of the production was the key to realising the director's search for an integrated work of art: Jarman conceived of this in artistic terms. The key to a good film was its design: 'when design is integrated into the intentional structure, and forms part of the dialectic, the work begins to sing. *Ivan the terrible* is the most perfect example.'[6]

Jarman's film of *The tempest* doesn't merely replicate the perception of alienation that runs through films like *Othello*. Instead it takes the alienated, grotesque perspective, the vision of a fragmented world ruled by the logic of a dream, and transforms it, through conscious references to the artifice of film and drama, into a positive affirmation of underground culture. It's important to note that Jarman chose *The tempest* because of what he felt to be its dream-like structure. This enabled him outwardly to ally his movie with the masques of the Elizabethan period.

Jarman felt that this period directly mirrored Punk England in the late 1970s. This idea was explicitly stated in his previous film *Jubilee* (1977) in which Elizabeth I travels through time to emerge in contemporary Britain. In *The tempest* the association of Prospero with Renaissance alchemists suggests a connection between figures like John Dee and Jarman himself. The implication is that the act of filming imitated the creation of the performance within the magical dreams of Prospero. The rediscovery of ancient myths and belief systems like alchemy and magic during the 1960 and 1970s was one of many nostalgic attempts to create a homogeneous and liberating counter-culture in the face of an alienating mass-consumer society. In many ways it echoed the evocation of mystical history in the Symbolist movement in the late nineteenth-century Britain. Jarman's choice of Elizabethan England is important because, unlike the rigid social totalitarianism of the 'merrie England' myth, it is usually constructed in popular culture as a contradictory, pluralistic society dominated by individuals (although, ironically, much of this myth is drawn from Victorian readings of Shakespeare).

*The tempest* was mainly shot in the Georgian wing of Stoneleigh Abbey. The dimly lit interiors give the film a strong Romantic quality, Jarman shot the exteriors through a blue filter to give them the unreal texture of a dream and to avoid any associations with what he referred to as 'tropical island' realism. Even so *The tempest* drew its static, painterly composition from the traditions of the British silent Shakespeare film: 'In *The tempest* we paint pictures, frame each static shot and allow the play to unfold in them as within a proscenium arch.'[7] By trying to use the symbolic and artificial texture of a masque the film imitated the structure of the Hollywood musical revue used in Warner's *A midsummer night's dream*. This coincided with the parodying of the film industry by underground cinema and Pop art's isolation of certain familiar cultural motifs. In the last sequence a group of teenagers in sailor suits perform an amateurish dance routine and then the goddess, played by Elizabeth Welsh, sings 'Stormy Weather'. The final shot contextualised this, and the rest of the play as a dream, by showing Prospero lying asleep in a chair. The last quote was from Shakespeare's text: 'We are such stuff as dreams are made on'.

In comparison Celestino Coronado's film of Lindsay Kemp's production of *A midsummer night's dream* (1984) is a collage of self-conscious references to other plays, movies and familiar images. At first sight the movie looks remarkably like the Warners film. The forest set has the same Gothic appearance as the wood in the earlier movie although the use of colour eliminates much of the brooding atmosphere. The Coronado-Kemp film also retained much of the episodic structure of the earlier version. There is a deliberate separation of performance styles; between mime, dance, ballet, singing and theatre. At the start of the film the capture and seduction of Hippolyta is performed as a part-ballet part-mime which takes place on a very obvious stage set. Similarly the relationships between the lovers are established during a protracted and silent game of blind man's buff which, in turn, becomes a dance. Apart from isolated quotes from Shakespeare which are read out on the soundtrack (as Theseus' thoughts) few of the players speak. Like *The tempest*, *A midsummer night's dream* is consciously theatrical. It uses costumes and techniques culled from the Elizabethan masque and also treats the play as a study in transgressive sexuality. Similarly, as in Jarman's film, its also questions accepted ideas about the homogeneity of the dramatic text by locating itself within a certain literary context. This is evident in the rehearsals of the rustics and in their pantomime performance of *Pyramus and Thysbe*. In the film this becomes mixed up with a slapstick version of *Romeo and Juliet*.

Jarman's *The tempest*, as an independent film made in the context of various transgressive movements within 1970s sub-culture, often deliberately challenges orthodox perceptions of Shakespeare. The extent of its success is debatable: as Anthony Davies suggests in an article for

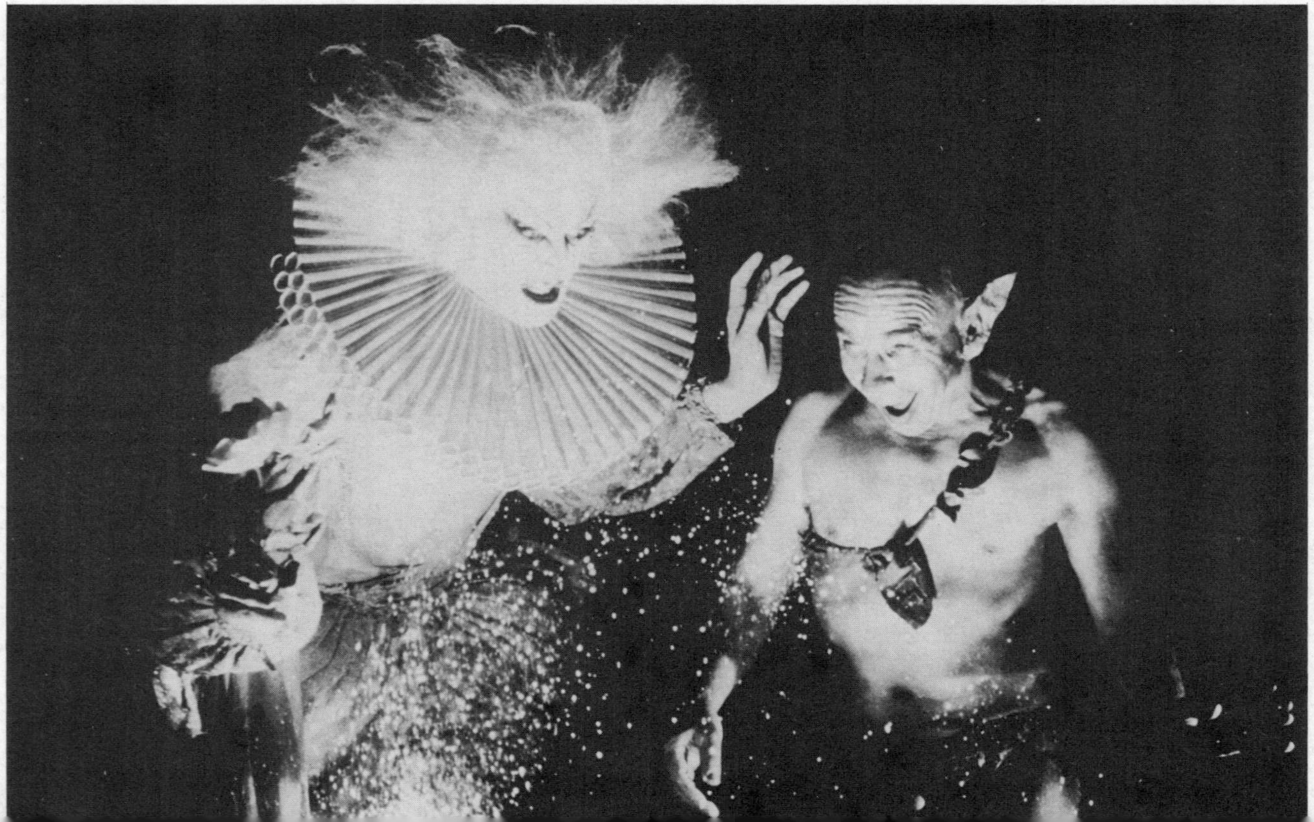

A midsummer night's dream (1984)

*Shakespeare survey*, even avant-garde movies affirm the orthodox significance awarded to Shakespeare's plays by their approach and treatment. It is true that some aspects of *The tempest* do interrogate accepted interpretations of the play. Jarman makes the relationship between Caliban and Miranda ambiguous. When Miranda is washing, Caliban bursts into the room gesticulating like a character from a *Carry On* film. Miranda throws him out only half-seriously; when he has gone she giggles. Even so this ambiguity is not especially radical, neither is the rejection of a narrative-based approach to the play and the substitution of a sequence of fragmentary dream images. This mystical, individualist approach places the film firmly within the tradition of the stagecraft of Appia, Craig and Reinhardt.

By comparing independent films like Jarman's *The tempest* and Coronado's *A midsummer night's dream* with Warners's film we can see how the theories of producers like Appia, Craig and Herkomer developed as a response to the economics of theatre and film production. The Symbolist and Expressionist stage designers working at the turn of the century sought to escape the vulgar materialism of the industrial society by discovering a mystical world of transcendent truth. In doing so they produced a theoretical framework for art which supported, rather than challenged, the accepted role of culture. Symbolism echoed its ideological roots by obscuring the real economic relationships in society. Therefore the relationship of its advocates with the means of production in the late nineteenth-century European and American culture didn't undergo any major change.

This continuing separation of the intellectual from the mechanisms of social change was addressed in two ways. On the one hand film makers like Welles adopted the mechanisms of the Freudian grotesque to articulate their position. They transformed their own feelings of alienation into a fragmented recreation of the perspectives of childhood, trapped in an absurd universe and victimised by unreasoning and authoritarian 'adults'. Although this position allowed them to adopt a maverick and often adolescent bohemianism it is, ultimately, a negative and introspective response to the alienation of the intellectual.

The other approach to the relationship between art and industrialism, within capitalism, occurs in Warners' film. Appia's theory of the *gesamtkunstwerk* was dependent on the acknowledgement and use of advanced technology. This appropriation of practical science was accompanied by the evolution of an aesthetics that adopted many of the values of industrial society: specifically the supremacy of artifice over the natural world and the use of a single, guiding artistic genius.

It's not surprising that Reinhardt's production of *A midsummer night's dream* and the theories of the 'theatre of light' should be so easily absorbed into the milieu of a large production company like Warner Brothers. Of the films discussed in this chapter the only one that came anywhere near to a truly radical articulation of the methodology of Symbolist cinema and theatre was Jarman's *The tempest*. Jarman's film operates on the borderline between two areas of counter-culture. On one side is the underground cinema that developed from Pop art and which was used to parody and interrogate the clichés and methods of Hollywood. On the other there is the transgressive and bohemian world of demi-monde gay culture. This provides Jarman with a positive perception of sexuality instead of the fraught and problematic attitudes of the grotesque perspective expressed in films like *Othello*. At the same time the anarchic and critical approach of underground film to Hollywood prevents *The tempest* from echoing Warner's celebration of conspicuous production. The film's radicalism largely stems from the fact that *The tempest* was made at the height of Punk, a movement that seemed to reflect the radical critiques of the underground cinema in its attack on bourgeois conventionality. Nevertheless, because Shakespeare's reproduction in British culture is so heavily determined and because Punk was never really a political movement, the final movie was ultimately received as yet another avant-garde interpretation of a great poet's work.

# PART THREE

# Shakespeare and the Russian intellectual

In Part III I want to look at the reproduction of Shakespeare in the cinema of Russia, specifically in the films of Grigori Kozintsev: *Hamlet* and *Korol Ler*. Here, for the first time, we encounter a director working in a society that has experienced a revolution. Kozintsev lived through the dramatic changes in Russia at the start of this century. The importance awarded to the role of the artists and writers in the promotion of socialism directly after the October revolution, and the development of Constructivism in the theatre and on film, seems to suggest that there is potential for a far more radical and interventionist use of Shakespeare in cinema; one which we can see operating in Soviet cinema. The extent to which this was realised in the works of Kozintsev, a director who experienced both the revolution and the stifling artistic and social oppression of Stalinism, will be examined in Chapter 6. In this chapter I want to concentrate on the social and historical background to the appropriation of Shakespeare in Russia before, during and after the revolution.

## Serfs and superfluous men

The sweeping changes that Peter the Great instigated at the beginning of the seventeenth century were part of an attempt to turn Russia into an enlightened Nation state. By ploughing the wealth of the nobility and the labour of the serfs into new industries, by severing the rigid control of the church and by forcing the wealthy into public service, the Tsar ensured that the focus on eastern and Byzantine society in Russian culture was shifted towards countries like France, England and Germany.

Tsar Peter's reforms were the culmination of a gradual influx of Western goods, ideas and influence since the time of Ivan the Terrible. Under his control what was, at best, an erratic process confined largely to the nobility and merchant classes, became a precise and totalitarian programme of change for the whole country. To a certain extent he was successful: the beginning of the century saw a flourishing iron industry established in the Urals and twelve academies were built at the new city of St Petersburg as models of enlightened government. The cost of these changes, implemented with autocratic and, at times, brutal efficiency, was the embitterment of the nobility and the increased brutalisation of the peasantry.

Not only were the nobility forced into public service but they had to bear the cost of the technological changes demanded by increased industrial output; paying for the new mines, smelting works, the army, etc. Peter created a 'Table of Ranks' for the civil service, a promotion ladder paralleled in the army and navy. Ascent to a higher rank was supposed to be by merit, though, given that most of the places were inhabited by the disaffected nobility with a resistance to any infringement of the noble order, the potential for corruption was infinite.

Inevitably the financial burden dumped on the shoulders of the landowners was transferred directly to their serfs. The beginning of the previous century had seen the steady increase on the powers of the owner and the concomitant loss of the rights of the peasantry. By 1649, when the time limit allowed for the retrieval of runaways was abolished, a landowner's serfs were entirely his property to dispose of as he saw fit. Peter the Great's reforms not only increased the alienation between owner and owned, but his attack on the church severed the links between the common people and their religious leaders. The creation of a quasi-bureaucratic body in charge of religion, which the clergy now had to serve, opened the way to the secularisation of Russian society. The priests, now finding themselves existing in tandem with the rest of the bureaucracy, began to compete with the gentry, thereby losing their links with the peasants.

The nobility was excused civil service in 1762. A class that had, up until now, been forced into the management of a vast economy and society no longer had to take part in actual state control. During the latter part of the eighteenth century the majority of the foreign influence that filtered down through Russian society from the court was French (although in 1786 Catharine the Great wrote *What it's like to have linen and a basket*, and adaptation of *The merry wives of Windsor*). Readings of Shakespeare during the eighteenth century followed the rigid aesthetic creed of classical literary theory. In an 'Epistle on poetry', published in 1748, Alexander Sumarokov invited his readers to meet the glorious writers Shakespeare and Milton, although he condemned Shakespeare for his vulgarity and boorishness. That same year his translation of *Hamlet* was produced by the Academy of Sciences. Sumarokov's version of the play was written in rhyming couplets, focusing on the conflict between Love and Duty. It had a happy ending in which the virtuous Prince triumphed over the corruption of the Danish Court and married Ophelia. In most cases stage performances of Shakespeare were taken from French translations.

The disjunction between the Enlightenment idealism in vogue at the Russian court and the realities of Russian society sparked off a move towards a more Romantic liberalism among certain members of the nobility. Alexander Radischev's descriptions of brutality and corruption in his *Journey from St Petersburg to Moscow* (1790) exacerbated this intellectual renaissance. The revolution in France drove a wedge between those who saw it as an abomination (including Catharine, who subsequently tried to destroy every link between Russian and French culture) and those who saw it as a beacon of hope for constitutional liberalism. Culturally the combination of the revolution and the war with Napoleon shifted interest away from French literature to German and English: Goethe, Schiller and Shakespeare. Lionel Kochan and Richard Abraham believe that Napoleon's invasion of Russia and the burning of Moscow were the events that crystallised the Romantic, revolutionary liberalism of the intelligentsia in Russia.[1] For the first time many of the nobility directly experienced the horrors of war and as a result some were brought far closer to the living conditions of the serfs than before. Also Russia's alliance with the rest of Europe widened contacts with other societies. Compared to some of these Russia could seem woefully barbaric.

The lack of any effective law of primogeniture had led to the dividing and subdividing of estates to a point where there was a large body of landless, educated and relatively wealthy people working in the army and in the civil service. These and others, formed a nascent class of intellectuals that had experienced direct contact with European ideas, literature and philosophy. They were sufficiently powerful to organise an abortive revolution in December, 1825, the aims of which were to abolish serfdom and introduce a constitution. The new Tsar, Nicholas I, responded by imitating Peter the Great, forming a ministry answerable to him which was placed on top of the civil service and equipping it with an effective secret police. By 1840, according to Kochan and Abraham 'the intelligentsia, as it was to be called, had become a tangible social reality, though it was no yet a class. In the absence of a "bourgeois market . . . providing a sufficient demand for trained intellectual labour and its products", the intelligentsia could only arise from the nobility and those members of other social groups who aspired to join them.'[2]

In the wake of Tsar Nicholas's authoritarianism a rift occurred within the intellectual movement, between those who were pro-Western and those who felt that Russia's salvation lay in a return to some unspecified, historical Slavonic culture. Russia's relative isolation from Europe before the reign of Ivan the Terrible, and her dependence on Byzantium as a source of religious culture, suggested the existence of some ideal, non-European and mythical agrarian democracy based on a Romantic perception of the small peasant community. The adulation of the peasantry by intellectuals is crucial to an understanding of the position of Shakespeare in Russian culture both before and after 1917. The notion of a unique historical Russian state gained even greater popularity when the revolutionary fervour of Western Romanticism dissipated in the abortive revolutions of 1848.

As in England Shakespeare was absorbed into the milieu of Romantic writing in Russia. Various factors made this inevitable, not least the rejection of Enlightenment culture during the war with Napoleon. Nicholas I's predecessor, Alexander, had lifted a ban on the import of foreign literature and literate Russians were exposed to the Shakespeare of the English Romantics. These intellectuals identified themselves directly with a need to reform society. The autocratic administration of the time provided no outlet for direct criticism, consequently literature itself was used as a way of evoking a revolutionary critique of the country's condition, albeit in a disguised way. Shakespeare was contextualised within this type of writing. The case of Pushkin is one example of this.

Initially Pushkin admired both the poetry and the political stance of Byron. Through his keen interest in the literary and radical implications of English Romanticism he discovered the plays of Shakespeare. He read the plays in strong Romantic terms, especially the tragedies, thinking of their characters as essays in passionate individualism. Renouncing the French dramatists he declared 'I am firmly convinced that our theatre ought to adopt the laws of the Shakespearean drama rather than the courtly conventions of the tragedies of Racine'.[3] Pushkin's discovery of Shakespeare also caused him ultimately to reject Byron's work. Given the fact that Russian Romanticism was concerned with using literature as a medium for direct intervention Byron's mysticism and his anti-heroic rejection of society seemed ultimately negative and irresponsible. Pushkin felt that Shakespeare's 'realism' evoked an unparalleled depth of character. The mysticism of Romantics like Byron was unable to address this.

This approach to the plays was echoed on stage. The actor Pavel

Molachov performed Nikolai Polevoy's translation of Hamlet at the Moscow Maly theatre in 1837. His interpretation of the part and the critical response to it (both then and for many years later) show how the character became emblematic of the position of Russian intellectuals. Molachov played him as an idealist and, almost, a Romantic revolutionary. His performance had an impressive effect on its audiences. It was after seeing Molachov's Hamlet that the journalist and critic Vissarion Belinsky remarked 'Hamlet! . . . Do you grasp the meaning of the word? It is great and profound: it is the life of man, it is man, it is you, it is I, it is everyone of us!'[4]

That the intelligentsia should have sought to associate themselves with Hamlet is not surprising. Their appropriations of the play allowed them to try and address both their positions as the scourges of corruption and the fact that they ultimately had little power. Hamlet, in Russian culture of this period, can also be read in the context of the 'superfluous man' of Pushkin and others: alienated and ultimately disaffected thinkers with plenty of grandiose, reforming schemes, but with no power and, in the end, no drive.

Turgenev's short story A Prince Hamlet of the Schigrov District illustrates this quite well. In it the narrator is invited to a dinner party at the home of a rich landowner. After meeting a succession of pompous and grotesque officials he finds himself sharing a room with another guest. This man, who ultimately identifies himself as the Prince Hamlet of the title, relates his life story. After receiving an education in philosophy and science at a German university he became involved with a group of political intellectuals (a 'little circle'). He returned to Russia to find his education, politics and, indeed, his whole tormented personality, irrelevant to life's realities. He drifted along for years before deciding to apply for an official position. When he told his ambitions to a local police inspector the sneering response he received revealed to him his true nature: 'That was the last drop; my cup overflowed, I paced up and down in front of a mirror. . . . The veil had fallen from before my eyes; I saw clearly, clearer than I saw my face in the mirror, what a fatuous, insignificant, and unnecessary man I was, and what an unoriginal one!'[5]

The reign of Alexander II was marked by the emancipation of the serfs in 1861. This deeply controversial move satisfied neither peasant nor landowner. The debates about the moral, social and economic implications of the abolition of serfdom had raged for several years; how would the landowners be recompensed so that they could afford to hire labour? How would the serfs survive with no patronage? In the end it was decided that the peasants would have to pay for any land that they took with them when they gained their freedom. Various complex and unjust methods of payment were introduced to try and ensure that the landowner lost as little as possible, while the serfs didn't actually starve or become brutalised into revolutionary activity. Redemption dues paid by the peasant to an ex-master could effectively saddle a family with a debt for life. Inevitably the early 1860s saw many instances of peasant rioting throughout the country. In the end neither the landowners nor the peasants benefited greatly from the emancipation. The former lost money, many going bankrupt as their land shrank and they found themselves unable to pay for labour. Many peasants were forced to grub an existence on far smaller, infertile tracts of land, living at a level of subsistence not far removed from starvation.

At the same time heavy industry continued to boom from the mid 1860s to the end of the 1880s, resulting in the development of a large, urban working class. Industry was subsidised heavily by the State and concentrated in large factories. The bourgeois entrepreneur class that controlled production of both the economy and culture in countries like England didn't exist in Russia: this situation 'is connected historically with the failure to develop an industrial and capitalist bourgeoisie, as distinct from a professional and intellectual one. The typical Russian bourgeois was not an independent entrepreneur or manufacturer, but some kind of professional, a bureaucrat or an administrator'.[6]

Without any direct involvement in capitalism and with little hand in the direct government of the country, certain factions of the intelligentsia continued to identify themselves and the future of Russia with an idealised Romantic vision of peasant life and the peasant commune. This populist movement had important ramifications for the development of Russian theatre at the turn of the century. It also had links with Mikhail Bakhtin's development of a positive theory of the grotesque in the 1940s when he equated peasant culture with that of the medieval carnival.

The appropriation of Shakespeare as a playwright who dealt with the problems of individual consciousness and morality accorded with the deep strain of introspective writing that flourished in Russia during this period. It is possible to trace connections between the Russian understanding of Shakespeare and the powerful and horrific dramas of alienation produced by writers like Dostoyevsky. Many grotesque motifs (a hostile universe, fragmented perception, the ennui of unchanging existence and the tyranny of an inflexible social code) became part of the introspective symbolism of works like Notes from the underground (1864), the fragmented and tortured outpourings of another 'unoriginal' man.

Books like these no longer dealt with society confronting the forces of unreason, but rather with the individual persecuted by the injustices of an incomprehensible and nightmarish world. Dostoyevsky perceived the alienating effects of urban bureaucratic society in terms of the disintegration of perception, human understanding and personal relationships. In order to communicate the resulting fragmentation of the individual consciousness he focused on the psychological condition of his protagonists. This (and the abstract and urban grotesques generated by his psychological reading of alienation) was closely allied with the cultural emphasis placed on Shakespeare's tragedies as character studies in the writings of people like Turgenev and Nikolai Leskov.

The assassination of Alexander II by extreme radicals in 1881 gave his successor, Alexander III, the pretext to strengthen absolutist control. Attempts were made to create a nationalist morality that would justify absolutist and totalitarian rule. Inevitably this not only set out to rigidly enforce social boundaries but was also extremely anti-intellectual. In response a quasi-revolutionary populist movement developed, within intellectual circles, that was dedicated to the education of the peasantry. In the 1890s one of the professed aims of the Moscow Art and Literature Society and the Moscow Art Theatre was to shoulder the responsibility of educating the peasants. In reality the theatre remained the province of the intellectual elite.

The work of Meyerhold was crucial to the development of both the Soviet cinema and Kozintsev's approach to Shakespeare. In 1895, disaffected with a tedious legal training, he became involved with Stanislavsky after seeing the Art Theatre perform *Othello*. In 1902 Meyerhold, unhappy with the Theatre's inability to abandon realistic acting methods and its mysticism, split with Stanislavsky. That year he formed his own experimental acting troupe. His aim was to try and engage the artist and his peasant audience in a meaningful and educational experience. His concomitant interest in the liberating power of fantasy is demonstrated by the fact that the troupe performed *A midsummer night's dream* six times while working in a theatre in the port of Kherson between 1902 and 1904.

Meyerhold wanted to combine the actors and the viewers in a shared experience, one equivalent to the Dionysian rituals of ancient Greece. These ancient celebrations, in which Meyerhold wanted to embody 'hidden life' using music and dance, were also regarded as significant because their prime motivating force stemmed from the duality of sex and death. As many Russian intellectuals retreated more and more from direct involvement in politics they turned to the private, introspective pursuit of meaning in such motifs as these. In his continuing efforts to break away from the mystical and excessively naturalistic elements of the Russian stage, Meyerhold turned increasingly to the rediscovery of primitive or early carnivalesque theatre forms. This work would take on added significance after the revolutions of 1917.

Tsar Nicholas II ascended to power in 1894. Towards the end of the century the nation became embroiled with conflicts in Asia, specifically concerning territorial disputes with China and Japan. Russia had come into contact with the Japanese as far back as the seventeenth century when explorers and cartographers came across each other on the islands north of Hokkaido. The sovereignty of these islands had always been in dispute. The need to quell unrest at home, and a Japanese attack on Port Arthur in 1904, seemed to give the Russian government sufficient reason to go to war. It did, and lost both the war and its navy. Within a year the first of many revolutions had begun.

The Russian intellectuals, those who read and watched Shakespeare on the stage, were effectively divorced from the mechanisms of state control. Their perceptions of themselves and of the art, literature and theatre they consumed, reflects this. However what is significant about their position in late nineteenth-century Russian society is that the development of industrial society had brought them no closer to the means of production or any freedom of expression. Government was still exercised by an absolutist state which appeared, at times, impenetrable to any encroachment by liberal humanism. Yet, because state absolutism was tied up with the development of capital, there persisted a sense of radical and interventionist power among artists and critic right up to the eve of the October revolution. Those who created the theatrical, literary and cinematic forms that Kozintsev used to construct his Shakespeare films were not only interested in the pursuit of psychological mysticism. They also felt themselves committed to the recreation, in art, of an idealised Slavonic community in which the intellectual and the peasant would engage in a mutually liberating carnivalesque.

## Revolution and Constructivism: Meyerhold and Eisenstein.

In the wake of the troubles of 1905 Tsar Nicholas set in motion the apparatus that would create the first Duma or consultative assembly.

This elected body was seen by many intellectuals as the route whereby the liberal humanist ideals of European governments would be introduced into the country. On the whole the population regarded it as an unrepresentative and fundamentally powerless body, a sop to the reformists which would do little to mitigate the tyranny of the state. This impression was reinforced when the Tsar promptly dissolved it , reinstated it with reduced powers the following year, dissolved it again and then repeated the process a third time. From 1908 onwards the Duma, when it was allowed to exist, had its powers continually eroded by the true government. Only the fourth Duma outlasted the Tsar.

The failure of the Duma was regarded by more radical intellectuals as a demonstration of the fact that the complex mechanisms of bourgeois government were ill suited to a culturally and economically backward country like Russia. What was needed was a complete social revolution along the lines propounded by Karl Marx, in which the proletariat would seize the means of production. The early twentieth century saw the growth of the Bolshevik movement. This party, of whom Lenin was a member, perceived the socialist revolution in Russia as two-tiered. First would come a bourgeois revolution in which the autocracy of the Tsar and the landowners would be overthrown by the proletariat in league with the peasantry. A liberal democracy would follow. The second stage would be the revolt of the proletariat who would not only remove power from the bourgeois rule, but also turn the peasant classes against themselves, using them as tools in the final class struggle. Lenin's argument implied a unification of the industrial proletariat with the dynamic socialist intellectual stance, and the subsequent relegation of the peasantry to the role of mute pawns: 'the proletariat must carry through to completion the democratic revolution by uniting itself to the mass of the peasantry, in order to crush by force the opposition of the autocracy and to paralyse the instability of the bourgeoisie. The proletariat must complete the socialist revolution by uniting itself to break by force the opposition of the bourgeoisie and to paralyse the instability of the peasantry and of the petty bourgeoisie'.[7] The peasant riots of 1905 merely served to create a class of small landowners from the agricultural workers. The rationale for the Bolshevik's support of the peasants was that their 'revolution' would help destroy the remnants of autocratic feudalism in Russia and pave the way for the brief capitalist democracy which the socialist revolution would, in turn, overthrow.

World War I brought the country's internal crises to a head. Disenchantment with the war and Russia's motives for entering into it were reflected by increasing strikes within the main industrial centres. It also led to the alienation of the peasants from the cities. The demands of war production meant that all the industries were channelled into the production of munitions, leaving no means of creating the commodities that the peasants usually received for the food they provided. Lenin believed that the revolution would be engineered initially by an intellectual vanguard. According to Kochan and Abraham, 37 per cent of the Moscow Soviet was composed of intelligentsia in 1917. The intellectual would have a direct and vital role to play in the formation of a truly socialist society. They would educate the proletariat of Russia, not merely in the essential skills of literacy and numeracy, but also to a full awareness of economic and social reality.

After 1917 Russia's relationship to the rest of the world, and the need to formulate an adequate socialist policy to address that relationship, was inextricably linked with the country's search for a successful economic and industrial framework. Ideologically the choice was between a rapid and uncompromising industrialisation of the country and the propagation of international socialism. Internationalism, while guaranteeing the freedom of Russia from the demands of the world economy, seemed a distant, utopian dream. Given the immediate threat to Russia from hostile foreign powers, waiting for the seeds of revolution to occur in Germany and elsewhere was too dangerous. Desperate food shortages and the crippled post-war economy meant that the first path was chosen. However it entailed the implementation of a capitalist economy by the state. The year 1918 saw the beginnings of a retreat into the adoption of state capitalism. Lenin described it as a step back before a great leap, and encouraged the imposition of labour discipline on the proletariat to ensure efficiency of production. Ironically, in order for Russia to survive in the world of the early twentieth century it not only had to defend itself, but it also trade with foreign, capitalist powers.

Of more pressing concern were the internal economic problems that followed the release of the peasant farmers or lumpen proletariat, and the concomitant difficulties of providing sufficient industrial output to meet the demands of a farming population freed from the obligations of forced rent. The rapid move in the Russian economy towards heavy industrialisation became the key purpose of the first five-year plan. Many critics have argued that the drive towards industrialisation, and the concomitant attempts to maintain Russia's position in the international market, meant that the years of Stalinist rule saw the transformation of Russia from a socialist to a state capitalist economy. Basically this means that the government took on the role of the exploiting bourgeois class, effectively dictating the working conditions of the proletariat who were ultimately no better off than under capitalism.

Ever since the revolution itself it had been recognised that the education of the workers and peasants was paramount if the new socialist state was to be successful. Initially, during the early 1920s, the move in the education system was towards the creation of a totalised, practical 'school'. People would be educated in a classroom that was nothing less than industrial society itself. The learning process would become socially useful labour in which all citizens would take part. The art theories that were formulated in Russia at this time reflected this. Constructivism, like its bourgeois equivalent, Futurism, sought to destroy the constraints of a liberal, rational perception of reality as fixed and immutable by using violent and fragmentary forms drawn from the machine age. This movement was typified in drama by the work of Meyerhold and Kozintsev's Factory of the Eccentric Actor. Reacting against the mysticism of Stanislavsky's Moscow Art Theatre, the aesthetes of the early years of the revolution set out to create an art that echoed, in its structure, content and mode of production, industrial factory-based labour.

Directors like Meyerhold, Kozintsev and Eisenstein drew on the artistic heritage of both grotesque Symbolism and Cubism. Late Symbolists like Edvard Munch and Gustav Klimt shattered the coherence of the realistic approach by distorting form itself, freely mixing flat, abstract patterns with naturalistic imagery and eliminating space with warped, two-dimensional compositions. Picasso, one of the founders of Cubism, developed his ideas of art from these painters. The whole project of Cubism, as Braque and Picasso conceived of it, was to fragment society's perception of reality and space and re-assert the two dimensional surface of the drawing, painting or photograph as the ultimate site of meaning.

Picasso's interest in the denial of any coherent artistic concept of the world, and his refusal to accept that human visual perception held any authority, corresponds to the disruption of realistic narrative in the theatre and cinema of Meyerhold and Eisenstein. Braque and Picasso broke up the surface of their pictures and in doing so they tried to imitate the processes of film. They showed the human figure or a landscape not just from one angle but from a whole range of possible points of view. In the end this meant that none of the fragmented and multifaceted images of the world held any authority over the others. The radical implications of this were enormous because they challenged the bourgeois individualist notion of fixed-point realism. The radical theatre groups that sprang up around Meyerhold sought to fragment the images,

sounds and text of the whole nineteenth century orthodox performance. Then by re-assembling these disparate elements into one unified
*gesamtkunstwerk*, they tried to forge a genuine revolutionary art. The Proletcult Theatre and FEKS (Factory of the Eccentric Actor) created social
realism on stage from pantomime, music, vaudeville, industrial noise
and Futurist architecture.

After the revolution Meyerhold openly dedicated himself to creating
a Socialist theatre. When all the Russian theatres were transferred to
state control in November 1917 over a hundred and fifty artists and
writers were invited to a conference on Soviet culture. Meyerhold was
among the five that turned up. A year later he produced the first Soviet
play, Mayakovsky's *Mystery-bouffé*. Transformed into a combination of
acrobatics, circus clowning and cubist imagery it received a mixed reception from its audiences (although the dangerously inconoclastic
Futurists approved of its violent and colourful forms wholeheartedly).
Nevertheless, by the early 1920s, Meyerhold became the director of the
RFSR Theatre No. 1, a company claiming to be the flagship of socialist
drama.

In the shadow of Soviet state capitalism the highly unprofitable RFSR
theatre soon closed. Meyerhold was put in charge of the State Higher
Theatre Workshop in Moscow in 1921 and it was there that he developed
his theories of biomechanics. The essence of this dramatic training was
the supremacy of the visual iconographic gesture over internal psychology. Among a whole plethora of sources (Japanese theatre, circus,
Futurism, Pavlovian behavioural psychology etc.) he included the theories
of Taylorism, using it to create an iconography of industrial labour. In his
first lecture at the Workshop Meyerhold stated that 'in future the actor
must go even further in relating his technique to the industrial situation.
For he will be working in a society where labour is no longer regarded
as a curse but as a joyful, vital necessity. In these conditions of ideal
labour art clearly requires a new foundation'.[8]

In 1921 Meyerhold was joined by Eisenstein, who had previously
worked as a designer in the Proletcult theatre. When he returned to the
Proletcult and later, when he worked with Kozintsev and FEKS, Eisenstein not only developed Meyerhold's concepts of biomechanics but
also drew upon the same Cubist and Futurist sources as his tutor. When
Eisenstein began to formulate his theories of cinema he expressed the
belief that the whole question of perspective was fundamental to the
construction of meaning in film. In his collection of essays *The film sense*
(1943) he quoted a passage from the writing of René Guillere which,
for him, summed up the difference between the scenery of the naturalis-

tic bourgeois theatre and the revolutionary stage designs that followed: 'In antique perspective the planes behaved much like the wings of a stage setting – receding in a funnel towards the depths where the vista closes on a colonnade or on a monumental staircase . . . In our new perspective there are no steps, no promenades. A man enters his environment – the environment is seen through the man. Both function through each other'.[9]

The unification of character and landscape was an important concept in the Expressionist theatres of Appia and Craig. Each element in a production was constructed as an extension and reflection of all the others; architecture, music, players etc. The destruction of 'natural' space (ie. the perspective-centred space of Renaissance art and the traditional nineteenth-century stage) was also central to Eisenstein's technique of shot construction. The elimination of the realistic theatre set with its receding objects and fake foreshortening opened the way for the evocation of a plastic environment manipulated through light. In the films of Eisenstein it also undermined the illusion of pictorial realism. It transformed the surface of the picture, shot or image from an impartial window on the 'real' world into a collage of signs.

Eisenstein thought of the film screen in this way and he composed his shots to create a visual pattern or collection of images. Instead of being bound entirely by a linear, narrative-based time scheme the eye would perceive the images in a sequence that was determined by the techniques of composition and associated meaning. These were the 'units of impression' that made up Eisenstein's 'montage of attractions', 'the art of plastic composition consists in leading the spectator's attention through the exact path and with the exact sequence prescribed by the author of the composition. This applies to the eye's movement over the surface of the canvas of the composition is expressed in painting, or over the surface of the screen if we are dealing with a film frame'.[10]

In his early career Eisenstein conceived of montage as part scientific, part artistic. Though the essence of montage was Symbolist (i.e. it was a sequence or arrangement of icons used to create a thesis or idea greater than the sum of their individual meanings) the significance of the imagery came from its shock value. The grotesque and disturbing juxtaposition of incompatibles was supposed to liberate the viewer into a new dialectical perception of reality. The process suggests the embodiment of the carnivalesque grotesque of Bakhtin; the humorous yet disturbing destruction of spatial coherence as a means of questioning bourgeois perceptions of the world. The effect was used directly in the noise bands and circus antics of the Proletcult theatre. Its most direct manifestation on film was the superimposition of images in *Strike* (1924). By the time he came to direct the first part of *Ivan the Terrible* Eisenstein was drawing elements from the Japanese Kabuki theatre, re-translating them into a mystical and, at times, exotic rediscovery of Symbolism. Even so, echoes of the earlier, more transgressive methods remain in the disturbing switch to colour in the last reel of *Ivan the Terrible part II*.

The conscious fragmentation of three-dimensional space, the destruction of narrative closure and the denial of the infallibility of the eye, canvas or camera had important political ramifications. The searching for a genuine revolutionary theatre and cinema widened the rift between the productions of Stanislavsky and the new self-styled proletarian theatres of Meyerhold and Eisenstein. Stanislavsky's work with Gordon Craig stemmed from an interest in the Expressionism of Appia and Wagner. This rather old-fashioned mysticism provided the others with a convenient aunt sally. In a period of social ferment, the vague and reified forms used to express mood in the paintings of the Symbolists and the sets of Appia were considered an inadequate challenge to hard-edged bourgeois realism. As far as Eisenstein was concerned, 'the Moscow Art Theatre is my deadly enemy . . . They string their emotions together to give a continuous illusion of reality. I take photographs of reality and then cut them up so as to produce emotions . . . I am not a realist, I am a materialist'.[11]

Eisenstein's search for a revolutionary, social realism in film can be seen as part of a process of self-definition. The rapid retreat into state industrialisation, which to some smacked of a return to the absolutist government of the Tsar, implied the cooling of the relationship between the intellectual artist and the state. Many intellectuals in revolutionary Russia sensed that they were committed to a social and political movement in which they could have only a token role. Eisenstein was fortunate, up until 1929, to be working in a sympathetic environment in the Soviet Union, one in which he could freely experiment with the radical, materialist movements of Futurism and Constructivism. After that the absolutism of Stalin, and the collectivisation programs, drove the intellectual artists toward the alienated perspectives manifest in Kozintsev's films, and a concomitant rediscovery of peasant culture.

## Stalin, Bakhtin and social realist Shakespeare

Meyerhold was one of the victims of Stalin's purges. Like many artists and writers his work was branded 'formalist' by a state committed to social realism. He was shot in 1940. Eisenstein also suffered: the second part of *Ivan the Terrible* was suppressed because of its 'excessive' concentration on the psychology of the Tsar and the third part was never completed. Kozintsev only survived by cautiously adhering to the requirements of the government censors. The period of Stalin's control spanned World War II. It began, roughly, in the late 1920s and ended at his death in 1953. During this time the experiences of those radical and revolutionary artists who survived the purges of the intelligentsia increasingly alienated them from Soviet society.

The years 1928 and 1929 saw widespread grain famines throughout Russia. To solve the food shortages, and to marshal the agricultural peasantry in the massive drive towards heavy industrialisation, the government, under Stalin' direction, set about the enforced collectivisation of the peasants. Stalin targeted the kulaks as the class that stood in the way of the adoption of socialist production methods by the agrarian economy. The term kulak ostensibly referred to the wealthier peasants; those who owned a small piece of land and who occasionally hired labour. In fact the word became a catchall reference to all those who were seen to oppose the state control of farming. As only a small fraction of the peasants were members of the Communist party in 1929 this branding of the 'uncooperative' as errant revisionists gave state bureaucrats carte blanche to brutalise the entire peasant population. The dispossession of the peasants from their land was carried out with cruel and arbitrary inefficiency. Not surprisingly many responded by repeating the 'burnt earth' policy used to stem Napoleon a hundred years before. Despite these pockets of resistance the dislocation and deaths of millions of peasants followed.

For many it was hard not to see, in the five-year plan of heavy industrialisation under Stalin's direction, the betrayal of both the workers and the peasantry. Attempts by more conservative writers and directors to invest the State's programme with humanist values were severely shaken by the enforced dictates of social realism. The imposition of this stultifying creed coincided with the creation of a single union of writers in 1934, a body intended to replace such radical groups as the Revolutionary Association of Proletarian Writers. The radical movements in education and art during the early 1920s, in which both areas of production were seen as integral components on the dialectic of social development, weren't sufficient to equip the population with the necessary skills to industrialise the economy. Consequently, in 1931, the Central Committee set out the framework for an education system that returned to the old autocratic, didactic methods of learning whereby children sat in a classroom and were taught by a teacher very much in authority.

The rapid industrialisation of the five-year plan, and the marshalling of art and education in the service of this economic drive led many disaffected artists to equate their suffering with that of the oppressed peasants. Although the misery of the latter far outweighed that of the former the simultaneous imposition of the industrial ethics of state capitalism on both groups led the artists to discover an apparent spiritual affinity with the agricultural peasantry. With both the intellectuals and the farm workers suffering persecution under Stalin there developed in the work of the former a hankering for a mythical populist culture. Like its counterpart in the nineteenth century, this invested a Romantic agrarian society with the values of an ideal commune. This time a serious attempt was made to use peasant culture as a sounding board for Marxist literary theory. Vladimir Propp's formalist study of folk tales and Bakhtin's work on the carnivalesque are two examples of this.

Bakhtin's theories of the grotesque differed radically from those of the European Symbolists. Moving back beyond the negative alienated writings of the late industrial age, this Russian critic used Rabelais's book *Gargantua and Pantagruel* (1532) to formulate a positive concept of the grotesque. The most familiar examples of Bakhtin's positive grotesque can be seen in the paintings of the Flemish artist Breugel the Elder, who specialised in depicting ridiculous representations of village proverbs and the continual struggle between the exuberance of peasant life and the orthodoxy of religion (*The battle between Carnival and Lent*, painted in 1558, shows 'Easter laughter' confronting the asceticism of the church). He also painted religious allegories populated by grotesque monsters; household utensils with arms and legs, cripples and composite beasts.

Bakhtin's location of the grotesque in peasant culture has its roots in the suppression of paganism by orthodox christianity in tenth-century Russia. The priests of the old religion were transformed into travelling players, and a culture of transgression developed around them as they wandered from village to village. According to Bakhtin the grotesque's liberating power lay in its inversion of the rational, authoritative world picture. It drew on three sources, the carnival, popular parody and 'debased' speech. These were combined to create a perception of the world that focused on the body. The head and face, representative of the intellect, was ridiculed and overcome by the revolt of the lower body, symbolised by the physical act of laughter: 'In grotesque realism . . . the bodily element is deeply positive. It is presented not in a private egotistic form, severed from the other spheres of life, but as something universal, representing all the people. As such it is opposed to severance

from the material and bodily roots of the world; it makes no pretence
to renunciation of the earthly, or independence of the earth and the
body'.[12]

Bakhtin's analysis of the grotesque is open to serious question. His
formalist analysis of the Renaissance carnivalesque is ahistorical and is
unable to account for the apparent shift from the positive, affirmative
grotesque to its negative, alienated equivalent in the seventeenth and
eighteenth centuries. The transgressive power of carnival as less interventionist than Bakhtin and others have implied: such motifs as the
fragmentation of the body had a strong religious significance that effectively suppressed much of the liberating power that manifested itself
on days of misrule.

Yet what is important about Bakhtin's book, which was written in
1940, is that its theories represent an attempt both to reinstate the value
of an idealised, non-industrial agricultural society as the site of affirmative
and revolutionary social practice, and to relocate the artist within this
framework. For Bakhtin *Gargantua and Pantagruel* represents what the
revolutionary artist should strive for; a liberating, transgressive proletarian art. Indeed, as the work of Kozintsev before and after Stalin implies,
the early Soviet artists did, almost, manage to achieve the radicalisation
of culture. Through their art the creative process recreated, canonised
and actually became an act of transgressive and liberating power. The
plays put on by Meyerhold and FEKS were constructed as anarchic
comedies and morality plays, circuses with acrobats and clowns. When
Kozintsev made *Don Quixote, Hamlet* and *Korol Ler* he drew on this tradition;
of factory art and pre-Stalinist cinema, and of Bakhtin and the victimised
intellectuals of the 1940s. Through it he sought to address his own
position in post-Stalinist Russia.

In the 1930s Shostakovich wrote an opera based on Leskov's short
story 'Lady Macbeth of Mtsensk'. Shostakovich's reputation as a radical new
composer began to develop with the premiere of his *First Symphony* in
1926; in 1929 he worked as a pianist for Meyerhold. His *Lady Macbeth of
Mtsensk* followed the original story quite closely. The 'Lady Macbeth' of
the title, Katerina Livovna, is the wife of an impotent factory owner.
Blamed by her ogreish father-in-law for her lack of children she starts
to have an affair with Sergei, a new worker. When they are discovered
by the father they murder him and her husband. Katerina and Sergei
then live together but the body of the father-in-law is discovered by a
drunken watchman. The couple are arrested and sent to Siberia. There
Sergei deserts Katerina for another woman and, in a fit of jealousy, the
abandoned wife kills both herself and his new lover.

The opera is a powerful study of the corrupting influence of greed and the oppression of women, contextualised within a capitalist economy. Shostakovich made certain significant changes to Leskov's story: he eliminated the sequence where the lovers murder Katerina's nephew and introduced a corrupt and ridiculous police force as the agents of the law. He also transformed a fairly innocuous scene; where the workers poke fun at Aksinya the cook, into a grotesque, mass choral piece; a parody of a work song, accompanied by Shostakovich's typically Modernist score. Although intended as a savage inditement of the dehumanising effects of bourgeois, decadent society, *Lady Macbeth of Mtsensk* was condemned in *Pravda*. It claimed that Shostakovich, cited as one of the great new composers of Soviet Russia, had produced a piece that debased and degraded humanity instead of affirming the positive values of social realism. It was the start of an uneasy relationship between the composer and the state during which he would continually have to answer charges of Formalism.

The official position of Shakespeare in Stalinist culture can be gauged by a booklet produced by Soviet news in 1947. *Shakespeare in the Soviet stage* was actually written during the war by Mikhail Morozov, a professor at Moscow University. The work was produced as a propaganda exercise, both in Russia and England, where it was prefaced by J. Dover Wilson. In his introduction Wilson goes through some remarkable theoretical gymnastics to demonstrate that Morozov's approach is both traditional and applicable to the condition of Russia and Britain in wartime. He transforms Morozov's insistence on the social reality of Shakespeare's characters into a general praise for Shakespeare's grasp of a non-specific human condition. Morozov's pamphlet is lacking in any depth of analysis, but this is not surprising given the intellectual climate within which he worked. What is interesting is the way in which he seeks to accommodate the Romantic idealism of Pushkin and equate it, albeit in a very cautious way, with the tenets of social realism: 'Shakespeare's realism was particularly close to Pushkin, as indeed it proved itself to be generally close to the Russian mind. . . . Truth in the presentation of life and man is what the Soviet playgoer and reader today value most about Shakespeare.'[13]

The book concerns itself mainly with descriptions of Shakespeare productions in Russia during the 1930s and 1940s. Few of these echo any of the Constructivist techniques of Meyerhold's theatre: they are, on the whole, conventional character-centred performances. Morozov sees this as a positive step because it reaffirms the social reality of Shakespeare's characterisation. The booklet also focuses on the heroic qualities of the plays; Morozov claims this to be necessary emphasis given Russia's involvement on the war. The general propagandist flavour of the work is echoed in the concentration on nationalist productions of the plays, not only those which emphasise a general Soviet patriotism but also those of specific regions: an Armenian *Othello* and a Tartar *King Lear* are two examples cited.

The most remarkable part of *Shakespeare on the Soviet stage* is the description of how Shakespeare is studied in Stalinist Russia and the links between the theatre and the educational establishment. Morozov devotes considerable space to the work of the USSR Theatrical Society (VTO):

The head offices of the USSR Theatrical Society are in Moscow. The VTO has also branches in all the larger cities of the RFSR ... [to which] actors always deliver their 'reports', consisting of extracts from the parts they are playing at the time, on which their colleagues are asked to pass judgement ... When, for instance, a theatre decides to put on *Hamlet*, the department will send it all sorts of illustrations dealing with this play and descriptions of how certain parts were performed by famous actors ... the local VTO branch will organise a thorough discussion of the performance after the first night. In this discussion the producer of the play and his assistants take part as well as the professors and lecturers of the local university, the dramatic critics, students and any member of the audience who wishes to express an opinion. A shorthand report of this meeting will eventually reach the VTO Shakespeare Department in Moscow.[14]

This represents nothing less than a massive centralisation and monitoring of Shakespeare production throughout the Soviet Union. The materials dispensed by the VTO were orthodox critical works, many of which were translated from English. Similarly the productions it encouraged and stewarded debates on, were straightforward character-centred narratives, with the actors' parts interpreted in terms of optimistic social realism. In Morozov's conclusion he emphasises the combination of the ideal and vulgar in Shakespeare's plays. This, and the interest in Elizabethan folk ballads and popular songs shared by many Soviet Shakespeare scholars, suggests a connection with Bakhtin's theories.

The so-called 'thaw' after Stalin's death represented a partial liberalisation of art in Russia. However those remaining radical artists and philosophers who had taken part in the revolution, and who had worked with Constructivism, were still alienated from the state. The realisation that they were little more than 'superfluous' men, and their subsequent alienation, was to colour the work of Kozintsev, especially his two Shakespeare films; *Hamlet* and *Korol Ler*.

In Russia, as in early nineteenth-century England, the people who displayed the greatest interest in Shakespeare's plays were the intelligentsia. A large body of landless intellectuals was brought into being with the formation of the Russian civil service during the reign of Peter the Great. In the wake of the Napoleonic wars they encountered the Shakespeare of the English Romantics. Like their British counterparts they used the plays to try to define their own role, and their relationship to the social realities of Russia.

Because Russia remained locked within a rigid political system of autocratic rule, and because the development of industry was effected through state intervention on a large scale, there was no burgeoning middle-class culture comparable to that in Britain during the first half of the Victorian era. Consequently literature retained many of the radical and subversive structures that were created during the late eighteenth century. Many writers, artists and philosophers continued to think of themselves in quasi-revolutionary terms; as free thinkers opposed to a despotic administration, Some of them, such as Dostoyevsky, joined 'little circles' of bourgeois radicals. Hence the Russian writers who appropriated Shakespeare were not so concerned with the pursuit of the reified ideals of art. Instead they wanted to try and address the social realities of their country. Their use of the plays bears this out: both Leskov's 'Lady Macbeth of Mtsensk' and Turgenev's 'A Prince Hamlet of the Schigrov District' locates two characters from Shakespeare's tragedies within specifically Russian geographic and historical moments.

Just after the October revolution artists like Meyerhold and Eisenstein transformed the theories of Symbolism, Futurism and Cubism into the radical and iconoclastic forms of Constructivism. Shakespeare had a relatively minor part in a movement that was dedicated to the destruction of bourgeois idealism in art and the siting of the creative process within the context of revolutionary labour. However, the imposition of the tenets of social realism under Stalin during the 1930s led to the concomitant marshalling of art in the service of a totalitarian government. The situation wasn't far removed from that under Alexander III. It's not surprising, therefore, that those artists who survived adopted a position similar to that of the pre-Revolutionary 'radical' writers. In many ways Kozintsev's use of Shakespeare represents a combination of the Romantic and liberal realism of writers like Turgenev and an idealistic rediscovery of the revolutionary potential of peasant culture, as articulated in Bakhtin's positive grotesque.

# Grigori Kozintsev's *Hamlet* and *Korol Ler*

The value placed on artistic expression in post-Romantic European and American capitalist society invests the position of the artist-intellectuals with a mystical authority while simultaneously distancing them from the actual mechanism of social change. In many of the Shakespeare films produced in the tradition of the 'theatre of light' this was translated into the language of psychological alienation; a helpless and deterministic angst. Despite its bleak manifestations this approach can be appropriated as a powerful method of self-identification: it justifies the separation of high culture from other forms of labour and isolates the artist as a unique genius. We can see the political implications of this in the case of Orson Welles. Despite his occasional political stances he rarely sought to interact consciously with politics. Apart from the occasional problems with financing, and brushes with state bureaucracy (which he turned to his own advantage), he was free to live out his self-appointed role as a bohemian artist. The Russian director Grigori Kozintsev, on the other hand, took part in a vast social revolution. He lived in fragmented and chaotic times and tried to construct from the material of his environment a positive and dynamic socialist art. Then, during the 1930s and 1940s he, like all the other directors in Russia, became subject to the rigid demands of state-prescribed social realism This dogma was not merely a set of rules about the form and content of art. Because its parameters were vague and ill-defined it demanded rigid self censorship on the part of the artist: 'the social realist artist would never know what was expected of his work, an explicit threat would hang above him'.[1] This setting of individuals against themselves paralysed many into rigid conformism or total inaction. After all, any film or book could be charged with Formalism and the accusation was notoriously difficult to refute. Welles could happily divorce the effects and sensations of alienation from their direct political and social origins: producing a psychological reading of *Othello* without fearing for his career or life. Kozintsev could not create art outside the tyrannical relationship between the state, revolutionary history and the intellectual without being in danger of criticism or even execution. Kozintsev's position as an artist has strong links with that of the nineteenth century Russian writers. His use of

Shakespeare coincides closely with their siting of characters and situations from the plays within specific moments in history. At the same time the state oppression of cultural practice and the brutalisation of the peasants during the 1930s manifests itself in a strong populist themes in Kozintsev's movies. The films draw heavily on the Bakhtinian grotesque; a positive affirmation of peasant culture that seeks to transform the liberal Slavonic Romanticism of the pre-Revolutionary writers into a radical carnivalesque. Yet, despite his strong commitment to the Russian tradition of character-based readings of Shakespeare, the worlds of Kozintsev's *Hamlet* and *Korol Ler* attempt to evoke, above all, the symbolic effect of history and social change. Through a synthesis of Constructivist film and drama techniques, carnivalesque motifs and the psychological realism of writers like Leskov, they avoid the introspective and ahistorical tendencies of earlier Russian interpretations. Because the tragic figures are inserted into worlds that are alien, intimidating and remorseless, the traditionally noble passions and flaws of Hamlet and Lear (indecision, metaphorical blindness, pride etc.) take on an absurd and self-indulgent quality. In the following sections we will see whether the result is truly revolutionary or whether Kozintsev's experiences of alienation under Stalin ultimately counteracts the radical elements in the films.

## FEKS

After the October revolution it was decided that one of the most important tasks was the mobilisation and education, through propaganda, of the scattered communities of the Soviet countryside. After 1917, and during the Civil War, railway carriages were equipped with film-making equipment and small printing presses and sent out across the vast rail network of Russia. These agit-trains took films, plays, pamphlets, posters and literature to outlying districts, stopping at villages, agricultural communities and war zones. Aboard the trains a handful of artists and writers filmed, developed and showed movies, wrote and performed short plays and distributed political material. Eisenstein worked on one, drawing satirical cartoons. Other agit-train workers included Kozintsev and his future companion Leonard Trauberg.

The work performed on the trains, while travelling from station to station, was to acquire a semi-legendary significance that emerged throughout these artists' later material. The agit-trains were seen to occupy a revolutionary role similar to that of the wandering fairs and

carnivals that sprang into being after the conversion of the country to
Christianity in the late tenth century. These roving groups of revolutionary artists likened themselves to the troupes of travelling players whose
presence challenged the authority of the orthodox church. Kozintsev
was to return, somewhat bitterly, to the image of the wandering theatre
in both *Hamlet* and *Korol Ler*. In a wider context Kozintsev, Sergei
Yuktevich, Trauberg and Eisenstein, drawing on their experiences on
the trains, tried to recreate the same dynamic conglomeration of agita-
tional art forms in their theatres and films. Bringing drama to the factories
was one idea: Eisenstein thought that plays performed amid the vast
machines would be the true embodiment of the Constructivist ideal of
art and factory labour. Other projects in the early 1920s included the
use of street theatre and carnivals.

In 1922 Trauberg and Kozintsev founded the Factory of the Eccentric
Actor, a theatre group dedicated to a form of revolutionary drama similar
to Meyerhold's. The key difference was that FEKS dedicated itself to the
total destruction of bourgeois drama and the reconstruction of art within
a revolutionary context. Much of Meyerhold's work involved the radical
reworking of classic texts by writers like Chekhov. While grotesque and
avant-garde, most of the contemporary plays he performed retained a
certain amount of allegorical coherence, a heritage of his involvement
with Symbolism in the pre-revolutionary era and a sign of his interest
in folklore and the traditional tales of the commedia dell'arte.

FEKS' approach to drama was far more violent. Its members collated
recognisable images and situations from artistic genres and made them
unfamiliar and shocking. This was achieved by removing them from
their context and juxtaposing them. In many ways this allies FEKS with
the work of the Dada and Futurist movement in European art. This
association was to prove dangerous as FEKS was criticised for its Futurist
leanings (this was a serious accusation given the strong fascist and pro-
war elements that flourished in the Futurist movement). Like its Italian
and French counterparts, FEKS developed a theory of anti-art that was
based on unsettling images, strange narrative forms, the total rejection
of earlier art and the adulation of machinery. The title of their first work
was *A gag in three acts: the electrification of Gogol*. FEKS performed this in 1922,
when Kozintsev was seventeen.

The chaotic and violent pace of the FEKS plays and films was taken
from the American silent comedies. These movies, in Russia at this time,
were seen in a radical context; as vehicles for the absurd imagery that
Kozintsev and his companions were searching for. The connection
between very early cinema and the mechanism of the Freudian dream-

work has already been discussed in Part II. The people who worked with FEKS were impressed by what they saw as a transgressive and fantastic dream logic in the frenetic urban slapstick of Charlie Chaplin, Buster Keaton and the Keystone Cops. This ridiculous, surrealistic humour was one of the main elements in FEKS revolutionary art. The intention of plays like The electrification of Gogol was to simultaneously ridicule and destroy bourgeois drama and cinema, and to construct a new, positive, vital art form. Both realism and mystical Symbolism were seen as anathema because their fundamental ethos was critical and introspective. Realism clinically dissected the world without offering any solution to its problems. Symbolism was heavily involved with mystical psychology. FEKS' art tried to take the components of these bourgeois genres and, by placing them together, reveal their methods of production and ideological positions. Hence the conscious acknowledgement of silent film technique, the disruption of coherent space, the introduction of clowns and acrobatics and (in extreme cases) the letting off of fireworks under the audience's chairs.

In her study of Kozintsev's work (Grigori Kozintsev, 1980) Barbara Leaming sees this critique of bourgeois film, theatre and literary styles as a form of intertextuality. For her Kozintsev would repeat this transformation, of Symbolist theatre, classic literary images and Hollywood stereotypes into a radical collage, in the films he made after the death of Stalin: Don Quixote, Hamlet and Korol Ler. Kozintsev was not only concerned with setting Cervantes' book and Shakespeare's plays in a historical and social moment but also with acknowledging the position of these texts within a certain critical tradition. In effect his films directly acknowledge the process whereby Shakespeare is constructed, in cinema, from a wide range of cultural materials. What Kozintsev tried to do was to consciously realign this tradition, removing Hamlet and King Lear from the clutches of the Symbolists, Romantics and Realists. In his writings on Shakespeare he engages with the old debate about the title of the book that Hamlet carries with him through Elsinore. Kozintsev suggested that it was written by William Shakespeare himself; a classically alienating FEKS technique which blows open the hermetically sealed diegetic world of the play (which, as far as bourgeois realism is concerned, is total, enclosed and believable). The idea of Hamlet reading the play Hamlet operates as a double metaphor: it reveals the nature of the text and the Prince's own character as artifice (Hamlet is an intellectual whose consciousness is literally embodied in words) and it imitates the process whereby Kozintsev constructs films through references to other texts.

Through FEKS Kozintsev and his companions tried to create a new avant-garde theatre wholly opposed to the hermetically sealed worlds of orthodox bourgeois drama, or the intellectual mysticism exemplified by Craig's Hamlet. Their theatre was based on shock; on the deliberate juxtaposition of traditionally incompatible codes of representation. Clowns, juggling, film and mime were mixed with ideas, emblems and narratives drawn from the experience of living in an industrial society: factory noises, robotic movements and the machine imagery of Futurism. No attempt was made to smooth over the differences between these motifs: meaning was derived from the combination of alien modes of discourse, a process that was both reminiscent of the Rabelaisian compilation of incompatible images and the grotesque paintings of artists like Ensor. Because much of the disruptive methodology of FEKS was adapted from the styles of American cinema, Kozintsev and Trauberg had little difficulty making the transition from theatre to film. Their first movie, The adventures of Octyabrina (1922) was a frantic, slapstick pantomime. However the promotion of Constructivist theories in the films of FEKS had little time to develop. In 1928 the first All-Union Party Conference on cinema voiced suspicion about the Futurist excesses of some film producers. Six years later the aesthetics of social realism became official party doctrine.

At first the movies that Kozintsev and Trauberg made under Stalin were well received. Their trilogy on the life of Maxim Gorky, produced in 1935, won the Stalin Prize. However during the 1940s the tightening controls imposed on artistic production meant that their work, like that of many others, was subject to close scrutiny; in 1946 the film Simple people was heavily criticised. Three years later both directors found themselves linked to an ill-defined section of society attacked by the state for their 'cosmopolitanism' (i.e. a refusal to acknowledge the national achievements of Russia). Although Kozintsev survived the years of Stalinist rule the eradication of the revolutionary idealism of the Constructivist movement had a profound effect on his perception of his role as an artist in the USSR. As a result his Shakespeare films not only retain elements of the FEKS interrogation of bourgeois realism and Symbolism but they also attempt to question the official VTO readings of the plays in the Russia of the 1940s and 1950s.

In his writings Kozintsev brands the use of Shakespearean characters and situations by critics like Morozov with the term 'Hamletism'. This refers to the unthinking use of the plays by authors anxious to vindicate the ideals of their own age and culture using Shakespeare's writings. Unfortunately Kozintsev's stance is dangerous because it implicitly attacks the use of characters like Hamlet as models of social types living in Russia at the turn of the century. His films show that he, at times, has difficulty separating the potentially radical integration of Shakespeare's characters in bourgeois Russian literature from the reactionary and conservative idealism of 1940s literary criticism. Yet this difference was crucial. Because the tenets of social realism demanded a positive reinterpretation of the tragic characters, Morozov perceived Shakespeare's plays as essays in passionate realism. At times Kozintsev seems unable to distinguish between this and the radical (albeit negative) critiques of bourgeois life in the writings of Turgenev and Leskov. Thus his Shakespeare films reflect the contradictions inherent in his position as a director who has experienced the social and cultural upheavals of Stalinism. He uses many of the motifs and structures of Constructivism to try and counteract the clinical and passive tenets of social realism. Yet in attacking 'Hamletism' he also attacks the pre-revolutionary appropriations of the plays in the service of radical social criticism. The irony is that, because he worked as an artist in a society run by a totalitarian government, his position is similar to that of writers like Dostoyevsky, Gogol and Turgenev.

Kozintsev's films, like the stories of his predecessors, rework Shakespeare's plays using the introspective and brooding psychology of the negative grotesque. Given his experiences during the 1940s it's not surprising that he, like Orson Welles, was interested in evoking an absurdist perception of the world. Like the Moor, Hamlet and Lear wander through landscapes that have no narrative, visual or spatial coherence. Their worlds are worlds that have dissolved into labyrinths and fragments. Othello is trapped by monolithic architecture and two-dimensional composition. In Hamlet the castle of Elsinore is never revealed in its entirety and the fragments we see have no coherent dimensions; the ghost of a father towers over his son like a giant, King Lear goes insane on a flat, featureless lake of dried mud. The radical heritage of FEKS allows Kozintsev almost to break away from this introspective and deliberately futile perception of the world. He used the vital and fragmentary aesthetics of pre-Stalinist Soviet culture to evoke the idealised world of Bakhtin's popular carnivals and to try and recreate the populism of the radical 'little circles' of the nineteenth century. The result is not entirely successful. Kozintsev's sense of alienation, when combined with his desire to create a radical reading of the plays, means that his theories often appear contradictory and self-defeating. In the next two sections we will see how this process occurs in his Shakespeare movies; Hamlet and Korol Ler.

## Hamlet (1963)

The works of writers like Turgenev show how the character of Hamlet had a special significance for Russian intellectuals. The Prince, a university student educated in metaphysics, qualifies as an archetypal 'superfluous man'. He is the rightful heir to the throne of Denmark and the fortunes of the country should be in his hands. Instead he is denied his role and alienated from the mechanism of power by his uncle. Tormented by his own indecision he ultimately falls victim to the complex web of intrigue on which Claudius bases his rule.

The Constructivist directors were opposed to the reproduction of 'classic' texts, preferring to write and stage contemporary works they felt were relevant to the aims of the revolution. Within post-revolutionary Russia Hamlet was still associated with the kind of treatment given to it by Craig and Stanislavsky in the Moscow Art Theatre production of 1912; a performance that many felt to be excessively cerebral and mysterious. Most productions of the early twentieth century reiterated this character-centred approach; following the tradition established by the Romantic actors Mikhail Schepkin and Pavel Mochalov.

In the late 1920s the state encouraged young communists to occupy the offices of incompetent bureaucrats and denounce the offenders to the Soviet people. Not surprisingly readings of Hamlet as the tale of a passionate, heroic character ferreting out corruption in the Danish state were encouraged during Stalin's rule. One attempt to challenge this orthodoxy was made by Nikolai Akimov who produced a radical version of the play at the Vakhtanyov Theatre in Moscow in 1932. His production was reminiscent of the anarchic iconoclasm of FEKS. In his version Hamlet was the ruthless schemer, scaring people with fake ghosts and cleverly engineering his way to power. Not surprisingly Akimov's production was criticised for being too 'formalist'.

When Kozintsev filmed Hamlet in 1963 he was working in the humanist tradition of the nineteenth century Russian critics. His movie imitated the attempts by Pushkin and Belinsky to create a humanist, socially aware understanding of Hamlet's position. He also used Laurence Olivier's 1947 film of the play to define his own response to Shakespeare's work. As far as Kozintsev could see Olivier's portrayal of Hamlet was a character study of the man's psychological state. The British actor's film perpetuated the English Romantic tradition by focusing on the Prince's search for spiritual and emotional fulfillment in a world that reflected the inner workings of his own mind. At the same time Olivier's Hamlet had a strong childlike quality; his indecision was the result of his victimisation and his inability to come to terms with his own psychological response to his father's betrayal and his mother's incestuous relationship.

Olivier's *Hamlet* owed much to the theories of the 'theatre of light'. For the movie Elsinore was designed as a large, chiaroscuro labyrinth. Large and non-functional its architecture traps the protagonists in a maze of walls and staircases. The camera drifts though these on seemingly aimless journeys, echoing the tortured wandering of Hamlet's consciousness. The opening shot shows Hamlet's funeral cortege on the sloping top of a tower. With its dramatic lighting and semi-abstract setting the shot is very reminiscent of the theatre designs of Gordon Craig. Yet, in contrast, the establishing shots of the Danish court, complete with Hamlet sprawled sullenly across a chair, look as if they have been transplanted wholesale from the Victorian stage. Olivier's film was a fragmented collage of styles: Expressionism mixed with Victorian imagery; long exchanges of heavily accentuated dialogue spoken in scenes shot using the techniques of silent cinema. It also drew heavily on familiar genre paintings for its imagery. The description of Ophelia's suicide is accompanied by a shot of her floating down a stream on a bed of flowers in exactly the same position, and with the same vacant expression, as Millais' Ophelia. The confusion of styles mitigates against any single perspective that would make Olivier's *Hamlet* the effective character study it sets out to be.

Kozintsev's *Hamlet* was intended partly as an antithesis to the English actor's psychological reading; a tragedy of a man caught in a climate of political corruption as opposed to one confronting his inner flaw. The landscapes of the two films bears this out. Olivier's Elsinore, despite its Expressionist construction, is a rigidly enclosed area. The camera's depth of focus, its occasional imitation of genre-art naturalism, and its frequent use of high-angle shots to establish scenes, awards it the authority of an impartial observer clinically picking its way through the Prince's psychological problems. Kozintsev's landscape is vast, limitless and only partially comprehensible. There is a strong feeling of subjectivity (which was to be repeated in *Korol Ler*) behind the drifting viewpoint; the impression that the action, characters and text are part of a vast and intricate dream world.

Kozintsev is at pains never to show the castle as a whole. Instead he gives the audience mere glimpses of its monolithic architecture from which they have to build up a perception of the geography. Yet this

Hamlet (1963)

geography, as created by the camera. is not only made up of blocks of complete and ruined masonry. It is also embodied in human, emblematic and textual motifs. In what seems to be a visual tribute to *Strike* shots of guards prowling through corridors are mingled with close-ups of large, slavering watch dogs. Elsinore is full of stairways. The confrontation between Hamlet and Ophelia takes place through the balustrade of one flight. In other scenes courtiers stand at various points on vast, worn steps; a visual metaphor for the ladders of power and the intricate 'Table of Ranks' of the old Russian bureaucracy. Other landscapes are bounded by fluttering tapestries, flambeaux, boulders and the boiling sea. 'The architecture of Elsinore does not consist in walls, but in the ears which the walls have. There are doors, the better to eavesdrop behind, windows, the better to spy from. The walls are made up of guards.'[2]

Hence the physical boundaries of the film are impossible to visualise because they are indissoluble from the imagery. Kozintsev is working in the tradition of Appia and Eisenstein, his use of architecture echoes the latter's elimination of spatial reality and the combination of the various elements of the drama (characters, setting, imagery, shot construction and editing) to create meaning. Eisenstein mingled the landscapes of the human body with the strange, grotesque architecture of *Ivan the Terrible*. Courtiers creep through impossibly low arches in a Kremlin dominated by Ivan's shadow, interiors oscillate between the grotesquely lush and a hard-edged Cubist world of light and dark, shapes and textures.

By creating a montage-based visual patchwork of images culled from the Constructivist theatre and Eisenstein's work, Kozintsev rejected the psychological introspection of Olivier's film. Because he was working within the tradition of Romanticism, as used in Russia, this results in a movie that parallels, to a remarkable degree, many of the settings and motifs of the early Gothic movement in eighteenth-century Britain. In Russia the move from radical Gothicism to the internalisation of the mechanisms of horror within the psyche was markedly different to that demonstrated by the novels of Maturin or Hogg. Even the most inward-looking tales of Dostoyevsky still retained a strong sense of the individual's position in society. Instead of the hallucinatory fantasies of the late Gothic and early Symbolist writers in Britain, Russian writers concentrated on creating grotesque and ridiculous parodies of Russian society.

One reason for this is that, although the Russian intellectuals and critics were still divorced from the mechanisms of power, the absolutist characteristics of government didn't change dramatically until 1917.

Consequently there was no pressure to retreat into the despairing and listless cult of ennui that many post-Romantic radical authors adopted in Britain. The mechanisms of alienation still had an obvious, concrete source. They could be placed (no matter how mistakenly) at the feet of an autocratic Tsar and his repressive government rather than be translated into a psychological reaction to indistinct and faceless market forces. In Stalin's USSR Kozintsev was in a virtually identical position to that of the artists labouring in the Russia of Alexander II. Their economic position was, in turn, broadly similar to that of writers like Walpole. It is no coincidence, therefore, that the massive architecture in *Hamlet* echoes the early nineteenth century British readings of the etchings of Piranesi; especially his sequence of fantastic prisons.

As well as drawing the ruins of ancient Rome, several times bigger than they actually were, Piranesi produced etchings of monstrous prisons which he called *Carceri*. These consisted of colossal interiors built from columns, stairways, arches, giant trophies and inexplicable machines. Writers like Walpole were influenced by these images because they embodied many of the textual effects of Gothic writing. Piranesi's prints showed partial glimpses of an incomprehensible infinity: arches within arches within arches stretching beyond the limits of vision. They had innumerable perspectives, they dwarfed humanity and each picture invited the viewer to create a multiplicity of fragmented narratives. These had, as their underlying theme, the oppression of an unenlightened government. 'But raise your eyes, and behold a second flight of stairs still higher: on which again Piranesi is perceived, by this time standing on the very lip of the abyss. Again elevate your eye, and a still more aerial flight of stairs is beheld and again is poor Piranesi busy on his aspiring labours.'[3]

In rejecting the inward looking Expressionist *Hamlet* of Craig and Olivier Kozintsev recreated much of the fragmented narrative and architectural texture of books like *The castle of Otranto*. Elsinore, glimpsed only in parts, and the vast countryside and seascape that surrounds it, imitate the Gothic perception of a hostile and infinite universe composed of awful and sublime forms. There is little doubt that the giant ghost in *The castle of Otranto* is derived from Walpole's reading of *Hamlet*. The vast spectre that haunts his castle is, at first. only perceived in fragments: a vast helmet that falls in the courtyard; a giant mailed hand on a bannister. Its appearance signifies the undeniable and unavoidable power of a symbolic, dynastic history which even the villain Manfred cannot deny. The ghost's final appearance is specifically to re-assert this and to indicate the rightful heir to the throne.

Kozintsev's use of the supernatural is very similar although, instead of manifesting itself as fragmented images, Kozintsev's ghost appears in its entirety from the very beginning. Hamlet, Horatio, Bernardo and Marcellus walk into a courtyard at night. Above them, in the lighted windows, move the shadows of the revelers. Suddenly Hamlet and his companions stagger back in the face of a powerful wind and the camera cuts to show the ghost towering up into the boiling night sky. While the context and appearance of the ghost is similar to Otranto's spectre, the physical space that it occupies makes the image elide into the iconography of the grotesque. It is impossible to determine the ghost's size. Hamlet looks up when he first sees it and the following shot of the wraith is taken from an extremely low angle. This suggests that it is enormous. The illusion is perpetuated, rather than dispelled, as it walks up a shallow flight of stairs. Dramatic lighting, slow motion photography and the indeterminate scale of Elsinore all contributes to an impression of enormous scale. But this is never explicitly stated. When the ghost strides below the battlements, and the tiny figure of Hamlet appears above it in a series of arches, it is impossible to tell whether the difference in scale is intended to be real, or merely the result of an extreme perspective. Finally, as Hamlet and his father confront each other and the ghost tells his son of the corruption in the Danish court, the tone is more intimate. But we never see Hamlet and the spectre together in their entirety, and the scale, though reduced, is still ambiguous.

In the encounter between Hamlet and the ghost of his father, Kozintsev creates a multi-layered evocation of dynastic power and tradition. The disruption of scale and the juxtaposition of the giant with a landscape whose boundaries are never fully defined is reminiscent of the final shots of *Ivan the Terrible Part I*. Ivan, frustrated by the corruption of the Boyars, undergoes self-imposed isolation. The people of Moscow come to his refuge to beg him to return. In a sequence of images Ivan's head is shown in close-up, looking down at a crocodile of figures stretched across the landscape. The shot is repeated, this time in extreme close-up, with Ivan's lowered face filling a third of the screen. The combination of the people in the snow and the huge profile (the actor's make up was based on that of the Japanese Kabuki theatre) creates a striking and sinister image of charismatic tyranny.

In Kozintsev's film the spectral giant and the cyclopean architecture rest in an uneasy alliance with the image of an enormous parent looming over, and threatening, the helpless, anxiety-ridden child. The former is intended to signify the inescapable and implacable weight of history. The sense of inevitability is crucial if the relationship between the individual and the world is to be seen as the site of political victimisation. However the visual evocation of a grotesque parent-child bond also implies a more ahistorical evocation of alienation. Part of Kozintsev's project in Hamlet is to redeem this sense of helplessness by using Bakhtin's positivist grotesque.

Kozintsev's film acknowledges the Slavonic populism of Bakhtin; a theme emphasised in the scene where Horatio and Hamlet meet by a ruined, burning village. He also combines Bakhtin's interest in peasant culture with the anarchic forms of Constructivism in an overt acknowledgement of multiple forms of art, using them to construct the film from disparate and fragmented discourses. Kozintsev's use of disruptive scale and the subversion of authority by the carnivalesque (specifically in the case of the players) reflects the playful destruction of orthodox mysticism by directors like Meyerhold. The play within the play is performed on a platform with the sea in the background. The makeup of the characters and their exaggerated performances parodies orthodox literary productions of the play and also suggests a conscious reference to FEKS.

This is made explicit in the scene where Hamlet confers with the travelling actors in a courtyard. Their conversation is punctuated by the cackling of hens, while above them, on a wall, stride the sentries. As Hamlet falls to musing, and his monologue is spoken on the sound track, the shot is framed so that he is surrounded by masks and props. Then the film shows him from the back, his figure shot through the covering of the cart. The sudden contraction of the dramatic space into the narrow confines of a theatrical store contextualises the text of Hamlet as a dramatic fiction. Kozintsev not only draws attention to the play as an artificial construct, a play within a play within a symbolic world of texts, but he is also referring to his earlier experience with the agit-trains and FEKS: acting on trailers and impromptu stages amid the chaotic world of revolutionary Russia.

Yet these positive Bakhtinian images are countered by the disruptive presence of the unknowable; of supernatural forces beyond human control. This causes the film to regularly shift its focus onto the impotence of a Hamlet who is incapable of reconciling his position in history. It's hardly surprising that Kozintsev, filming Hamlet in the post Stalinist 'thaw', should have placed his student Prince in such a strange and disturbing world. The works of the exiled Soviet director Andrei Tarkovsky evoke a similar theme. His film of Stanislaw Lem's Solaris (1972) used the mechanism of the fantastic to similar effect. Orbiting above a world covered in a vast, intelligent and totally incomprehensible ocean a small group of intellectuals confront a host of figures and images recreated from their memories.

It is, above all, the sense of political history that marks Kozintsev's *Hamlet*. Shirking the determinism of Olivier's character-centred reading, Kozintsev perceived Hamlet's purpose as the destruction of a corrupt Machiavellian court and his tragedy as a 'tragedy of conscience'.[4] That the conscience of an intellectual should be so important is, in itself, a revealing comment on Kozintsev's perception of himself and his work. Hamlet's indecision and final death proceed from his involvement in a historical process which has little room for intellectual honesty. The final sequence makes clear the overall insignificance of his motives and deeds: his killing of Claudius has merely cleared the way for the militaristic order of Fortinbras. The last words of the film are 'the rest is silence'. Hamlet's body is then picked up and carried down a flight of steps, soldiers milling around the improvised bier. The corpse is soon lost in the crowd and the final image is of the castle's shadow cast on a heaving sea; an image which like Solaris itself, signifies 'the change of tides, the boiling of chaos, and again the silent, endless surface of glass'.[5]

In *Hamlet* the juxtaposition of incompatible images and impossible architecture works in a similar way to the collation of disparate art forms in the performances of FEKS. While the result iterates, to a certain extent, the positive, transgressive qualities of Bakhtin's grotesque, Kozintsev's approach, emerging from the long night of Stalinism, reflects the alienated populism of writers like Dostoyevsky (whose answer to the oppression of the Tsar was a plea for old, Slavonic, Christian values). Yet in the end Kozintsev's historical position has more in common with Pushkin's and Bakhtin's than with Dostoyevsky's. Multiple images and montage techniques enabled him to use Shakespeare to rediscover partially an art form that acknowledged history as a dynamic process, instead of embedding the play in the fossilised dogma of social realism.

## Korol Ler (1969)

Kozintsev's film of *King Lear* offers a study of the corrupting processes of absolutist power that reproduces many of the discourses present in Sergei Eisenstein's three-part study of the reign of Ivan Gronsky. There are strong similarities and differences between *Korol Ler* and the two extant parts of *Ivan the Terrible*. These are highly significant given the historical and social position in which Eisenstein and Kozintsev worked. Both films, in attempting to display the manifestation of totalitarianism

Korol Ler (1969)

within the character of the despot, suggest that the directors are trying to come to terms with the traumatic period of Stalin's rule.

Eisenstein's films, made during World War II, seek to address, and partly justify, the effects of power upon the individual ruler. The gradual changes that take place in Ivan's character mirror the social and political transformations that determine the nature of his rule. At the start of the first film he is a noble and heroic youth. In the final image of the second part his hunched figure and mask-like face are grotesquely accentuated by the violent colours of the final reel. His last words, following the abortive attempt on his life, are 'a Tsar must be ever watchful!'[6] Ultimately both movies are ambiguous, offering both an apologia and a criticism of Stalinism which Eisenstein tried to weave into a dialectical relationship. Given the content and treatment of Eisenstein's two films it is not very surprising that Part II was heavily criticised for its apparent concentration on the psychology of Ivan's character, and that Part III was never finished.

Eisenstein preferred the tragedies of Webster and Marlowe to those of Shakespeare: he felt that their excesses of violence and emotion were more dynamic and potentially radical than Shakespeare's plays. This statement implies a rejection of the liberal humanist tradition into which Shakespeare had been inserted in Russia before and after the revolution. For Kozintsev, on the other hand, this tradition was significant in the context of his position as an artist during the post-Stalinist 'thaw'. It is in Korol Ler that Kozintsev's adoption of the theories of Bakhtinian populism find their most sophisticated expression. By integrating them with elements of the Japanese Noh theatre he almost succeeds in producing a radical, albeit austere reincarnation of the mechanisms of Constructivism within a Shakespeare play.

Kozintsev published his diary of the making of Korol Ler as King Lear: the space of tragedy in 1977. The first part of it is devoted to his trip to Japan and his encounters with the Japanese Noh theatre. In 1928 a troupe of actors from Japan's Kabuki theatre visited Russia. Eisenstein went to a performance and saw within its rigid pre-determined forms the key to his theory of montage. Kabuki theatre, unconcerned with naturalism, created meaning through an explicit conglomeration of symbols; masks, stances, images and music. The influence of the Kabuki, and of Japanese art as a whole, can be seen in the cinematic composition of Ivan the Terrible, and the stylised makeup worn by Nikolai Cherkassov in the title role.

After seeing how Akira Kurosawa used the structures of the Noh theatre (an older, more aristocratic form of drama) in his film of Macbeth,

Kumonosu jo, Kozintsev rejected the colourful and melodramatic style of the Kabuki (which Kurosawa has referred to as a 'sterile flower') in favour of its more austere and operatic ancestor. This was not only a stylistic move: it suggests a closer affinity between the position of Kozintsev and Kurosawa (a self-styled liberal humanist) than between Kozintsev and Eisenstein. In the work of Meyerhold and Eisenstein the techniques of the Japanese theatre were used in the context of the populist grotesque of the revolutionary 1920s theatre. Kozintsev's film, made long after Stalin was dead, uses the stylised techniques of the Kabuki and the Noh to recreate the Romantic humanism of the pre-revolutionary intellectuals. The key to the reformist position lies in his attitude to the Noh mask and the way he uses it to divorce the figure of Lear from the historical and social forces behind his tyranny.

In the Japanese Noh theatre the main characters wear a mask (or Nohmen) which signifies their roles. The masks don't represent specific characters, instead they stand for certain generic types: a young woman on the edge of madness; a demon; the ghost of an aged man etc. The relationship between an actor and the mask is highly ritualised and parallels the shamanistic ceremonies of the early Japanese religious festivals. Actors put on the mask in a small room set apart from the Noh stage, called the 'mirror room'. After he has been helped into his costume (all Noh actors are men) the player takes the mask that represents his character and studies it. Then in front of a mirror, he puts it on. At this point the traditions of the Noh hold that the soul of the mask enters the soul of the actor in a form of aesthetic possession. From then on, with his own features concealed by those of the Nohmen, the actor is the character signified by the mask.

Kozintsev used the concept of the Noh mask to define the relationship between Lear and power; between humanity and the masks it assumes as it engages in social practice. Here Kozintsev treads on dangerous ground. Hamlet's uneasy assumption of the persona of a social rebel is set within the context of a world built from the Gothic and grotesque imagery of corrupt power and politics. In Korol Ler the focus is less upon the mechanism of social rule: the intertextual references to the Noh hint at a strongly spiritual mystification of Lear's character. Kozintsev's movie suggests a disturbingly reified concept of the relationship between the individual and politics which he emphasised with his remark that 'Lear tears off the mask of power, and throws it away. Only then does his face become visible; suffering has made him beautiful and human.'[7]

The influence of Noh can also be seen in the use of landscape in Korol

Ler. Korol Ler possesses little of the massive Gothic impedimentia of Hamlet. The architecture of the castles is low, indeterminate and incomplete. The landscapes are flat and featureless: vast expanses of dried mud, sand and reeds. Kozintsev tried to use this minimalist terrain in the same ritual way as the Noh, transforming empty areas into symbolic representations of dramatic space. The landscapes of Korol Ler contract or conflate distance according to the dictates of the drama. The terrain becomes a battlefield or a place of refuge or spiritual awareness depending on the role (or mask) adopted by the character within it (madman, king, beggar, fool etc). While shooting the film Kozintsev came across some boulders lying in the dried bed of a prehistoric lake. He had these removed and placed in precise positions on the mud flats where the movie was being made. The intention was to reconstruct, as a landscape, the pattern of the rocks in a Buddhist garden that Kozintsev had visited while in Japan. This had a double effect. Like the sand garden the barren landscape was intended to reflect the consciousness of the character who looked upon it, or experienced it. Traditionally such a landscape signifies the attainment of enlightenment; a state of wisdom achieved by meditating or experiencing its spontaneity. At the same time he created a world that oscillated between a realm of brutal and harsh realism and a terrain composed of symbols: the scattered rocks are reminiscent of giant gravestones.

In Korol Ler, as in the Noh, the diegetic space barely exists in a concrete, physical form. Its reality and meaning depends entirely on the definition placed on it by the tragic characters it surrounds, especially Gloucester whose imagined leap from the cliff takes place in the totally empty wilderness of a vast mud flat. Such an approach to landscape is ambiguous. It has radical possibilities in so far as it suggests that environment, and reality, are called into being by the communal ritual of drama that the Noh embodies. However, the emphasis on individual reconciliation in Kozintsev's film transforms this thesis into the classically liberal argument that a landscape is a blank page that can reflect a person's state of consciousness. Kozintsev, by using the Noh, is also replicating the spiritual and transcendental precepts of Buddhism as embodied in an austere and elitist dramatic form (as it is reproduced in Japan and, for that matter anywhere else). From this it is easy to see why Eisenstein and the radical theatre producers of the 1920s preferred the artificial forms of the popular Kabuki theatre. In using the spatial structure of the Noh, and by playing on its associations with Buddhism (a state of being associated with insanity) Kozintsev was working more within the traditions of Stanislavsky's Moscow Art Theatre, and the fluid, Expressionist architecture of the 'theatre of light'. It's not wholly surprising that Kozintsev, in his writings, should make the connection between Craig's production of Hamlet and his own methods of film production.

The film is partly, not wholly, redeemed through the contextualisation of the tragedy within a non-specific history, and the echo of the carnivalesque that appears in the crowds of wandering beggars that drift through the film. The role of these cripples as both audience and chorus to the tragedy of Lear is reflected in the character of the fool. This figure, played by Oleg Dal, is both a nostalgic tribute to FEKS and the equivalent of the chorus and orchestra that accompany a Noh play. The noise of his bells was deliberately used to challenge and disrupt the dramatic rhetoric of Lear the king. His flute, on the other hand, is played in imitation of the atonal and minimal Noh music.

Despite the fact that Kozintsev tried to create the same transgressive juxtaposition of incompatible narratives and images in Korol Ler, the hermetically sealed and highly overdetermined aesthetic structure of the Noh (because it relies so much on unfamiliar images and concepts) fails to surface as a sufficiently powerful discourse. Kozintsev's perception of its symbolic and aesthetic mode of representation becomes bogged down in a dangerously ahistorical imagery of character and inner self. Hence the implication that the misfortunes of the king and Edgar can transcend the boundaries of social and political relationships.

A major problem during the production of the film was the search for a suitable King Lear. The guidelines that Kozintsev followed, and his final choice, demonstrate the extent to which his perception of the king was based on a humanist understanding of the relationship between the individual and power. The actor Yuri Yarvet was chosen: his appearance in the film is far from majestic. He looks like a small, frail, slightly angelic old man. When he first appears at the start of the movie it is without the pomp and ceremony of a ruler. A little door opens and, his face covered by his fool's mask, Lear comes into the room and warms himself by the fire. Kozintsev's vision of the king is articulated within a specific tradition. Yuri Yarvet's appearance and performance is very similar to that of Solomon Mikhoels in the production of King Lear performed by the State Jewish Theatre in Moscow in 1935. Mikhoels saw the situation of Lear as a conflict between subjective and objective perceptions of reality. Lear's fall from power and his madness represented a recognition of the real nature of the world, and could therefore be understood as a liberation from the blinkered preconceptions of power. This approach, the equation of Lear's madness with the acquisition of true knowledge, has a double-edged meaning which neither

Mikhoels nor Kozintsev fully came to terms with. On the one hand Lear's madness places him outside society in a position that allows him to recognise the true material relationships that condition people's lives. Kozintsev achieves this by introducing the mad Lear to the straggling crocodile of beggars and destitute peasants that weaves its way through the film. Lear becomes one of the outcasts, his experience of their suffering operates on the level of a populist, Romantic reconciliation between the ruler and the peasant. Yet at the same time the recognition by Lear, of the true nature of reality divorces him from those mechanisms of power that reproduce, and are reproduced within, that reality. Ultimately Lear's position, like Kozintsev's, is that of the impotent intellectual who, while capable of reconciliation with those who suffer, is unable to mitigate that suffering on any level other than through personal, sympathetic experience.

*Korol Ler*, in reconciling the ruler with the peasants, cripples and lowest of the low, represents an attempt to absolve the responsibility of both the despot and the intellectual from the perpetuation of brutal totalitarianism in Stalinist Russia. In adopting this approach Kozintsev is reproducing both the populism of the late nineteenth century and the mystification of peasant culture inherent in the work of formalist critics like Propp and Bakhtin. His use of the austere and highly spiritual Noh theatre to effect this implies a move away from the radical Constructivism of FEKS and a step towards a resigned, humanism in which he seeks to reconcile himself, and his position, with a brutalised world.

Kozintsev's two films, *Hamlet* and *Korol Ler*, are among the films that come closest to realising a radical reproduction of Shakespeare in the cinema. Lenin saw the marshalling of the left-wing elements in the Russian intelligentsia as a vital move in securing the success of the proletarian revolution. This enabled many artists and writers to realise the Romantic dream of creating a vital, populist culture that combined the carnivalesque of folklore with the violent and absurdist forms of Futurism. The work of Meyerhold, Kozintsev and FEKS sought to achieve this through the rejuvenation as art as labour.

The creative freedom of artists in the early 1920s was short lived. The Constructivist approach to drama gave way to a state-imposed doctrine of positive and nationalistic realism. Kozintsev and others found themselves in virtually the same position as the avant-garde writers of the pre-Revolutionary years. This confirmation of the helplessness of the intellectual persisted well after the death of Stalin. Consequently Kozintsev's films represent the uneasy alliance of Constructivist techniques and the Romantic vision of the radical intellectual. The result is a transformation of the interventionist theatre of FEKS into the idealised carnivalesque of Bakhtin on the one hand and the reified spiritualism of the Noh on the other.

In the late nineteenth century Shakespeare had been used to address the relationship between the individual and the realities of life under a totalitarian autocracy on a very personal level. His works were all but abandoned during the 1920s. When they did re-appear it was to either support the doctrines of social realism, or to articulate the problems of isolated intellectualism. This suggests that the enshrining of Shakespeare in British Romanticism, and the transmission of associated readings of his plays to different cultures, effectively precludes his cinematic re-appropriation in a radical context.

# PART FOUR

# Hamlet on a bicyle:
# Shakespeare in Japan

Every one of the films looked at so far has come from a European, American or English studio. Although each movie represents a specific understanding of Shakespeare, and the assimilation of his plays into a unique historical and social moment, there are common areas of influence. The extent of the British Empire before World War II ensured that the perception of Shakespeare embodied in the Victorian theatre was widely disseminated outside England; hence the heavily determined 'British' atmosphere of the American-backed BBC series. Similarly Romanticism, Modernism and the theories of Wagner and Appia had a profound effect on the cultures of many nations. For those critics intent on judging Shakespeare film according to Anglocentric ideals these links are useful. With Japan the Western critic treads on unfamiliar terrain.

Japan was fortunate enough to escape invasion during the mid nineteenth century and, despite the rapid programme of 'Westernisation' at the beginning of this century, managed to preserve its developing culture from political or ideological interference until after 1945. Consequently orthodox criticism has difficulty coping with Kurosawa's films *Kumonosu jo* and *Ran*. It either attempts to recreate the movies according to the tenets of British Shakespeare studies or retreats, baffled, into silence. The reactions of Jorgens and Peter Brook to *Kumonosu jo* illustrate this confusion quite well. We have already seen how Jorgens dismisses the 'influence' of Japanese art and theatre as being responsible for little more than the movie's beautiful imagery. For his argument he uses the traditional reading of the play as a study concerning the opposition between society and an evil natural world. He concludes that 'the central polarity in *Throne of blood* is between the forest and the fortress'.[1] By discarding what seems peripheral to this theme he has, in effect, re-made the film in the image required by traditional literary criticism. That such an interpretation would appear baffling to a Japanese audience (whose cultural background makes a far less oppositional distinction between nature and society) is not important. Politically this reinforces the notion that each and every film is, and should be seen to be, aspiring towards the essential English reading of the plays. This not only confirms Shakespeare's 'universalism' (different cultures appear to derive the same message from the text) but it suggests that the rest of the world must defer to the Anglocentric understanding of Shakespeare. Brook claimed that the film was 'a great masterpiece, perhaps the only true masterpiece inspired by Shakespeare, but it cannot properly be considered Shakespeare because it doesn't use the text . . . So what may be the best Shakespeare film doesn't help us with the problems of filming Shakespeare.'[2] Kurosawa's work hovers uneasily on the edge of the genre of Shakespeare film, exiled into the realms of incomprehensibility or only acknowledged because it contains a few recognisable elements from an Anglocentric understanding of the plays.

A materialist analysis of Kurosawa's *Macbeth* necessitates a greater awareness of the cultural position of the film. Most critiques have searched for similarities between Western readings of the play and Kurosawa's. Yet they fail to acknowledge how the Japanese have absorbed and appropriated Shakespeare into their own culture. The Japanese don't share the same attitudes towards feudal betrayal and heroic tragedy as the English. Their codes of representation on the stage and in film are radically different to those of Hollywood. Shakespeare had a very precise political meaning for the first Japanese translators and Kurosawa's own liberal humanism has informed his approach to foreign literature. In ignoring these factors critics are suggesting that they are unimportant.

This attitude is very disturbing. If the ideal Shakespeare performance preserves the unadulterated text then any production in a foreign language is automatically inferior. Even if the culture is so similar to that of Britain that the meaning is preserved (the contextual meaning as well as the basic translation of the words) the poetry is still lost. In the case of *Kumonosu jo* the absence of the text is sufficient for some critics to discard the film entirely. Yet to analyse the movie fully as a Japanese Shakespeare film we need to begin with the cultural and social traditions of Japan, and that means moving back into medieval history.

## Japanese feudalism and the tragic hero

Towards the end of the eighth century the court-based administration of Japan, structured according to Confucian models adopted wholesale from China, began to break down. Land (a vital commodity on islands

where only a fraction of the country is arable) fell under private owner-
ship and possession became hereditary. This had certain practical
benefits: a continual administration through a number of generations
ensured the consistent and efficient farming of the land. Politically it
meant that a number of large landed families and religious institutions
influential at court took over the running of the economy.

The next five hundred years of Japanese political history saw a succession
of provincial families rising to challenge and replace the official
court. Their names and the heroes they fostered are familiar to all
Japanese; the Taira, Fujiwara and Minamoto (Genji) clans. The continu-
ously shifting political background of the middle ages, punctuated by a
series of bloody civil wars, brought the figure of the samurai and his
lord into the forefront of the power struggle. It was in the culture of a
society dominated by the warrior-lord bond that Japanese theatre began;
the Noh came into being during the violent fifteenth century. Japan
didn't experience any form of social or political stability until 1600 when
Ieyasu Tokugawa seized control of the country.

Before the ascension of the Tokugawan military government the various dynasties struggled to be recognised as the 'official' court clan. It
was a time of shifting alliances and, in the complex and often treacherous
diplomacy of the period, whole families were eradicated. Betrayal from
within, as well as outside enemies, posed a continual threat and it was
not unknown for samurai to change sides several times during a battle,
depending on who was winning. As in European feudalism the power
of the head of a dynasty depended on the favour of his vassals. Honour
and obligation, ethics that are stressed time and time again in Japanese
culture, rarely stood in the way of a retainer who felt himself to be
unjustly treated by his master. The phrase ge koku jo (literally, 'the low
defeats the high') was coined in this era and was used specifically to
refer to the slaying of a lord by one of his own samurai who wished to
take his place.

Hence, in the culture of the era, the mark of a true Japanese hero was
his sincerity to his ideals, to the lord of the clan and, ultimately, the
symbolic figure of the Emperor. The most emphatic expression of this
spiritual dedication was suicide. By disembowelling himself the loyal
retainer demonstrated that his motives and loyalty were pure. Unfortunately the treachery and Machiavellian diplomacy that had characterised
Japanese politics for seven centuries left little room for such ingenuous
honesty. Consequently the sincerest heroes in Japanese culture are also
the the most tragic. Ivan Morris, in The nobility of failure: tragic heroes in the
history of Japan (1975), describes a canon of dedicated samurai who have

become powerful cultural symbols, not because of their heroic prowess but because they are all, to a man, abject losers. The doomed figure is such a persistent motif that the Japanese have a phrase, *hoganbiiki*, which signifies sympathy with a losing side. It literally translates as 'sympathy with the Lieutenant' and refers to the famous warrior Yoshitsune Minamoto who held that rank at the apex of his career. The most renowned tragic hero in Japanese history, he committed suicide in 1187. Morris catalogues the most famous examples of the heroic failure; from Prince Yamato of the fourth century, who was mortally wounded by the god of Mount Ibuki and died alone on the plain of Nobo, to the young men of the Special Attack Forces who piloted flying bombs and aeroplanes into American warships in a futile attempt to rescue Japan from defeat in the last few months of World War II.

## The Meiji revolution and Japanese Shakespeare

In 1720 the ban on all occidental books, imposed at the beginning of the seventeenth century, was lifted by the Shogun Yoshimatsu Tokugawa (although books of Christian philosophy were still rigorously prohibited). Scholars, anxious to learn from the West, seized upon Dutch books of cartography, science and navigation. In the wake of this 'Dutch learning' came less practical influences in the form of art and literature. In the early nineteenth century there appeared a few oblique references to a barbarian playwright called Shakespeare. There were no translations of the plays available in Japan at this time; the little information that was available was confined to Japanese translations (usually taken second-hand from Dutch) of English Grammars. In 1841 Rokuzo Shibukawa translated a Dutch version of Lindley Murray's *English grammar*, misreading the author's comments on Shakespeare as actual play titles. Consequently Shakespeare was credited with a drama called *Inventive mind*.

The first actual quotation from a play, Polonius's advice to Laertes from *Hamlet*, appeared in a translation from Samuel Smiles's *Self help* written by Masanao Nakamura. This also appeared in an anthology of Western sayings, *Taisei meigen* (1874), written in the style of Chinese Confucian aphorisms. There are other unsubstantiated rumours about the influence of Shakespeare in Japan prior to 1853. It's been claimed that the Kabuki play *Kokoro no nazo toketo iroito* ('A tangled love-story with a happy ending') resembles *Romeo and Juliet*. However it is only with the opening up of Japan's borders in the mid nineteenth century that Shakespeare became a significant part of the subsequent intellectual and cultural revolution.

In the 1840s and 1850s the Western world began to turn its attentions back to Japan. The US government was especially keen on opening Japanese ports to shelter its ships. Frustrated by the country's isolationism they finally decided to force the Shogunate's hand. In July 1853 Commodore Perry sailed a fleet of 'black ships' into Tokyo bay and, under the shadow of their guns, demanded a trade treaty between Japan and the USA. The Tokugawan government, thrown into a state of confusion, agreed and allowed the Americans to use Shimoda port near Tokyo and Hakodate in Hokkaido, the northernmost island. Within two years further treaties had been signed with seventeen other nations. The move (which had involved the unprecedented step of asking the advice of an Emperor who had been little more than a figurehead for nine hundred years) split the country. On the one hand there were the conservative isolationists who wanted no truck with the barbarian West. Opposed to them were the people who recognised that negotiated treaties (no matter how biased they were towards the economic interests of the Western powers) at least provided some security against the ruthless exploitation visited on the Chinese during the 1850s.

The government's inability to deal with the crisis, and the unequal treaties they negotiated, led to their downfall. Over the next fifteen years they tried to rescue an economy that was seriously disturbed by the introduction of Western trade. It was too late. Anti-government forces seized power on 3 January 1868, the Shogun resigned, and the Emperor was reinstated as the ruler of Japan. So began the Meiji era. Although his restoration was the avowed purpose of the rebellion the Emperor's influence on politics remained unchanged. Japan now found itself to be a backward nation in an industrialised world. Ever conscious of the threat of colonisation it set out frantically to modernise itself under the banner fukoku kyohei ('a developing country and a strong army'). This phrase shows that one of the most immediate benefits sought for through the imitation of Western capitalism was the ability to build up military strength capable of repelling any invaders. By 1905 Japan had amassed sufficient naval might to destroy the Russian fleet at the battle of Tsushima.

Japanese society was anxious to rid itself of the antiquated and rigid past and learn about, and adopt, the ways of the West. This fascination of 'enlightenment' affected every facet of Japanese culture. Up until 1870 Japan had used China as the model of civilisation, adopting that country's philosophy, system of government and arts for its own use. Now it was the turn of Europe. The writings of the West, now freely available in Japan, provided insights into a fascinating and radically different world.

In the first few years after the revolution many short, narrative adaptations of Shakespeare were published, often taken from Lamb's *Tales*. Japanese writers automatically read these in terms of the dramatic styles they were familiar with. Thus, at first, motive, action and resolution were given a sound moral basis in the tradition of the didactic Japanese fiction of the time. One example is 'an adaptation of the story by Shakespeare of England' called *The strange affair of the flesh of the bosom* (1877). In this version of Lamb's *The merchant of Venice* Portia became Kiyoka ('Scent of purity') and Shylock was Yokubari Gapachi ('Stubborn closed fist'). The tale finished with a Confucian moral: 'this story shows the swift turning of the wheel of Heaven's retribution and how woe will come to him who, out of cupidity, causes suffering to others, whereas he who bears affliction for his friend will be rewarded with good fortune'.[3] Short versions of *Hamlet* and *King Lear* were also published with correct emphasis given to the triumph of virtue over vice. In 1882 and 1883 three professors at the Government Institute in the new capital of Tokyo (later the University of Tokyo) published two collections of Western poetry in Japanese translation: *Shintai shisho* and *Shintai ka*. The aim of the collections was to help create a new poetry for Japan. Gray's 'Elegy', Tennyson's 'The charge of the light brigade' and Longfellow's 'Psalm of life' appeared in the books. Also included were three speeches; from *Henry VIII*, *2 Henry IV* and *Hamlet*.

At first Japanese intellectuals who embraced the ways of the West tended to think of it as a unified whole. Many of them assumed that occidental morality was a universally applicable system. The more 'radical' members of the pro-European Minyusha group ('Friends of the nation'), having avidly read the works of Mill, Spencer and Rousseau, concluded that a society based on an industrial democracy represented the final stage in a long and arduous social evolution. This implied that Japan, still clinging to its feudal and autocratic past, was lower down on the evolutionary ladder than other Western nations. 'Westernism', as a universal social goal, was a historical stage toward which Japan had to move in order to take its place with pride among the other empires of the world. This belief also explains the tendency in Japan to assume that Shakespeare's writings, because they belonged to this ideal culture, contained truths that were 'universally' applicable. British critics have been loath to dispel this notion.

After the initial reformist enthusiasm had died down certain cultural and social difficulties became apparent. The problem of Japan's self-image began to loom large in contemporary thought. The industrial and economic superiority of the foreign nations, with their colonies and powerful armies, was obvious. What became less evident was the superiority of their ethics and culture. Even so, some writers in Japan could still quite cheerfully declare 'we stand before Westerners exposing our weak and inferior civilisation; it is rare that we can hold our heads high and peer down on other races as they do'.[4]

This acute sense of cultural inferiority, coupled with an anxious desire to embrace European and American culture, now left many Japanese with a profound identity crisis. To begin with there was the problem of imitation. Japan, in order to compete with the West, had to dispense with its own antiquated traditions and imitate its 'betters'. Yet to do so was to deny Japan's individual characteristics as a nation. To some young Japanese this opportunity to rebel against the ancient regime was a godsend. Others found the dilemma less easy to resolve and attempted to create a new, modern, but essentially Japanese society.

For the young intellectuals of the Meiji era such acute difficulties operated on a very personal level. These students faced a cultural and social dislocation that had never been experienced by any Japanese before 1853. Up to a certain age their education had been traditional. They were taught in the community schools founded during the previous era where they were instructed in the fundamental Confucian tenets: filial piety; duty to one's parents and love of the Emperor as the divine ruler of Japan. In the household the father was the boss and it was assumed that the first son would carry on with the family business. Then, almost overnight, a generation's expectations changed. The new government brought in a series of reforms that destroyed class-based job restrictions and introduced colleges based on America models. Now many young men went to universities where they were schooled in a system of morality that opposed everything they were used to. Suddenly the prime virtues were individualist, not community or family-orientated. The emphasis was upon self-reliance, determination and personal action.

Few found it easy to cope. The change disrupted the relationship between the young and old, one writer remarked: 'today's elders are unfortunately a troublesome burden'.[5] There was a spate of nervous breakdowns and suicides. Towards the end of the nineteenth century the suffering intellectual starts to appear in Japanese culture. A spate of books, popularly known as 'I novels', tried to address the question of what it was to be Japanese; usually by transforming the character's dilemma into a peculiar personal obsession. Finally, the culturally traumatised students of the Meiji era found mirror images of themselves in the characters created by Chekhov, Ibsen and Shakespeare. The reasons for the inclusion o f Shakespeare in this canon are understandable. For the Japanese the emergence of the individual, breaking out of the constraints of a community-orientated feudal society into the moral and intellectual independence of the Renaissance, was a vitally significant motif. Their reading of Shakespeare, channelled through the works of writers and critics like Lamb, made the seemingly Romantic and character-centred plays appear directly relevant.

The first complete translation of the works of Shakespeare was a direct product of this intellectual angst. Yuzo Tsubouchi's initial encounter with the plays occurred when he was a student. He was asked to write an essay on *Hamlet*, analysing the character of Gertrude. Following the tradition of Japanese critical studies he adopted a moralistic stance; criticising Hamlet's mother for her unnatural behaviour. To his distress his work received very low marks. As with so many of his contemporaries he suddenly became acutely aware of the incompatibility between his own intellectual heritage and that of the West. Consequently he set out to revaluate Japanese attitudes to literature. His translations of Shakespeare's works, a project that lasted forty years, were an integral part of his attempt to catalyse a literary renaissance in Japan.

The first play he translated was *Julius Caesar*. In Tsubouchi's eyes this was an undeniably political work; in 1882 the leader of the Liberal Party was attacked and badly wounded by an assassin. Two translations of *Julius Caesar* appeared within the space of a year. The first was published in a political paper and then later issued as a book called *A mirror of Roman vicissitudes*. Tsubouchi's version was *Shizaru Kidan: jiyu no tachi nago no kireaji* ('Emperor Caesar: the sword of liberty displays its sharp blade').

Although many of Tsubouchi's friends were heavily involved in politics he lacked any firmly articulated views. This is not surprising: characteristically the sensations of angst experienced by the new generation stemmed partly from their inability to create a unified movement and thereby change society. This is reflected in the confused beliefs expressed in *Shizaru Kidan*. Tsubouchi began the translation by denouncing tyranny and ended by attacking republicanism. Consequently he has been cast in the role of a Romantic writer torn between literary and political alliegances. Tsubouchi's confusion may not necessarily have been the fruit of a tormented soul. Unsure of his precise motives for translation it is evident that he was still torn between traditional Japanese culture (heavily bound up with Confucianism and Emperor worship) and what he felt to be the radical potential of Shakespeare.

Other writers followed in Tsubouchi's footsteps. The general pattern was for the plays to be transformed into stories with Japanese characters and settings. In 1885 an eleborate adaptation of *The merchant of Venice* was staged in Osaka. It was called *All for money* and at the start of each scene narrative speeches explained the action to follow. Robun Kanagaki's *Hamlet* (1886) was set in fourteenth-century Yamagata and published in a newspaper. Jono Saikiku turned *King Lear* into a novel called *Three daughters* and the writer who called himself 'Chikuyo sanjin' was influenced by Shakespeare in his *Taisei jowa sofuwen* ('A love story in the Western manner'). It was set (and performed) in Osaka in 1892, just after the inauguration of the new parliament.

At the same time there was a growing awareness of the critical tradition used to analyse Shakespeare in Europe. Tsubouchi had already been made painfully aware of the disparity between his own approach to *Hamlet* and that of his tutor William Houghton. The appointment of foreign teachers specialising in their own cultures at the newly formed colleges became standard practice. Between 1872 and 1876 James Summers taught Shakespeare as part of a general class at Tokyo University and in 1883 W. D. Cox published a book called *Shakespeare and the English drama*. The study of Shakespeare in Japan began to fall in step with the teachings of the West. Quite reasonably it was assumed that the English had a better understanding of the plays than anyone else. Japanese scholars resolutely set out to learn and imitate the Victorian empirical approach to literature. The year 1901 saw the publication of the first book written by a Japanese author on Shakespeare. It was an account of his life; the twenty-first volume in a series called the *Biography of universal history*. Yoshio Nakamura, naming his work *Shakespeare*, concentrated on the playwright's life in Elizabethan England. Typically Nakamura compared the state of literature in Japan with that of Renaissance England and lamented the fact that the Meiji Restoration, for all its similarities to the cultural rebirth of the sixteenth century, had failed to produce any great writers.

Occasionally the combination of didactic Western scholarship with traditional Japanese learning yielded bizarre results. Takakeiro Kimura, writing as late as 1915, advanced the theory that *Hamlet* was set at the mouth of the Ganges. His reasoning was as follows: Hamlet bears resemblance to many mythical heroes from ancient religions; archaeological evidence shows that many of these myths originated on or near the mouth of the Ganges; thus the events of the plays must also take place in the same region. This author used the same deductive reasoning to less alarming effect in *The ancient history of Japan, based on a study of world history* (1912) in which he compared Hamlet to a number of historical and fictional Japanese heroes.

Shakespeare was also making his presence felt in the Japanese theatre. Tsubouchi had already written several Kabuki plays that were inspired by the English playwright. During the last few decades of the nineteenth century there evolved a strong bond between progressive Liberal politics and several burgeoning drama movements. A group of actors and writers, interested in new and socially relevant forms of drama, created a revolutionary movement called 'Shimpa' which claimed direct descendancy from Western styles. In fact 'Shimpa' differed from the more sycophantic readings of European culture in that it constructed, through a symbolic recreation of the West, its own unorthodox cosmopolitanism. The company performed Shakespeare and, after the assassination of the president of the municipal Assembly in 1901, they arranged special productions of *Julius Caesar* in Tokyo and Osaka. Their most enthusiastic member, Otojiro Kawakami, journeyed abroad to get some first-hand experience of the Western theatre. His subsequent performances were obviously influenced by the grandiose performances of English and American actor-managers. Several strange legends surround his career. It is claimed that in one scene of his production of *Hamlet* the Prince arrived on stage riding a bicycle.

By the start of the twentieth century the Shakespeare tradition in Japan had divided into two specific trends. The radical intellectuals of the 1870s and 1880s had used his plays to tackle questions concerning their own identity and the emergence of Japan as a modern nation state. As the Meiji era progressed they became more and more aware of their own political impotence and their search for social fulfillment became increasingly expressed in existential and psychological terms. Shakespeare's popularity with this movement was replaced by the more introspective writings of Chekhov, Ibsen and Japan's own 'I' novelists. The other movement in Shakespearean studies was more conservative; a drift away from the radical appropriation of the plays towards an academic interest in them as subjects for literary analysis. This more Westernised approach is exemplified in the career of Tsubouchi. His attitude to his translations had noticeably changed as he worked his way through the plays. Less concerned with revitalising Japanese literature he concentrated more and more on scholarly and accurate word-for-word renditions.

The painstaking recreation of the complete works of Japanese was also the motive behind Masayasu Tozana and Wasaburo Asano's translations of the entire works (although they only completed ten plays). They began in 1905 when Japan was at war with Russia and clearly winning. Tozana and Asano, captured by the nationalist feeling of the time, saw their work as symbolic of the general progress Japan was making as a civilised nation. Despite the more conservative and scholarly nature of their work they still sought for parallels between Shakespeare's age and their own: 'in their general preface the two friends marvel at the serene atmosphere in which they have been able to pursue their labours. The result, they claim, will mark for later generations the high tide of the national spirit. To the intrinsic value of their work, however, they attach less importance: as the literature of the Elizabethan age rose to its climax in the second half, so the most flourishing period of Meiji literature might be expected in ten, twenty or even thirty years time; and it was for that day that they were working, to the best of their ability, by introducing foreign literature.'[6]

In the 1900s two groups formed around Tsubouchi. First came the Literary and Art Association, then, six years later, the Literary and Dramatic Society. This second group organised the first complete and unadulterated performance of a Shakespeare play in Japan. The confusion that surrounded the rehearsals of their Hamlet is revealing. Tsubouchi was still torn between his alliegance to European cultural idioms and a sense of Japan's own literary heritage. Two English drama teachers coached the actors but Tsubouchi was deeply dissatisfied with the results. Three days before the first performance he told the cast to forget what they'd been taught and to try to make the production more 'Japanese'. The result was not particularly successful.

In 1913 the break-up of the troupe consolidated the differences in approach among Japanese intellectuals towards Shakespeare and European drama in general. The traditionalists among the group returned to the styles of the Kabuki. Kaoru Osani, dubbed the 'Gordon Craig of the East', teamed up with the left-wing actor Sadanji to form a theatre which specialised in plays by Ibsen and Gorky. Another group, the Mamei Kai ('the nameless club'), tackled such plays as Macbeth and Othello but broke up during the 1920s. By now Shakespeare had lost his radical appeal and was supplanted by the more exciting works of the Symbolist and Modernist playwrights.

In the cultural revolution of the late nineteenth and early twentieth centuries the foundations of Japanese Shakespeare as a cultural, dramatic and literary tradition were firmly established. Recreated from the components of the traditional Japanese theatres, plays like Julius Caesar, Hamlet and King Lear provided many Japanese people with a medium for expressing the problems of cultural identity. Hamlet dealt with the dilemma of the young intellectual divorced from political power in a world undergoing a profound and rapid change. King Lear touched on the sudden uselessness of old people in an industrial democracy. Finally works like Macbeth, Julius Caesar and the history plays tackled the nature of political power, liberalism and tyranny. They allowed the dramatists of the period to challenge their own burgeoning ideology into universal statements on feudalism and democracy. They did this by recreating contemporary events (such as assassinations) in the distant past of faraway countries.

Most importantly Shakespeare signified the apex of an era of cultural development in European history. His works were emblematic for many Japanese who sought to create a parallel renaissance in their own country. The plays were transmitted by the British as a cultured expression of civilised patriotism. The emphasis on individualism and sentiment in the writings of contemporary Western critics made the plays appear especially pertinent to those Japanese scholars trying to locate their own identities in a rapidly changing world. They read Shakespeare as a writer who expressed the complexities of motivation and who shattered the simplistic moral equations of traditional Confucian learning. Hence they used the medium of translation to try and formulate a new code of ethics. In all cases the Japanese intellectuals were able to 'read' Western culture according to their own codes of meaning with little interference from colonial ideology. Once we recognise this then Tsubouchi's, Asano's and Tozana's claims that Shakespeare translation was a patriotic activity are understandable. Furthermore it underlines the crucial fact we must bear in mind when dealing with Kurosawa's films: Shakespeare in Japan is, and always has been, an essentially Japanese tradition.

## Reaction and defeat: Japanese Shakespeare as an institution

Kurosawa's position as a politically aware artist in twentieth-century Japan means that his beliefs and attitudes are closely related to those of the Meiji intellectuals. However at least thirty years lie between the last radical appropriation of Shakespeare in Japan and Kurosawa's film of Macbeth. The extreme nationalism of the 1930s and 1940s meant that the plays of Shakespeare, like all other non-Japanese writings, were banned. After the war, when the US administration paved the way for a sudden

upsurge in American-style colleges, Shakespeare in Japan became very much an academic discipline studied using Western literary values and systems of analysis. Nevertheless, the political climate prior to 1945 is important because of the way in which it coloured Kurosawa's career and beliefs. Similarly the consecrating of Shakespeare as 'worthy foreign literature' taught in English departments provides the cultural context against which the significance of *Kumonosu jo* and *Ran* can be judged.

In Japan dates are based on a dynastic calendar that corresponds to the reign of the Emperor. Thus when the Emperor Meiji died in 1912, and his son became the next ruler, the Taisho era began. This period saw the ground laid for a democratic system of government which was finally achieved in 1925 with the repeal of the voting tax. The law had stated that only those men who paid a certain amount of tax were eligible to vote. After being reduced from 15¥ to 3¥ this guideline was scrapped all together, theoretically introducing universal sufferage for the male population.

It has been suggested that democracy was only achieved because of the conflict of interest between a number of powerful civil and military bodies all anxious to retain their administrative powers. The court officials still demanded certain rights even though the implementation of a truly democratic government meant that the Emperor would have little influence on the running of the country. The civil bureaucracy and the army also wanted to make sure that their political interests were secure. Finally various intricate connections existed between the new, large industrial businesses, who had combined into powerful lobbying groups called *zaibatsu*, and the Diet. The problems of democratisation were still seen as ethical ones. Democracy was regarded as a necessary step towards civilisation but Japan had no traditional indigenous code of morality to support it. At the same time the sudden aggressive nationalism that was sweeping China, and the racist attitudes of the West towards the Japanese, drove more and more of the population to the comforts of right-wing nostalgia.

Even so Japan's 'Westernisation' proceeded at an ever increasing pace. Yet the building of new, modern urban landscapes and the disappearance of traditional lifestyles concealed a deepening economic crisis which reached a head in the mid 1920s. Various solutions were offered to alleviate the situation; these boiled down to two basic alternatives: trade or war. For a time the government threw itself at the mercy of the international market. Unfortunately it fared badly and, by the start of the 1930s, many of its inhabitants were very conscious of Japan as a nation discriminated against by Europe and America. The Chinese 'threat' showed no signs of disappearing and, as far as the international community were concerned, the Japanese were lumped together with the rest of Asia as the 'yellow peril'.

The rise of nationalism in the 1930s was partly defensive and partly the result of a misreading of the source of industrialism's ill effects. The greatest support for the new right came from farmers and country dwellers. The concentration of business in the cities had resulted in the rapid development of a dual economy. The country depended on the agricultural workers for its livelihood but they were socially and financially discriminated against. The enervating effect of Western luxury on the urban rich was cited as one of the key arguments for a return to the austere and nationalistic samurai lifestyle that was still supposedly practised in the farming communities. The military exploited the situation by attempting a number of minor coups. Many political assassinations were attempted during the 1920s and 1930s and the perpetrators were often venerated as sincere and tragic heroes. Traditional suspicion of the powerful business conglomerates and their parliamentary lackeys was played on by right-wing groups anxious to emphasise the sincerity of the dedicated soldier towards his country and the Emperor. Ironically it was a faked sabotage attempt by the Japanese army in Manchuria that started the war with China in 1937 (they blew up a railway and blamed it on the Chinese). By this time the country was in the grip of a military-based fascist administration determined to purge the nation of 'effete' and 'decadent' Westernism. For the next eight years anything associated with America or Europe was firmly suppressed.

In 1946 the Japanese started to reconstruct their shattered cities under the watchful eye of General Douglas MacArthur; the Supreme Commander of the Allied Powers (in Japan his nickname was 'the blue-eyed Shogun'). There was a severe backlash against the military ambition and expansionism of the 1920s and 1930s. The US administration encouraged this by suppressing any manifestations of militarism. Martial arts were banned as were any books or films that glorified Japan's feudal past. Indeed the term 'feudal' became a general term of abuse used to describe all manifestations of bull-headed authority from bank managers to politicians. The war had seemingly destroyed the last hold of traditional Japanese ethics on the country's culture.

Yet this second social revolution also caused great psychological upheaval, especially among the young. The old Tokugawan and Confucian values had gone for good but there seemed little of any worth to replace them with. The young generation of post-war Japan found themselves caught in as great a dilemma as their nineteenth-century predecessors. It was true that they no longer felt tied to the constraints of a family-based Confucian ideology. However the countries of the West didn't appear to have any coherent philosophical system that Japan could use. Despite the grandiose claims made for liberal democracy it had still spawned Nazism. All the countries of the world had their poor, oppressed and destitute. The developing Cold War further cast doubt on the prestige of the West, especially in the first country to suffer the effect of a nuclear attack.

MacArthur wisely decided to rule by proxy through the Japanese authorities, leaving the society to perfect the parliamentary structure begun in the 1910s. He also encouraged the transformation of the education system so that it followed the style of American campuses. More university places were made available for Japanese students, re-absorbing the intellectual into the mainstream of society. It also narrowed the gap between English, American and Japanese approaches to Shakespeare. One sign that the Anglocentric concept of the plays had a far greater hold on intellectual circles after 1945 was the numerous attempts to translate the texts into idiomatic Japanese.

It would seem reasonable to assume that the less precise a rendition the more 'open' it is to radical appropriations. Several experimental translations were made in the 1970s in which fools and gravediggers make jokes about Nissan and Toyota. These may appear in keeping with the aims of the Meiji writers because they are creating a Shakespeare that is contemporary and relevant. Translation theory suggests that this is not the case. A translation from Elizabethan English to modern Japanese is a political act because it glosses over the problems of ideological, cultural and sexual difference. The writers of the Meiji era transformed the entire plays into Japanese or symbolically 'Western' artifacts which could then be used as powerful and radical challenges to traditional Japanese theatre and literature. The new translators tried to preserve the form, content and meaning of Shakespeare's text. Their work presupposes that a hidden language of meaning exists above and beyond English and Japanese and is accessible from both: 'A translation from language A into language B will make tangible the implication of a third, active presence. It will show the lineaments of that 'pure speech' which precedes and underlies both languages.'[7] The existence of this transcendent language supports the traditional claims that the truths of Shakespeare's art persist above and beyond history. It is worth pointing out that radical student theatre groups in Japan in the 1970s used traditional Japanese drama to challenge the bourgeois conventionalities of their country's orthodox 'Western' theatre.

Shakespeare never recovered the popularity lost with the Meiji discovery of the European Modernists. In the 1950s Shakespearean studies became part of a growing academic curriculum. Students were taught his works as they learnt to speak his native tongue. Consequently they were exposed to the European cultural assumptions about his plays at the same time. The consolidation of this Anglocentric critical framework became complete when, instead of setting the actual texts straight away, the tutors began to wean their pupils on narrative summaries.

Thus a pattern was established that has persisted to the present day. Japanese students are introduced to Shakespeare via Lamb's *Tales* or other condensed 'stories'. Peter Milward, lecturer at a prestigious Catholic University in Tokyo, has written two anthologies: *Shakespeare's tales retold* and *More Shakespeare tales retold*. These are sold as standard texts for EFL teachers. It is only during the third and fourth year that students approach the plays themselves and then, at that stage, 'the usual method of teaching English authors in general and Shakespeare in particular is a somewhat laborious process of translation'.[8] It is rare for any student to be encouraged to read a critical study. This is a far cry from the radical enthusiasm that the writings of Shakespeare engendered in the minds of Kawakami and Tsubouchi. Certainly it demonstrates the ideological efficiency with which the Anglocentric reading of the plays is disseminated in Japanese universities. In the case of Kurosawa his education and experience of foreign writers occurred during the uncertain pre-war period and still carried much of the revolutionary associations of the Meiji era. Nevertheless the political situation in the 1950s had a profound effect on the films he produced, even if the standard approach to Shakespeare at that time was infinitely less original and dynamic than his own.

# Kurosawa's Kumonosu jo and Ran

## The Noh theatre

The oldest type of drama in Japan is the Noh. Before the fourteenth century there was no indigenous Japanese theatre, only a tradition of *saragaku* or 'miscellaneous performances'. Mime, songs acrobatics and magic acts were presented for public entertainment outside temples on festival days. Actors would don animal masks and dance in small open-fronted booths to the accompaniment of a small orchestra. At the same time there were agricultural and religious ceremonies called *dengaku* or 'field performances'. In these an area of a field was roped off and designated as a sacred space. A god was invited to descend into this area to bless the land in a fertility ritual that celebrated the relationship between humanity and the spirit world.

This concept of supernatural descent and possession was developed through the Noh in three ways. As in the *saragaku* the Noh actor, in putting on his mask, allows his soul to be merged with, and transplanted by, the soul of the being that his costume represents. Similarly possession by an angry ghost, god or demon appears time and time again as a major theme in the plays. Characters are perpetually invaded by animistic forces from the spirit world; these beings force their hosts to transcend the social order through madness. Finally the ceremony of invoking a god who then descends to possess a man and, via him, spread good luck survives in the ritual which begins a day's performance of the Noh.

The design of the Noh theatre developed from the architecture used for small shrines and sacred dance halls. The stage is made of unpolished wood divided into three areas. Most of the drama takes place on the main stage. On the left hand side is a section where the chorus kneels. The orchestra sits on a back stage in front of a wall. On this there is a painting of a Japanese pine tree. The whole assembly is connected to a second, concealed room (the 'mirror room') by a covered bridge.

Noh was the traditional entertainment of the high-ranking samurai, their lords and the Emperors court. Noh has few similarities with post-Renaissance Western drama. It continually makes the process of its own production explicit. There is no conflict between this and the content and structure of the plays themselves. Meaning is achieved through the portrayal of a spiritual rather than secular realism. Traditionally the Noh performance lasted all day and would consist of five plays dealing with a god, a man, a woman, madness and, finally, a demon. In the evening the presentation would end with a song of thanksgiving. This song implied the beginning of a new sequence at a later date. Interspersed with these serious works were short comic plays called *kyogen*.

In the Noh plays there is rarely a plot. The majority deal with a particular event, usually taken from one of the medieval chronicles. Many plays describe an encounter between a ghost and the real world. The latter is usually embodied in the form of a travelling priest. This type is called *mugen* ('a dream of a ghost'). The others, *genzai* or phenomenal Noh deal with straightforward events in the legendary past. The two categories are not absolute. There are many plays that combine the two or deal with different, though related subjects. The drama is centred on the role of the *shite* or main character. The *shite* is the god in a god play, the woman in a woman play, the ghost in a *mugen* etc. Apart from one or two exceptions the *shite* always wears a mask. The second player is called *waki*. Travelling priest and court official are typical *waki* roles and in this capacity the player consciously or unconsciously generates the reason for the *shite* to appear. As a whole the *waki* takes a passive role after the first encounter.

The five plays of a day's performance follow a very definite pattern. The first drama, the god play, often shows the descent of a god. The story is taken from chronicles written in the early eighth century which freely mix painstaking historical detail with legend and myth. The stories are familiar to most Noh audiences. The majority of second category plays 'are *make shura*, battle pieces that depict the pathos of the hero in defeat, showing both the misery and glory of death.'[1] These plays deal with angry ghosts. A ghost is usually a soul that is still tied to earth (supernatural vendetta is largely confined to demons from hell). For its past sins this spirit must wait for the necessary prayers before it breaks free of the eternal cycle of fate. Then, and only then, can it attain Buddhahood. In the Noh theatre the ghosts spiritual torment is internalised. A warrior's fate becomes one of eternal reincarnation as a spirit forced to relive and endure the mental agonies of its previous existence. Having first manifested itself in a human incarnation in order to make contact with the *waki* the ghost appears in the dream of the latter and re-enacts its death. The play ends with the ghost appeased, having achieved enlightenment through the prayers of the mortal and (by implication) all those who watch the performance. In these Noh plays time is continually disrupted. The plays follows a linear time scheme (the *waki* embarks on a physical and spiritual journey that ends with a reconciliation between him and the spirit world) and a cyclical one (the events of the ghost's past are repeated in the dream). The dividing line that separates vision and reality is hazy and in many cases the *waki* doesn't realise he has dreamed until he wakes. The *mugen* plays also allude to the structure of the Noh as a whole, especially its repetition of highly stylised sacred drama through a series of five performances.

The third kind of Noh portray women distracted by love, or beautiful women whose looks have faded with age. They also deal with ghosts. In the five-play cycle madness Noh appear fourth, at the position which signifies the final stages in a destruction and transformation. Again Noh madness is a form of possession and it has its dramatic roots in the dances of the *sarugaku*. In Japanese culture madness is associated with a form of higher wisdom. Someone who goes insane is denying the 'illusions' of the material world. The Noh imposes another outlet on women by constructing madness as a viable 'alternative' to sexuality. Madness affords the only escape for the woman wracked by her own sexual and emotional needs. It can punish or it can exorcise the 'hidden demon'. A large number of Noh show a princess or priestess turning into a monster which is then banished from Earth.

Finally there are the demon plays. The founder of Noh, Zeami Motokiyo, specified two types of demon: 'steady' and 'unsteady'. The 'unsteady' demon represents the erratic evil within the human spirit. Such monsters have strong connections with the Madness plays because they represent wilful and uncontrollable transgressions of the social order; signified through possession. Rage, jealousy and insanity transform the *shite* into a hideous and magical demon which then appears in the second half. The 'steady' demon is a true monster who leaves hell to terrorise the human world and who must be exorcised.

The majority of the plays were written in the fifteenth century against a background of bloody feudal war. They are suffused with a sense of things long past and the unattainability of heroic or spiritual ideals. The plays harked back to an idealised and mythical age of bravery: the eleventh century and the period before the vicious civil wars.

## Narrators and genres in Japanese cinema

Japanese cinema began at the same time as its European and American counterparts. The rapid industrialisation of the country during the late nineteenth century ensured that any new technology was seized on with enthusiasm. In 1896 several of Edison's Kinetoscopes were imported into Japan. A year later a programme of films by the Lumiére brothers was shown in public. By 1897 both the Vitascope and the Lumière Cinématographe had appeared. Audiences were able to see projected film for the first time. Cinema was initially 'read' by the Japanese using the symbolic codes of the puppet theatre (or Bunraku). The characteristics of this type of drama made it an ideal 'ancestor'. The puppet plays were silent because the dolls couldn't speak; they expressed meaning through gesture and stance. At the same time a narrator, physically separated from the world of the diegesis, declaimed the narrative. He mediated between the audience and the play by explaining what was happening 'on stage' at any given moment. His presence in full view of the audience enforced the impression that the performance was an artificial construct.

The cinematic equivalent of the Bunraku narrator was the *benshi*. He wasn't just a lecturer whose task was to educate an otherwise bewildered audience. He supplied the viewers with an interpretation of the image. Through him the movie became a text or field of signs rather than an unmediated slice of life. The *benshi*'s approach to European and American films highlights the difference between late nineteenth- and early twentieth-century Western realism and the symbolic Japanese theatre. The influence of the *benshi* on Japanese cinema was crucial. They emphasised the fact that, like the indigenous theatre, film was there to be 'read' as a collection of symbolic images, not passively experienced as a transparent window on the real world. Because of the *benshi* most Japanese films still retain a separate, didactic line of discourse that mediates between the audience and the events of the diegesis. It can take the form of an actual narrator (as in Kurosawa's *Ikiru*) or an obvious and stylised disruption of the narrative (as used in the films of Nagisa Oshima).

The existence of a narrator external to the events unfolding on the screen meant that films made in Japan had no need to adopt narrative-based methods of editing. In the West there was a continual move towards perfecting the 'flow' of the story or plot and eliminating any

disruption of the illusion. At a time when the Western camera was beginning to-consolidate this naturalism by penetrating filmic space (the
fictional area beyond the screen in which the narrative was set) Japanese
directors were quite content to keep their cameras static. The machines
faced the set at an angle of ninety degrees, the viewpoint of an imaginary
audience. Makino Shozo's Chushingura (1913 or 1917) is a typical example.
Shozo used a few changes of camera angle and close-ups in the film
and was obviously aware of Western methods of narrative editing. He
was simply not interested in adopting these non-Japanese styles.

Furthermore Japan created a national cinematic idiom at an early stage
in film history before Hollywood dominated world film production.
Thus certain stylistic devices which were discarded elsewhere have persisted in Japanese films. The use of the hard-edge wipe and the general
lack of gentle dissolves in many works is often cited as evidence of
Japanese cinemas primitive style. Hard-edge wipes draw attention to
the physical construction of the frame through the brief juxtaposition
of two incompatible images. Dissolves are supposed to make the shift
of scene as unobtrusive as possible (though they are no less artificial).
Burch believes that the Japanese hard-edge wipe derives from the use
of sliding screens in their architecture to manipulate, conceal and reveal
space. It is also reminiscent of the long curtain pulled across the Kabuki
stage at the beginning and end of each performance.

Japanese cinema has very definite genres, a direct continuation of theatrical
practice. *Jidai geki* are films set in the past, dealing with the fortunes of
lords and samurai. *Jidai geki* usually embrace the idealism of the medieval
period: their stories deal with the opposition between honourable
samurai and corrupt officials, the glory of bravery and sincerity and the
problems of duty versus feeling. Inevitably these themes have been
mobilised in support of liberal and right-wing ideologies. The work of
Kurosawa and his 'teacher' Kajiro Yamamoto represent opposite ends
of this political spectrum. *Gendai geki* deal with modern life in Japan and,
for this reason, are more often used to address political questions. The
so-called 'golden age' of Japanese cinema coincided with a number of
economic crises and a growing discontent over the apparent injustices
of industrial capitalism. *Gendai geki*'s roots lie here and in the radical plays
of the 1920s. Despite the gradual tightening of state censorship during
the 1920s many films reiterated the political stance of the liberal theatre.
These were called *keiko eiga* or tendency films. However their reliance
on 'modern' Western methods of film making meant that they were
seriously hampered in their attempt to formulate any radical critique.
By the early 1930s the *keiko eiga* had become transformed into harmless

comedy or *rumpen mono*: films about the less politically sensitive lumpen-proletariat. It's important to recognise the characteristics of the different kinds of Japanese movies, and to understand how they relate to Kurosawas work. Outwardly both his Shakespeare films are *jidai geki*. However their articulation of Kurosawa's liberalism draws heavily on the structure and style of the radical *gendai geki* and *keiko eiga*.

## Kurosawa, liberalism and protest

In his third film, *Tor no o o fumu otokotachi* ('They who step on the tiger's tail', 1945) Kurosawa formulated many of the stylistic and philosophical structures that would dominate his later works. The movie was based on a Kabuki play *Kanincho*. This deals with an episode in the life of the tragic hero Yoshitsune Minamato in which he and his servant Benkei swap roles; disguising themselves to avoid capture by hostile government troops. After they have successfully outwitted the guards at a border post Yoshitsune is recognised beneath his porters clothes by an officer. To try and preserve the disguise Benkei, the real servant, beats his porter for being too slow. The officer is so overcome by the pitiful sight (which contravenes practically every feudal ethic) that he allows Yoshitsune to escape.

The film was finished just after the surrender of Japan and was dutifully banned by the American censors for championing the ideals of feudalism. Yet, by including the comic actor Enoken in the role of another servant, Kurosawa was criticising Japan's militaristic traditions. Yoshitsune and the monk Benkei are familiar folk heroes enshrined in the tragic canon of Japanese culture. The introduction of a 'common man' caught up in, yet isolated from, the mythical events around him highlights the abstract and cold idealism of the samurai legends. The casting of the female impersonator 'Peter' as the fool in *Ran* is another example of Kurosawa's wish to debunk transcendent hero worship. In the last scene of *Tora no o o fumu otokotachi* the comic porter is left sleeping on a moor by the two heroes. He wakes up and, finding himself alone, pathetically mimics the dance that is usually performed by Benkei at the end of *Kanjincho*.

The concept that truth and morality are purely relative man-made notions lies behind the film that made Kurosawa's name internationally famous. *Rashomon* was based on two unrelated stories by the nihilist writer Akutugawa Ryunosuke: 'Yabu no naka' ('In a grove') and 'Rashomon'. Rashomon is the entrance to Japan's ancient capital Heian Kyo;

in the story the upper part of this once-magnificent piece of architecture has become an unoffical mausoleum for the victims of poverty and starvation. Kurosawa's film begins in the ruins of the capital. It is raining and a woodcutter, a peasant and a priest are huddled under the broken gate. The city has been destroyed in the feudal wars. It is an age of misery and ruin: 'I heard that demons used to live in the castle here by the gate, but they all ran away, because what men do now horrified them so!'[2] The priest and the woodcutter have been witnesses at court. The case was that of a murder and a rape. The solution was unimportant as all three participants: the woman; the bandit who raped her and the dead samurai (who speaks through a medium), confess to the killing. What has totally shattered the woodcutters and priests faith in the world is the fact that none of the accounts of the incident tally. Rashomon is composed of a sequence of narrative flashbacks which recreate each version in turn.

Certainly the idea of relative morality was an appealing one in the troubled political climate of Japan in the late 1940s when neither nationalism or democracy appeared to have 'worked'. Yet Kurosawa didn't just challenge the idea of universal truth or question uncertain values by showing four versions of the same incident. The structure of the film, and the use of perpetually shifting and disruptive camera shots, suggest that it is reality rather than truth that is being challenged. More specifically Rashomon was challenging those Western concepts of empirical reality that were being imposed on Japan as a precursor to the country attaining political maturity in the eyes of the Americans.

Like Yoshitsune and Benkei the murdered man and his wife in Rashomon are a traditional feudal unit. Tajomaru the bandit, the Enoken figure, is completely the opposite to the archaic restraint and self-possession of the samurai. He leaps about, grimaces and generally overacts. The bragging of a grotesque and riotous conqueror and the tragic loneliness of his humiliated victim had an obvious appeal to the Japanese in the late 1940s. Their confused relationship with MacArthur's administration and the question of their own political destiny was reflected in the films chief concern: is there a genuine reality? Analytical reasoning (the court and the 'impartial' camera) can't supply the answer. The bandit's and the samurai's accounts are coloured by their individual arrogance. The possible solution seems to lie with the woodcutter who, hiding in the bushes, saw the whole incident. His version comprises the final sequence. Then even this 'truth' is shattered when he is implicated in the theft of the missing murder weapon.

Given Kurosawa's own humanistic idealism, and the mood amongst

Japanese intellectuals at the end of the war, the ending of Rashomon is not as incongruous as has been claimed. The three men hear an abandoned baby crying and the woodcutter offers to bring it up with his own children. The priest (whose faith in man is restored by this charitable act) watches him walk away from the ruins with the child in his arms. The rain stops. In the wake of Hiroshima, Nagasaki and the saturation bombing of Tokyo it is hardly surprising that a Japanese government official should have claimed that 'the significance [of Rashomon] for the current situation in Japan is widely accepted'.[3]

In Japan and the West Rashomon was used as the starting point for the rediscovery of a new national cinema. The accessibility of the work to European notions of Existentialism left Kurosawa in a curiously ambivalent position. He was dubbed with the epithet of 'the most Western Japanese director', a title that has clung to him throughout his career. Yet the concept of relative truth swallowed up by the pragmatic necessity of war was already clichéd by the time Rashomon went on general release. Although it allowed Japanese culture to regain some of the respectability lost in the eyes of the Allied nations it was regarded primarily as a beautiful example of Oriental mysticism.

By the mid 1950s the sense of political uncertainty expressed in films like Rashomon had decreased. Kurosawa's works show a growing sense of resignation coupled with humanist optimism. Both Ikiru ('Living', 1952) and Shichinin no samurai ('The seven samurai', 1954) were more positive of their affirmation of Kurosawa's personal liberal philosophy. Shichinin no samurai imitates many of the themes of Rashomon, translating the peasant-samurai conflict into a wider pseudo-historical context. At the same time the implicit critique of the samurai ethos constructed through the character of Enoken is made explicit with the introduction of Kikuchiyo; a farmers son who pretends to be samurai. The overall atmosphere of this, Kurosawa's most famous movie, is far from nihilistic. The samurai defeat the bandits, losing four of their own in the process. The historical perspective is implicit in the fact that these casualties are shot: an identical representation of the passing of the feudal age occurs at the end of Kagemusha when the entire Takeda army is mown down by concentrated musket fire. Ultimately in Shichinin no samurai the future is placed in the hands of the commoners.

By 1952 relations between America and Japan were strained. The older Americans who had been stationed in US bases just after the war were replaced by raw draftees; youngsters who easily provoked the disfavour of the very etiquette-conscious Japanese. The incident that provoked most anger was the testing of the hydrogen bomb on Bikini atoll in

1954. A Japanese fishing boat was caught in the fallout and when the crew sailed home they were found to be suffering from radiation sickness. The Americans were indifferent and even accused the fishermen of spying.

The film Kurosawa made just before Kumonosu jo, Ikimono no kiroku ('Record of a living being', 1955) was his personal statement about the continual testing of nuclear weapons by the superpowers, and a study of his and his country's inability to protest. It reflects the political uncertainty of the era and the impotence of the individual in the face of social and cultural upheaval. Nakajima is an old man who is terrified of nuclear war. Convinced that nowhere in Japan is safe he tries to persuade his family to emigrate to Brazil. Their response is to have him certified as incompetent and, through the combination of their cruelty and his fear, he ends up in a hospital for the insane. As well as demonstrating the futility of individual action Ikimono no kiroku displays many of the attitudes expressed towards old age in post-Meiji Japan. According to the film the old, once venerated, are held in contempt. They can only express their wisdom through madness. Ikimono no kiroku is the antithesis to the generalised humanism of Shichinin no samurai. It works as a study of the lone political consciousness; of the intellectual in a changing world that has no room for thinkers.

Ikimono no kiroku is also an important work because Kurosawa used it to explore new film-making techniques. In many ways the highly structured result, with its extremes of contrast and its use (and critique) of a pseudo-documentary style, echoed that of Rashomon. The ending, in which the hero passes a woman carrying a baby on a flight of stairs, certainly imitates, in a more ambiguous way, the optimism of Rashomon's final shot. Toshiro Mifune's mannered performance as the seventy-year-old Nakajima is reminiscent of the Kabuki acting methods and it disrupts the impartial and supposedly 'realistic' narrative. In Kumonosu jo this growing fascination with the mechanism of cinema and the pessimistic attitude towards politics, war and change became even more striking. Although the subject matter was about as different as it possibly could be, Ikimono no kiroku anticipated many of the characteristics of Kurosawa's first Shakespeare film.

## Kumonosu jo (1957)

Kumonosu jo was released by Toho films in 1957. Kurosawa had wanted to make the film for some years but was unable to get the necessary financing. *Shichinin no samurai* had exceeded its budget by the time it reached completion and Toho were very wary about allowing its director to make another expensive period film. *Kumonosu jo* means 'The castle of the spider's web' (although it was released in the West as *Throne of Blood*) and Kurosawa insisted that the fortress of the title be built from scratch and then destroyed. In this light it is perhaps not altogether surprising that Toho should have its doubts about the film. It was only after much deliberation that Kurosawa was allowed to proceed with the shooting.

*Kumonosu jo* begins amid a wasteland of lava hills. In a series of shots the camera tracks across this misty landscape before focusing on a ruin and a funeral post that reads 'The Site of Cobweb Castle.' A chorus sings:

Behold, the ruins of a castle
Inhabited by deep-rooted delusion.
Perpetually haunted by spirits.
The ruins show the fate
Of demonic men with treacherous desires.
Life is the same now as in ancient times.[4]

The political significance of *Kumonosu jo* is obvious from the beginning. Like Rashomon gate the fragments of the keep are the remnants of an era characterised by destruction, war and cruelty. This time, however, Kurosawa is not dealing with the question of relative truth or the possibility of redemption in an ambiguous and evil world. *Kumonosu jo* tackles the method by which cruelty and ambition prevails and concludes that these are both inescapable forces; untouchable and incomprehensible to those mortals trapped in their snares.

Outwardly the film can be read as a straightforward critique of the militaristic ambition that led Japan into the tragedy of World War II. Yet if this is all the movie is primarily concerned with then *Kumonosu jo* is a curiously dated film. It is reiterating issues that Kurosawa had examined in earlier films like *Rashomon*. The answer lies in its relation to *Ikimono no kiroku*. *Kumonosu jo*, like the earlier film, is partly a study in political impotence. Kurosawa's *Macbeth* constructs a study of social uncertainty and historical repetition, concluding that the individual, no matter how much she or he comprehends the 'system', is ultimately divorced from self-perpetuating political 'necessity'.

The exact period in which *Kumonosu jo* is set is unclear but the uniforms, settings and political situations in the film place it during a generalised fourteenth or fifteenth century; the time of the civil wars. In his film Kurosawa returns regularly to the notion of treachery. In the world of

Kurosawa's Macbeth, General Taketoki Washizu, the crime is commonly practised. In fact most of the key figures in the movie have betrayed, or betray, their rightful leader. At the beginning of the film another samurai of the clan, General Fujimaki, has tried to defeat Washizu's lord. Later, when Washizu is reluctant to kill his master his wife, Lady Asaji, points out that 'the same lord . . . he himself ascended the throne by killing his previous lord, as you well know'.[5] Finally Washizu's downfall is due to a revolt by his own men. They, in turn, betray their rightful leader. There is never any suggestion of social or religious sin among all this betrayal. At this period, as in the self-contained world of Kumonosu jo, morality was a matter of expediency. If a betrayal was a success then the triumph mitigated any breach in the feudal code. Given the historical situation Washizu is fitted more to the role of the tragic hero than the ambitious sinner. He lacks the confidence to kill his lord without conscience and he is incapable of living up to the medieval ideals of sincerity and honour. In his way the film criticises both the tenets of feudalism and the hypocrisy of an ideology that is wracked with political uncertainty but which demands total commitment from its followers. Kurosawa uses Macbeth to demonstrate the effect of these pressures on one individual.

Taketoki Washizu belongs to an age ideal for heroic failures. He is already living in the shadow of such giants as Yoshitsune Minamoto. Yet the tragic hero, already an anachronism in medieval Japan, is doubly so in the world of Kumonosu jo. Washizu's problem is neatly encapsulated in the phrase giri nin jo ('obligation versus feeling'). He strives to maintain his loyalty to his lord and in doing so he commits himself to the self-destructive morality embraced by characters like Yoshitsune. His life is dominated by an ever-increasing tension between this and his own instinct for self-preservation. As his wife recognises; if Washizu remains faithful in an age that has no time for sincerity then he will perish.

There are obvious connections between Kurosawa's choice of Macbeth as a play pertinent to his age and Tsubouchi's reading of Julius Caesar. The traditional concept of the sincere yet doomed hero failed to take into account the complexities of motive and the moral and social position of men like Washizu. Western literature seemed to provide a way of interrogating these two hazy areas. Certainly Kurosawa and Tsubouchi were living at a time when the educated individual no longer felt part of a cohesive society. Kurosawa found it particularly hard to express himself through film under the ever-watchful eyes of the wartime censors. After 1945 the wholesale influx of American-style education provided little scope for the Japanese to embark on any rigorous academic

self-analysis. With Macbeth Kurosawa was able to study the feudal character as a complex individual rather than as an ideal symbol of tragic
sincerity or corrupt evil. The film he finally produced also tackled the
uneasy relationship between these heroic figures and the 'common
man', between the leaders and those who watch from the wings: Enoken, Kikuchiyo and Nakajima the mad old man. In Kumonosu jo this rogue
character is Kurosawa himself, the liberal humanist, and the audience
who watch the film.

In portraying the politics of ambition as an inescapable machine; a
perpetual wheel of events that catches up good and evil, corruption
and sincerity and grinds them into a grey, indistinguishable mess,
Kurosawa's film reiterates the classically liberal assumption that the
structures of politics exist independent of people. The image of the
cobweb, as in Cobweb Castle and the surrounding Cobweb Wood, had
been used in sixteenth-century Japanese art to represent the snares of
a corrupt shogunate. Kurosawa's use of the metaphor is less precise.
Washizu's lord is not the shogun, neither is he a king with a divine claim
to power. He is just another warlord who has made his way to the
centre of the web to become ruler for a while. During the course of the
film he will be briefly replaced by the next usurper; Washizu. All that
remains constant is the cobweb; in the form of the forest and its supernatural inhabitants. The implication is that it is the political system that
creates evil, not the characters caught up in it.

Kurosawa's statement on the inescapability of the system and its continued existence in the world long after Washizu has perished echoes
the conclusion of Ikimono no kiroku. In the previous movie he suggested
that, in the wake of the international situation, the individual was incapable of changing the order of things and could only go insane through
frustration and rage. Kumonosu jo is an expression of the disaffected intellectual's vision of political power as a force that is alien and unstoppable.
The only course left to those who experience this vision is an appreciation of the futility of their existence before the juggernaut of politics.
As Burch remarks; in many ways Kurosawa, during this period, was
anticipating the helpless angst of the politically motivated directors of
the 1960s who could only assume a Goddardian cinematic insanity to
be heard.

As Kurosawas Macbeth follows on from Ikimono no kiroku so, in many
ways, Shichinin no samurai and Kumonosu jo represent opposite ends of the
spectrum. The former suggests a generalised solution to the strife of the
middle ages in the activities of an idealised peasantry. Its condescending
attitude to the farmers, a comic lumpenproletariat who discard the

samurai like a dirty shirt once they are no longer needed, belies an
attempt to skate over the problems that Kumonosu jo directly acknowledges (albeit without offering any effective solution). The remaining
four samurai are left to wander conveniently out of history. Washizu,
on the other hand, is trapped both in history and in an eternal political
situation constructed, like the dream Noh, from the past and recycled
eternally.

Kumonosu jo is a movie that directly acknowledges its artistic and cultural
roots. Indeed the director deliberately set out to make a film that would
recreate Macbeth using the Noh theatre. At all levels Kurosawa drew
symbols and images from this, the oldest of Japanese dramatic forms,
and from art, literature and music. Both the content and structure of
the film are based on the traditional forms of the Noh. It's easy to see
how the five-section or five-play sequence from the Noh can used as a
template for the Japanese Macbeth. The interaction between the human
world and the supernatural, the descent of a god into the sacred performance space, corresponds to the first encounter with the witches. As
in the Noh they call attention to the play as an artificial construct. The
witches tell both Macbeth and the audience a rudimentary outline of
the plot. The hero's exploits in the first battle and his character as a
brave and fearless soldier embraces the themes of the warrior plays.
Lady Macbeth is prime material for a woman play and, as in many of
this type of Noh, her role involves a gradual elision into that of a character
from a madness play. Her insanity proceeds from an inability to reconcile ambition with guilt; an echo of the classic duty-affection dilemma.
Mythologically she is the victim of an 'unsteady' demon which, in her
case, manifests itself in her sleepwalking. Macbeth's own distraction at
the sight of the ghost of Banquo imitates many of the themes of the
madness Noh; especially that of the possession of a character by the
ghost of one she or he has wronged. Finally Macbeth himself is the
disruptive 'unsteady' demon who is exorcised from society at the end
of the play.

Overall Kurosawa's film is constructed like a mugen Noh in which
the audience (and by implication the director) adopt the viewpoint of
the wandering priest or traveller who experiences the ambiguous dream
amid the ruins of a past age. In the original screenplay the fragments of
the castle are dominated by a 'sobbing pine tree' that rustles against a
stone wall; a visual reference to the pine tree painted on the rear wall
of a Noh stage.[6] In the final version of the script the chorus sings:

Behold, within this place now desolate

Stood once a mighty fortress,
Lived a proud warrior
Murdered by ambition
His spirit walking still.[7]

During the chant the camera focuses on the sacred space delineated
by the grave marker and its surrounding fence. The mist swirls across
the screen and then retreats to show the castle intact. This emulates the
manipulation of space and time in the Noh theatre. We see a religiously
significant area, the screen is then 'emptied' and we jump back in time
to when Cobweb Castle was still standing. Cinematically the space has
dilated. The area marked out by the post and fence has become that
which it signified; the site of the castle. At the end of the film the first
sequence with the castle and the grave marker is reversed (again the
pine tree figures prominently in the original screenplay). The audience
has travelled full circle, like the priest awakening from his dream.
Throughout the film Kurosawa uses both the mist and the hard-screen
wipe to transform depth and to condense or conflate time and distance.

Kurosawa employs the strictly demarcated boundaries of the Noh to
entrap characters and eliminate any single, coherent point of reference.
The tale of Washizu is visually contained by the sequence with the
funeral post and the mist. Washizu himself is often placed within an
area that is surrounded or confined; either by people, ghosts, animals
or architecture. The most emphatic example of this is in Scene 14. Lady
Asaji is goading Washizu, challenging him to murder his lord and assume
power. Washizu stands in front of a screen which has been drawn back
on either side. Beyond, in the courtyard, a horse is being exercised. As
Washizu stands and glares at Asaji we see the horse turn in the left-hand
space, gallop behind the screen and reappear, circling round, on the
right. Washizu appears trapped in a rigid composition; movement-still-
ness-movement. At other times Washizu is lost within a forest, encircled
by demon warriors and surrounded by his own, treacherous men.

There is a coherent pattern in Kurosawa's use of Noh. Washizu's fate
is inscribed within a cyclical and inescapable environment of mist, violence and highly stylised camerawork. Spiritually his circumstances and
the political forces he represents are caught up in the wheel of fate. The
wasteland in which the film is set, the jumble of lava slopes that surround
Mount Fuji, give the situation mythic significance. Like the ghost in a
Noh play Washizu appears trapped in Naraku, the warrior's hell. Yet
this is not the only theme of Kurosawa's first Shakespeare film. In fact
Kurosawa's interest in Noh outstrips the pessimistic political critique of
Kumonosu jo, betraying the extent to which his interest in film production

and its methodology eclipses his occasionally didactic liberalism. The use of the Noh to define character in Kumonosu jo suggests another facet of the films attitude to tragedy and tragic fate; one in which Shakespeares Macbeth is read as a play about the mechanism of drama and the nature of Japanese heroic legends.

Before the filming began each of the main actors was shown a Noh mask and asked to use it as the basis for their characters. Chieko Naniwa (who played the forest spirit) was given the demon mask Yamanba. Isuzu Yamada (Lady Asaji) had the mask Shakumi: this shows the face of a woman whose beauty is no longer young and who is teetering on the edge of madness. Finally Kurosawa gave Toshiro Mifune a mask called Heida. This is the face of a valiant warrior. Throughout the film many of the actors assume positions derived from the relationships between the points on a Noh stage. Lady Asaji walks with the heel to toe shuffle of a Noh actor and her gestures, when washing the imaginary blood from her hands, imitate the stylised movements of the theatre.

Using the Noh Kurosawa constructed a system of characterisation that was extremely complex. The actors whose roles are comparable to that of the shite all assume the expressions and characteristics of their masks all the time, except for Washizu. It is only at certain points in the film that he mimics the expression of his mask; baring his teeth and glaring. If we consider the traditional notions of possession as constructed by the Noh then a very specific and precise pattern can be seen in this selectivity. Women are the agents of evil in Kumonosu jo. Lady Asaji, in keeping with Kurosawa's other villains, is a total, compete and impenetrable character. She assumes the face Shakumi throughout the film and sits and walks just like a Noh actor. Kurosawa enforced her mastery over her husband by deliberately choosing an actress who was considerably older than Mifune. As Japanese society values the relationship between mother and son very highly this choice traps Washizu in a double bind. He is married to a dangerous and demonic woman who could also double for his mother. Asaji's expression doesn't change until she goes insane; then she merely substitutes one mask for another. She is possessed by her dramatic role, by an unsteady demon, and she in turn 'possesses' Washizu.

The role of the forest spirit is also bound up with this notion of an uncontrollable and demonic invasion. She occupies a sacred space of her own, a reed hut, and she speaks in the hollow voice of the medium from Rashomon. Only Washizu's face fluctuates, suggesting that the extent of his 'possession' by ambition, fate and the warrior spirit Heida is not complete. The assumption of the Noh mask varies according to the extent to which each character follows the dictates of their fate. Washizu only pulls the face of Heida when he pursues his destiny. His expression is transformed into that of the mask when he kills Tsuzuki, when he is trapped in Cobweb Wood, when he sees Miki's (Banquo's) ghost and when he is surrounded by demon warriors in the mist. Finally, with his body riddled by the arrows of his own archers, his expression becomes fixed as that of a brave and admirable warrior.

In his *Macbeth* Kurosawa seems to be suggesting that the fate of Washizu is not merely that of an ambitious, complex soldier. It is also the tragedy of a character trapped within a legend; forced to act out an impossible role according to a 'plot' over which he has no control. Washizu is locked in what is basically a heroic fiction. The imprisonment takes on a bleak and nihilistic form as the protagonist is doomed to act out a myth according to the cruel dictates of a medieval ideology, in cinema houses for as long as the film is shown.

In this way *Ikimono no kiroku* and *Kumonosu jo* are perhaps the bleakest expressions of Kurosawa's liberal pessimism. In the second film the camera adopts the viewpoint of the individual conscience which sees the world dominated by deterministic political forces. Kurosawa has read *Macbeth* as a study of possession and futility: there is no redemption or reconciliation; no attaining of Buddhahood in his first Shakespeare film. Instead the dream of the wandering priest has become the inescapable and ever-present nightmare. The film represents an impasse in the liberal view of politics in Japan during the late 1950s.

## Ran (1985)

Kurosawa's film of *King Lear*, *Ran*, marks his second encounter with the tragedies of Shakespeare. Outwardly *Ran* is similar in theme and approach to *Kumonosu jo*: the director has made Lear into the cruel warlord Hidetora Ichimonji, and both films portray the horror of treachery and bloodshed. Yet *Ran* and *Kumonosu jo* are very different films. *Kumonosu jo* is deeply pessimistic, *Ran*, despite the carnage and suffering, ends with an optimistic critique of the traditional concepts of transcendence, insanity and forgiveness. Kurosawa's *Macbeth* refused to permit a reconciliation between the suffering intellectuals and their perception of politics. His *King Lear* suggests that a solution can be found by abandoning mystical and self-indulgent angst and coming to terms with the 'real world'.

This reformist position has been in evidence in Kurosawa's films since

Kumonosu jo (1957)

the late 1960s. Significantly it became most noticeable after 1971, the year in which Kurosawa attempted suicide. While it is dangerous to ascribe simplistic motives to this act, on one level, as a formalised act of rebellion, Kurosawa's self-destructive behaviour could be seen as the culmination of the highly individualist liberal protest he began in the 1940s. His behaviour afterwards, and the three films he has produced since then (*Dersu Uzala* (1975), *Kagemusha* ('The shadow warrior', 1980) and *Ran* ('Chaos', 1985)) suggest that this interpretation is partly correct. Kurosawa, previously hostile to publicity, began to appear in whisky commercials and give interviews.

Despite this seemingly more practical and outgoing attitude to his work the production difficulties that had plagued him since *Shichinin no samurai* continued. His reputation for awkwardness (which he deliberately cultivated as a result of his humiliating experiences working with Twentieth Century Fox on *Tora, tora, tora!* (1969)) and expensive projects meant that no Japanese production company was prepared to finance his films. *Dersu Uzala* was funded by the Soviet Union and Kurosawa co-produced the movie with Mosfilm. George Lucas and Francis Ford Coppola financed *Kagemusha* and will do the same for his new film *Yume* ('Dreams'). *Ran* was only completed with funding from a French-backed business conglomerate.

After the failure of *Dodesukaden*, a low budget comedy made in 1970, Kurosawa returned to concentrate on spectacular and politically uncontroversial period films. Consequently none of his subsequent films came anywhere near the bleak, precisely realised political critiques evident in *Ikimono no kiroku* and *Kumonosu jo*. Instead the isolated individual in *Dersu Uzala* was the eponymous Siberian hunter. Kurosawa used this old man's reverence for nature to formulate a gentler antidote to the evils of mercantile capitalism than Nakajima's madness or Enoken's sarcasm. Joan Mellen, in describing Kurosawa's affinity for Dostoyevsky, suggests the extent to which *Dersu Uzala* represents a liberal compromise with the director's earlier political beliefs: in '*Dersu Uzala* Kurosawa finds an ideology equivalent to Dostoyesky's Slavophilism in a pantheistic belief in the magnificence of nature and in an embarrasingly archaic adulation of "natural man"'.[8]

Outwardly *Ran*, with its remorseless representation of the brutality of feudal warfare, is far less optimistic. The similarity between the world of *Kumonosu jo* and the traditional warrior's hell, Naraku, is echoed in *Ran*. Here the evocation of this nightmare world of burning landscapes and storms of arrows is far stronger (the movie was filmed almost entirely on the lava slopes of Mount Fuji). The imagery of hell is especially powerful during the long siege of the third fort. The lack of noise and the eerie music give it the unreal quality of a nightmare, compounded by the recurring image of Hidetora sitting in the keep, surrounded by flames, while his soldiers are massacred in the chaotic battle outside. The references to Naraku in *Ran* suggest that, like *Kumonosu jo*, the film follows the pattern of the ghostly Noh. It shows, in a 'vision' the tragic doom of a warrior. However, whereas in *Kumonosu jo* the overall structure is modelled on the Noh, in *Ran* Kurosawa uses the traditional imagery of the plays as a series of motifs. Certain structural similarities do persist but they are used with less consistency than in the earlier film.

Certainly in *Ran* the delineation of the dramatic space and the dream that will occur within its boundaries, is less powerfully stated. The opening shots are similar to those of *Kumonosu jo* in their evocation of the Noh. This time the 'sacred area' is the enclosure erected around Hidetora Ichimonji's hunting party. However, the camera, instead of moving laterally, jumps inward in a series of brief shots before showing the Lord, his Fool, the three sons and the guests. The composition of the group is reminiscent of the Noh, a motif that is emphasised by Tatsuya Nakadai's mask-like makeup and the Fool's comic dance. But, instead of remaining 'within' the performance space all the protagonists (except for Hidetora himself) and the camera leave the enclosure. When Hidetora emerges, some time after the others, he claims to have had a horrible dream. In *Kumonosu jo* the audience experience the 'vision', in *Ran* only Hidetora is the dreamer. The visual references to the Noh are definitely there, but the imagery is distanced from the viewer.

In general the five-play pattern can be picked out in *Ran*, although the sequence is not rigidly adhered to. The god play, in which a deity appears on earth, has its structural counterpart in Washizu's encounter with the forest spirit in *Kumonosu jo*. In *Ran* there is no supernatural episode. However, the scene in the Cobweb forest, where Washizu and Miki stumble across the hut of the spirit, has its counterpart in the later film. Hidetora, the Fool and a loyal samurai find a hovel in the wilderness. Inside, dressed in a Noh costume, is Hidetora's stepson, Tsumuramu, whom he had blinded after vanquishing the boys clan. Tsumuramu plays a flute, a direct reference to the warrior Noh *Atsumori* in which the ghost of a samurai is disguised as a flute playing reaper. It is at this point that Hidetora, realising who the blind man is, loses his last shreds of reason. In both cases an encounter with a Noh character, seated in a hut that resembles a Noh property, occurs as a vital turning point in the tragedy. The third category of Noh, in which a woman is driven to madness by her own unfulfilled desires, is displayed in the career of Lady Kaede in

Ran. Similarly the concept of possession, whichis integral to the Noh understanding of madness, is present in Kumonosu jo, but is largely absent in
Ran. Insanity is transcendent: Hidetora becomes like a child, separated
from the horrors of the world he has helped create.

Overall, Ran, made thirty years later, is far less experimental in its
approach to Shakespeare than Kumonosu jo. As indicated above, much of
this is to do with its position in the canon of Kurosawa's films. Its closest
forebear is Kagemusha (1980), a movie that carries much of the same
elegiac attitude to suffering, militarism and ambition. The overwhelming
theme of both Ran and Kagemusha can be summarised by the term mono
no aware, the Japanese phrase used to express sadness at the transience
of earthly hopes and dreams. The use of the Noh, and specifically the
Noh symbols of madness, in Ran is closely allied with this concept. This
is primarily because Ran addresses the folly and impotence of old age.

Traditionally the madness of the elderly results from the bitter sense
of uselessness experienced by old people. Hidetora, his face made up
to resemble the mask worn by actors playing the aged in the Noh,
confronts the same incompatibility between his desire (to be honoured
as Lord) and reality as the many old characters in the Noh. Furthermore
there are parallels between Nakajima from Ikimono no kikoro and Hidetora,
especially in the sequences where both fathers are forced to abase themselves before their families (actions that would be unbearably degrading
for a Japanese parent to perform). The difference is that while the earlier
film is pessimistic Ran carries a strong positive message. This is because
Hidetora's transcendental madness is represented as undesirable
escapism.

This theme is strongest in the relationship between the Fool and
Hidetora. The Fool, played by the female impersonator 'Peter', has
strong associations with Sambaso, a comic figure whose dance is used
to exorcise visiting gods at the beginning of a day's Noh performance.
When Hidetora first becomes mad he sees an imaginary army composed
of the phantoms of his dead enemies. At this point the Fool, dancing
and singing a Noh song, mocks him with a semi-burlesque display. Later
when the insane Lord wanders through the ruins of Tsumuramu's castle
the Fool's attitude is surprisingly cynical. Although his remarks conceal
his deep loyalty he treats the old man like a child: shouting at him and
commanding him to leap from a high wall. Kurosawa seems to be imply-
ing that the madness that provides Hidetora with a certain uncom-
prehending and a transcendent peace is a false luxury. This impression
is compounded by the fact that Hidetora, unlike Lear, is suffering for
his own atrocious crimes. The root of his madness is not the cruelty of

his sons but his own blindness and complacency. Unable to cope with
the truth he becomes an imbecile.

Those elements of the Noh used in *Ran* appear as isolated motifs: in
Tatsuya Nakadai's makeup; Lady Kaede's walk and in the encounter
with Tsumuramu. What is especially noticeable is that the blind
Tsumuramu's behaviour, which in the confines of his hut is charged
with all the traditional symbolism of the Noh, appears pitiful and childish
in the outside world. Hidetora's madness and Tsumuramu's sightless
retreat from the world (both of which are traditionally associated with
spiritual transcendence and reconciliation) are wholly inappropriate
weapons against the tragic violence of feudal Japan. Significantly
Tsumuramu's sister, still living with the clan, has achieved the inner
peace that her brother, for all his isolation, has failed to reach, The final
image of the film sums up this theme. After Hidetora has died the Fool
rails the gods for their cruelty. Tango, the samurai persecuted for his
pragmatism, points out that man is cruel, not the gods. Then, as the
funeral procession makes its way across the wilderness, the camera, in
a series of jump cuts, moves in on Tsumuramu. The blind man is tapping
his way towards a cliff edge. He stumbles and jerks back from the gulf.
The scroll of Buddha falls from his hand to lie, opened, on the ground.
The camera then draws back, showing the tiny figure in the midst of a
barren landscape. According to Kurosawa this is an optimistic image
because it underscores the futility of trying to withdraw from reality.

*Ran* and *Kumonosu jo* represent different studies of the themes of
militarism, tragic madness and reconciliation that have fascinated
Kurosawa throughout his career. *Kumonosu jo* is an intensely artificial film
that recreates *Macbeth* as the tragedy of a man trapped in a fictional world.
*Ran*, on the other hand, is an open-ended film that acknowledges the
potential for change; if only by suggesting that engagement with reality
is preferable to spiritual escapism. There is a strict contrast between the
realistic attitudes of characters like Tango and Saburo and the often
self-indulgent behaviour of Tsumuramu and the mad Hidetora. This
duality is echoed by the intermingling of Noh motifs and images with
straightforward (and sometimes rather pedestrian) camerawork.

Kurosawa's second Shakespeare film suffers for its optimism. On the
whole *Kumonosu jo* is the stronger film. *Ran* is often reminiscent of
*Kagemusha* but it lacks its powerful imagery. By re-casting *King Lear* as
an actual historical figure Kurosawa has sacrificed the political mythology of *Kumonosu jo* for a more realistic portrayal of medieval Japan.
Despite his claims that *Ran*, like *Kagemusha*, is relevant to modern Japan

the film fails to make the precise connection between militarism, intellectual impotence and political necessity evident in the previous film or his *Macbeth*. This is not altogether surprising given that, when he made *Ran*, Kurosawa intended it to crown his life's work. For this reason a certain amount of reconciliation between the artist, his work and society is to be expected and this is demonstrated by the image of Buddha appearing at the end of the film. Furthermore in the character of Hidetora Ichimonji, another 'mad old man' like Nakajima, there is the implied criticism of the younger Kurosawa from a 'mature' and more 'realistic' viewpoint.

In general it would have been surprising if Kurosawa had used *King Lear* to construct a radical thesis comparable to that in *Kumonosu jo*. Shakespeare is now firmly enshrined in orthodox Japanese culture. With few exceptions modern theatre presentations are either in the tradition of English and American 'academic' productions or they attempt to achieve a kind of elegant cosmopolitanism by copying European avant-garde styles. Kurosawa's *Ran* is not as derivative as these but it does represent return to the liberal idealism of *Ikiru* or *Dersu Uzala* and a personal rejection of the creed of the suffering, politically aware intellectual. At the time of writing Kurosawa has begun work on another film. Called *Yume* ('Dreams') it is intended to be a fantasy film consisting of the dreams of nine Japanese people. It would appear that Kurosawa has abandoned entirely his role as the voice of the fraught liberal conscience.

# Shadows in the mirror

## Shakespeare and film

The case studies in this book have demonstrated how the production of Shakespearean cinema is inextricably linked to the appropriation of his plays by a specific class within a precise historical and social moment. It is this group of critics, writers and theorists who, in England during the early nineteenth century articulated the critical precepts that are the basis of orthodox literary and film criticism. The idea that the isolated genius of the poet was the fount of true art, propounded by writers like Coleridge and Wordsworth, was further developed in the theories of the New Critics. During the 1920s they created a type of textual analysis that combined this concept of high culture with the belief that the act of writing and reading are two separate and distinct activities.

Writers like I. A. Richards and F. R. Leavis believed that a poet, playwright or novelist creates a work of art which reflects her or his own perception of reality. The sensitive reader or astute critic is one who, on approaching the work, understands it as a true representation of the verities of existence. By careful concentration on the text this perceptive reader experiences the same emotions and feelings as the writer did at the time of creation. 'The poem, self-contained and closed, constitutes a pattern of knowledge which leads to a philosophy of detachment. Rising above the vicissitudes of the world "poems remain and explain", and New Critical readers encounter in solitude the paradoxes of human experience which lead to a wise passiveness.'[1]

The passive consumption of the text and the truths it embodies is not only advocated as the correct way of approaching Shakespeare's plays but it is also implicitly cited as the ideal method of translating them on film. The criteria that writers like Jorgens, Ball and Manvell use to judge Shakespeare films suggest that each play is a total, enclosed work of art: Shakespeare invested his poetry with a specific set of meanings and the director's task is to articulate these, to act as a mediator between the meaning of the text and the audience. The emphasis is wholly on the passive recreation of an 'original' rather than any intervention in the way the text is reproduced. Linked with this is the notion that film should be a transparent medium for the communication of Shakespeare's art. If a film appropriates or changes the play then it is justifiably open to criticism for its lack of fidelity to Shakespeare's work or the director's failure to show proper reverence for an English classic.

At best this approach is theoretically unrewarding. Because it judges every film according to how well it articulates Shakespeare's 'intention' the debates it fosters are sterile and repetitive. The reason for this is that the truths that the plays supposedly embody are, in fact, the expression of the ideology that has institutionalised Shakespeare in the literary and educational establishments of England. Far from being eternal, classless and meaningful to all cultures they endorse the ethics of a certain class in a specific country at a precise point in its economic development. Therefore the producers and critics of Shakespeare film, working within a liberal, humanist tradition, are faced with the dilemma of supporting the attitude that Shakespeare is universally applicable to all while simultaneously attempting to suppress movies that seem to differ from Anglocentric readings of the 'essential' text.

This is reflected in the frequency of arguments that take as their main premise the idea that a Shakespeare film is an act of translation. This approach condones those changes that are necessary for basic comprehension or artistic expressiveness (from the stage to celluloid, from English to Japanese) but suggests that the final product still reflects the fundamental poetic truth of the source text. Directors and critics have been discussing the ability of the 'language' of film to reflect Shakespeare's poetry since the nineteenth century. Before that Lamb tackled the same argument in reference to the theatre.

The idea that a film must be judged as a passive reading of the text enforces the idea that literature is a commodity to be consumed within a capitalist economy. To challenge the processes whereby the analysis of a text or film is constituted as an act of passive consumption we need to isolate and recognise the various elements manifest in the work for what they are: signifiers within a complex and contradictory system of signs. The approach of the Romantic and New Critics has tended to reinforce the belief that a play, or film, is a passive and transparent window on reality. Shakespeare's plays show, through art, the emotional and psychological conditions of a number of characters living in archetypal, recognisably real settings. The reconstruction of English history during the mid Victorian era lent weight to the belief that Shakespeare was a chronicler of the British past. By depicting believable people in familiar situations he articulated the truth of the human condition. A fundamental step to appreciating the plays in this way is the acceptance that what is being read, or viewed, is a representation of reality transformed though the skill of the playwright or director.

Semiotics, the study of signs, has radically undermined the belief that this kind of art functions as an impartial window on the world. Semiotics, when applied to art, suggests that what is constructed within a text is a system of signs. These signifiers are artificial, polyvalent codes of representation that are 'read' by the audience and used to construct meaning. Whether their reception of the text is conscious or unconscious depends on the social and historical context in which the art is created and consumed and the level of intervention that is permitted within a particular ideology.

Japanese theatre and film acknowledge the means of their own production and the signs they use have very specific and instantly recognisable meanings: a man raising his hat over his head and lifting one foot shows great determination; a woman biting a handkerchief is distraught. In British Shakespearean cinema the methods by which signs like these are reproduced are concealed in order to retain the illusion of reality. Nevertheless the signs are as artificial as the Kabuki or the Noh although their connotations are less precise. The figure of Hamlet, with his blond hair and tight, black clothes, sitting slumped in a chair at the Danish court has a very definite set of meanings associated with Victorian images of melancholy, high art, Byronic angst, British culture and so on.

The reproduction of Shakespeare in British society is linked to the promotion of a certain set of class values as natural and eternal. This is why the artificial nature of the codes of representation used in Shakespeare film and drama is obscured or suppressed by orthodox criticism. The films and plays discussed in this book depend heavily on archetypal structures culled from other areas of cultural practice and most of them are intertextual in that they recreate previous texts. Yet these relationships are mystified.

Early semiotic theory, as created by writers like Roland Barthes and Kier Elam, tended to be ahistorical. While attacking the homogeneity of the classic realist approach it often failed to address the economic and ideological forces that constructed meaning within a text. Instead it invested sign systems with a structural coherence independent of their historical context. An acknowledgement of the material reasons behind the use of the signs present in Shakespearean cinema is essential to a full understanding of the way in which the plays are reproduced within cultures as varied as Russia, Britain and Japan. Marxist theorists like Chanan and Burch, in applying a theory of ideology to a semiotic deconstruction of film, have begun to reveal the way in which meaning is created within the cinema of Western, Anglo-American capitalist cultures.

The deconstruction of cinema and orthodox film theory within their historical contexts has important ramifications for Shakespearean cinema. When this approach is applied to the films that are part of the accepted canon it reveals how the reproduction of the plays is dialectically linked to their appropriation within literary culture by a certain class. Those writers who demand the passive understanding of the 'eternal' text are working within a tradition that actually appropriates and reconstructs the plays in accordance with the ethics of Victorian industrial society. Their use of Shakespeare invests the texts with meanings that are pertinent to their existence as the producers and consumers of art in a culture that reiterates the concepts of individual subjectivity, the inevitability of progress, the ethics of a liberal economy and so on. This book has looked at how these intellectuals recreated Shakespeare in Britain, and how their readings of the plays were then transmitted to similar groups in North America, Russia and Japan.

As well as revealing instances of cultural appropriation the deconstruction of Shakespeare films made over the last ninety years also allows us to discover the broader historical and material processes that determine the reproduction of the plays within a certain society. The movies that exist both inside and outside the accepted canon of Shakespeare cinema are not simply translations from a poetic text to the language of film. Each movie is composed of a multiplicity of discourses which are taken from a variety of sources: theatre, art, cultural perceptions of tragedy etc. These varied sources are often heavily determined; the myth of the Japanese tragic hero or the lush material splendour of the Busby Berkely revue are two examples. It is vital to understand the way in which these areas shape a particular society's reading of Shakespeare at a given point. These elements are not just used as dressing to make a film more palatable to the less artistically minded members of an audience; they are the temmplates used to re-appropriate Shakespeare as a meaningful part of a country's culture.

## Shakespeare and the intellectual

Studies of cinema and society which focus on the material evidence of history show that a film of a Shakespeare play needs to be studied as part of a specific culture at a certain point in its economic development. What also needs to be acknowledged, in the case of Shakespeare, is the significance of the writer and his plays. Why should a Japanese or Russian director make a film of a Shakespeare play in the first place? What significance do the plays of a sixteenth-century British playwright have for an audience in Tokyo or Moscow and what are the political reasons for the reproduction of the Shakespeare mythology outside England?

What we are dealing with is the appropriation of Shakespeare by alienated intellectuals attempting to come to terms with the disruptive effects of the rapid expansion of capital. Shakespeare in Russia, Japan and England has been adopted as writer emblematic of a certain group of people whose relationship to the means of production becomes, at best, problematic with the development of an industrial economy. This use of the texts, and the characters within them, is echoed in film representations of the plays. Interpretations of Shakespeare by isolated and gifted artists are adopted as symbols of cultural merit in highly organised and labour-intensive productions. This process can be seen operating in Barker's *Henry VIII*, Warner Brothers' *A midsummer night's dream* and the Time/Life BBC series of videos.

Despite protestations that the popularity of Shakespeare in countries outside the Anglo-American sphere of influence is proof of Shakespeare's universal art there are more concrete reasons for the use of his works by intellectuals in foreign cultures. In Russia and Japan we can see how the readings of the pre-revolutionary intelligentsia and the Meiji intellectuals were determined by the nature of the translations and critical works that were exported to these countries. Not surprisingly the medium through which Shakespeare was transmitted was the literature and philosophy of the Romantic movement.

Shakespeare's 'renaissance' in England corresponded to the search for a national culture that would both mitigate and endorse the ethics of industrial capitalism. The reason that so many artists threw themselves wholeheartedly into this project was because the production of culture had become inextricably caught up in the economic framework of a burgeoning laissez-faire market. Shakespeare's works were significant in this context for a variety of reasons. To begin with, his plays, and his own position, were seen as symbols of a new national awareness of the heritage of the British middle classes. At the same time his histories and tragedies, to an audience used to narrative character-centred literature, appeared to address the relationship between the individual and the remorseless mnechanisms of the state.

The readings of the plays popular on stage and in the critical writings of people like Lamb and Walpole drew on the imagery and structures of the Gothic novel. This genre tried to tackle the horrors of industrial society using a number of mechanisms. It combined studies of psychological oppression with the cult of the sublime; contextualising it within a mythical and Romantic vision of history. In this context Shakespeare's plays were understood as wild, passionate tales of brutality in which characters were motivated by extremes of emotion and threatened by the supernatural agents of dynastic tyranny. Like the Gothic novel they transplanted this perception of an uncontrollable and hostile world into the past.

At this point the idea of Shakespeare's genius was at its strongest. The writers and artists of the Romantic movement sought to mystify their relationship to the means of production by investing the creative act with a transcendental significance. This involved the separation of the poetic text from its reproduction on the stage and in art and its isolation as the ideal source of meaning which only the individual could comprehend through an isolated act of consumption.

In England Shakespeare's plays were rapidly absorbed into the mainstream of nationalistic culture. The boom in printed versions of his plays and the activities of businessmen like Josiah Boydell contributed to this. The image of the transcendent genius whose works were emblematic of a new historical consciousness was aptly suited to the ethics of Victorian society. Conversely, because of his close connections with middle-class perceptions of history, Shakespeare became less suited to the articulation of the alienation that the more radical Romantics experienced during the mid nineteenth century. The reproduction of Shakespeare on the Victorian stage and in British silent cinema confirmed his role as a bastion of national culture. The transmission of this perception of Shakespeare to other cultures corresponds to the rapid expansion of the British Empire during the Victorian period. Yet although they were now contextualised within the orthodox reproduction of imperial ideology both at home and in the colonies many of the humanist elements emphasised by Lamb and others remained.

Thus when the writers and artists in Russia and Japan started to come into regular contact with the plays they were received and understood in this context. The swing away from French culture to German and English occasioned by the Napoleonic wars meant that Russian writers and critics discovered the works of Shakespeare via the writing of Byron, Coleridge and Lamb. In Japan the intellectuals of the Meiji period experienced Shakespeare's plays as character-centred narratives in which the development of the plot was occasioned by the spiritual and psychological dilemmas of the protagonists. The economic situation of Russian and Japanese society determined the way in which Romantic readings of Shakespeare were appropriated. Both countries had developed, or were developing, capitalist economies. In both cases this took the form of a remorseless, centralised transformation of society. In fact Japan's rapid 'modernisation' was a direct response to Western expansionism, being chiefly sparked off by the government's fear of colonisation.

In Japan the modernisation programmes of the late nineteenth century produced a group of intellectuals schooled according to Western philosophy and ethics yet whose cultural roots were traditionally Japanese. These students, unable to come to terms with their position in society, saw their sense of alienation reflected in the character-centred narratives of the Romantic Shakespeare. They were created by the new age but they had no control over the mechanisms of power and hence little self-determination. Kurosawa belongs to this tradition as his Shakespeare films demonstrate.

There are strong similarities between these Meiji intellectuals and the 'superfluous' men of mid nineteenth-century Russia. However the latter were already linked with an established tradition of liberal dissent. Tsarist Russia was governed by an autocratic state and it lacked a fully formed laissez-faire market. The intelligentsia, composed of landless nobles, students and civil servants, weren't allied to the interest of a growing middle class. This had a dual effect. It resulted in the perpetuation of a strong radical movement, which expressed itself as a Romantic populism, while removing its adherents even further from the mechanisms of power than the British Romantics or the Meiji students. On the one hand this enabled people like Meyerhold to throw themselves wholeheartedly into the revolutionary ethic of the Bolshevik movement. On the other hand it meant that the re-introduction of totalitarianism under Stalin forced artists like Kozintsev back into an idealised perception of the relationship between the thinkers and the serfs.

The lack of direct colonial rule meant that the writers and artists who experienced the cultural aspects of international trade could appropriate Romantic Shakespeare for themselves and use it to address their own relationship to society without their response being conditioned by a colonial ideology. The films of Kozintsev and Kurosawa represent attempts to reconcile the intellectual with both the state and society. They use the traditions of the Romantic readings of Shakespeare to internalise the effects of oppression and power on the individual. Even so there are still attempts from within Anglo-American culture to create a world-wide cultural hegemony based on the orthodoxy of New Criticism. The targeting of an international market by Time/Life, Morgan

Guaranty and the BBC is symptomatic of this. Fortunately the chances of its success are limited. In the intellectual movements of countries like Russia and Japan Shakespeare already has a strongly determined and long-established role. Nevertheless projects like the BBC Shakespeare, with their glib re-assertion of the mythology of the universal bard, contribute to the continuing suppression of radical and interventionist readings of the plays both in England and abroad. This can only be challenged by the conscious deconstruction of Shakespearean cinema and by relating the films to their specific cultural moments.

# Notes

## Introduction

1 Jack Jorgens, *Shakespeare on film* (London: Indiana University Press, 1977), p. 1.
2 David Robey, 'Anglo-American new criticism', *Modern literary theory*, Ann Jefferson and David Robey, eds. (London: Batsford, 1982), p. 69.
3 Alan Sinfield, 'Give an account of Shakespeare and Education, showing why you think they are effective and what you have appreciated about them. Support your comments with precise references', *Political Shakespeare: new essays in cultural materialism*, eds. Jonathan Dollimore and Alan Sinfield (Manchester: Manchester University Press, 1985), p. 138.
4 Charles Eckert, *Focus on Shakespearean films* (New Jersey: Prentice Hall Inc, 1972), p. 2.
5 Robert Hamilton Ball, *Shakespeare on silent film: a strange eventful history* (London: George Allen & Unwin, 1968), p. 88.
6 Jorgens, p. 6.
7 Graham Holderness, 'Radical potentiality and institutional closure: Shakespeare in film and television', *Political Shakespeare: New essays in cultural materialism*, eds. Jonathan Dollimore and Alan Sinfield (Manchester: Manchester University Press, 1985), p. 186.

## Chapter 1

1 W. Moncrieff, quoted in Joseph Donohue, *Theatre in the age of Kean* (Oxford: Basil Blackwell, 1975), p. 50.
2 George Coleman, in Donohue, p. 50.
3 Quoted in Donohue, p. 19.
4 Turner Morton, 'The art of gesture', *Pearson's magazine* (April 1901), p. 289.
5 James Smith, *Melodrama* (London: Methuen, 1973), p. 16.
6 George Rowell, *The Victorian theatre, 1792-1914* (Cambridge: Cambridge University Press, 1978), p. 13.
7 John Stokes, *Resistible theatres: enterprise and experiment in the late nineteenth century* (London: Paul Elek Books, 1972), p. 6.
8 Bulwer Lytton, in Michael Chanan, *The dream that kicks: the prehistory and early years of cinema in Britain* (London: Routledge & Kegan Paul, 1980), pp. 138-9.
9 Horace Walpole, Preface to the second edition of *The castle of Otranto* (1765), in ed. Mario Praz, *Three gothic novels*, (Harmondsworth: Penguin, 1981), pp. 44-8.
10 Walpole, *The Castle of Otranto*, p. 60.
11 Samuel Taylor Coleridge, *Biographia literaria* (London: Dent, 1974), p. 180.
12 Charles Lamb, 'On the tragedies of Shakespeare, considered with reference to their fitness for stage representation', in E. Tillyard, ed., *Lamb's criticism* (Cambridge: Cambridge University Press, 1923), pp. 35-6.
13 Charles Lamb, *Tales from Shakespear* (n.p.:n.p., 1807), p. 6.
14 Charles Lamb, *Tales from Shakespear*, p. 7.
15 Michael Booth, *Victorian spectacular theatre 1850-1910* (London: Routledge & Kegan Paul, 1981), p. 140.
16 Quoted in Booth, 1981, p. 31.

17 Herbert Beerbohm Tree, 'Henry VIII and his court', quoted in J. C. Trewin, *The Edwardian theatre* (Oxford: Basil Blackwell, 1976), p. 134.
18 Quoted in Booth, 1981, p. 132.
19 Tree, 'Script for *The tempest*', in Trewin, pp. 134-5.

## Chapter 2

1 Chanan, p. 126.
2 Raymond Williams, 'British film history; new perspectives', eds. James Curran & Vincent Porter, *British cinema history* (London: Weidenfeld & Nicolson, 1983), p. 10.
3 Chanan, p. 125.
4 Quoted in Ball, p. 22.
5 Ball, p. 23.
6 Quoted in Ball, p. 30.
7 Quoted in Ball, p. 42.
8 Henry Barker, Publicity brochure for the Tree/Barker *Henry VIII*, Feb. 1911, p. 1.
9 Rachael Low, *The history of British film 1906-1914* (London: George Allen & Unwin, 1949), p. 225.
10 Titles for the F. Benson/Co-op Cinematograph Company production of *King Richard III*, 1911.
11 Neil Taylor, 'Two types of television Shakespeare', *Shakespeare survey*, Vol. 39 (Cambridge: Cambridge University Press, 1987), p. 52.

## Chapter 3

1 Kenneth MacGowan, *The theatre of tomorrow* (New York: Boni & Liverwright, 1921), p. 179.
2 J. K. Huysmans, *Against nature*, trans. Robert Baldick (Harmondsworth: Penguin Books, 1979), p. 36.
3 Chanan, p. 249.
4 Friedrich Schlegel, in Macgowan, p. 14.
5 Quoted in Stokes, p. 73.
6 Adolphe Appia, *Music and the art of the theatre*, Robert Corrigan & Mary Dirks (Florida: University of Miami Press, 1962), p. 98.
7 Appia, p. 22.
8 Hubert von Herkomer, in Stokes, p. 88.
9 Herkomer, in Stokes, p. 105.
10 Gordon Craig, 'Conversation with Konstantin Stanislavsky', in Lawrence Senelick, *Gordon Craig's Moscow Hamlet* (London: Greenwood Press, 1982), p. 68.
11 Grigori Kozintsev, quoted in Senelick, p. 190.
12 Franz Kafka, 'Letter to his father', *Wedding preparations in the country and other stories*, trans. Ernst Kaiser & Eithne Wilkins, (Harmondsworth: Penguin Books, 1982), p. 38.
13 Gaston Melies, quoted in Ball, p. 34.
14 Chanan, p. 32.

## Chapter 4

1 Leo Braudy, 'Genre: the conventions of connection', *Film theory and criticism: introductory readings*, second edition, eds. Gerald Mast and Marshall Cohen (Oxford: Oxford University Press, 1979), p. 454.

2 Andrew Bergman, 'Frank Capra and screwball comedy, 1931-1941', Mast & Cohen, p. 762.
3 Nick Roddick, *A new deal in entertainment: Warner Brothers in the 1930s* (London: British Film Institute, 1983), pp. 23-4.
4 Roddick, p. 105.
5 Derek Jarman, *Dancing ledge*, Shaun Allen, ed. (London: Quartet, 1984), p. 188.
6 Jarman, p. 172.
7 Jarman, p. 194.

## Chapter 5

1 Lionel Kochan and Richard Abraham, *The making of modern Russia*, second edition (Harmondsworth: Penguin Books, 1983), p. 155.
2 Kochan and Abraham, p. 165.
3 Alexander Pushkin, quoted in Mikhail Morozov, *Shakespeare on the Soviet stage*, trans. David Magarshack (London: Soviet News, 1947), p. 12.
4 Vissarion Belinsky, quoted in Morozov, p. 15.
5 Ivan Turgenev, 'A Prince Hamlet of the Schigrov district', *The hunting sketches*, trans. Bernard Guerney (Geneva: Edito Service, 1969), pp. 301-2.
6 Kochan and Abraham, p. 195.
7 E. H. Carr, *The Bolshevik revolution*, part 1 (Harmondsworth: Penguin Books, 1979), p. 67.
8 Meyerhold, quoted in Edward Braun, *The theatre of Meyerhold: revolution on the modern stage* (London: Methuen, 1986), p. 165.
9 Réne Guillere, quoted in Sergei Eisenstein, *The film sense*, trans. J. Leyda (London: Faber, 1977), pp. 81-2.
10 Eisenstein, p. 148.
11 Eisenstein, quoted in Peter Wollen, *Signs and meaning in the cinema* (London: Secker & Warburg, 1972), p. 65.
12 Mikhail Bakhtin, *Rabelais and his world*, trans. Helen Iswozsky (Cambridge, Mass.: M.I.T., 1968), p. 19.
13 Morozov, p. 13.
14 Morozov, pp. 59-60.

## Chapter 6

1 Barbara Leaming, *Grigori Kozintsev* (Boston: Twayne Publishers, 1980), p. 57.
2 Grigori Kozintsev, *Shakespeare: time and conscience* (New York: Hill and Wang, 1966), p. 255.
3 Thomas De Quincey, *Confessions of an English opium eater* (Harmondsworth: Penguin Books, 1979), p. 106.
4 Kozintsev, *Shakespeare: time and conscience*, p. 243.
5 Ibid., p. 253.
6 Sergei Eisenstein, *Ivan the Terrible Part I* (Central Cinema Studio, Alma-Ata, 1944).
7 Grigori Kozintsev, *King Lear: the space of tragedy* (Berkeley: University of California Press, 1977), p. 62.

## Chapter 7

1 Jorgens, p. 157.
2 Peter Brook, in 'Finding Shakespeare on film: from an interview with Peter Brook',

*Focus on Shakespeare films*, Charles W. Eckert, ed. (New Jersey: Prentice Hall Inc., 1972), p. 37.
3 Quoted in Minoru Toyoda, *Shakespeare in Japan: an historical survey* (Tokyo: Iwanami Shoten Press, 1940), p. 20.
4 Inoue Tetsujiro, in Kenneth Pyle, *The new generation in Meiji Japan: problems of cultural identity 1885-1895* (California: Stanford University Press, 1969), p. 21.
5 Pyle, p. 7.
6 Toyoda, p. 46.
7 George Steiner, *After Babel – aspects of language and translation* (Oxford: Oxford University Press, 1977), p. 64.
8 Peter Milward, 'Teaching Shakespeare in Japan', Shakespeare quarterly, Vol. XXV, p. 230.

## Chapter 8

1 Kunio Komparu, *The Noh theatre: principles and perspectives*, trans. Jane Corddry and Stephen Comee (Tokyo: Weatherhill and Tankosha, 1982), p. 40.
2 Akira Kurosawa, dir., *Rashomon* (A Daiei Production, 1950), scenario by Shinobu Hashimoto and Akira Kurosawa, English subtitles by Donald Richie.
3 Quoted in James Davidson, 'Memories of defeat in Japan: a reappraisal of Rashomon', ed. Donald Richie, *Focus on Rashomon* (New Jersey: Prentice Hall Inc, 1972), p. 127.
4 Akira Kurosawa, Hideo Oguni, Shinobu Hashimoto and Ryuzo Kikushima, original screenplay for *Kumonosu jo*, trans. Hisae Niki, in Hisae Niki, *Shakespeare in translation in Japanese culture* (Tokyo: Kenseisha Ltd, 1984), p. 155.
5 *Ibid.*, p. 167.
6 *Ibid.*, p. 155.
7 Akira Kurosawa, Hideo Oguni, Shinobu Hashimoto and Ryuzo Kikushima, final screenplay for *Kumonosu jo*, trans. Donald Richie, in Donald Richie and Joan Mellen, *The films of Kurosawa*, second edition (Berkely: University of California Press, 1984), p. 117.
8 Richie and Mellen, p. 197.

## Conclusion

1 Catherine Belsey, *Critical practice* (London: Methuen, 1980), p. 20.

# Further Reading

## General

*a) Shakespeare and film*

Ball, Robert Hamilton, *Shakespeare on silent film: a strange eventful history* (London: George Allen & Unwin, 1968).

Eckert, Charles, *Focus on Shakespearean films* (New Jersey: Prentice Hall Inc., 1972).

Jorgens, Jack, *Shakespeare on film* (London: Indiana University Press, 1977).

Manvell, Roger, *Shakespeare and the film* (New York: A. S. Barnes & Co., 1979).

*Shakespeare survey*, Vol. 39 (Cambridge: Cambridge University Press, 1987).

*(b) Film theory*

Mast, Gerald & Marshall Cohen, eds. *Film theory and criticism: introductory readings*, second edition, (Oxford: Oxford University Press, 1979).

Nichols, Bill, *Ideology and the image* (Bloomington: Indiana University Press, 1981).

Wollen, Peter, *Signs and meaning in the cinema* (London: Secker & Warburg, 1972).

*(c) Literary theory*

Belsey, Catherine, *Critical practice* (London: Methuen, 1980).

Dollimore, Jonathan and Alan Sinfield, eds., *Political Shakespeare: new essays in cultural materialism* (Manchester: Manchester University Press, 1985).

Jefferson, Ann and David Robey, eds., *Modern literary theory* (London: Batsford, 1982).

Kott, Jan, *Shakespeare our contemporary*, trans. Boleslaw Taborski (London: Methuen, 1967).

## British Shakespeare film

*a) Shakespeare and narrative*

Butler, Marilyn, *Romantics, rebels and reactionaries: English literature and its background, 1760-1830* (Oxford: Oxford University Press, 1981).

Lamb, Charles, *Lamb's criticism*, ed. E. Tillyard (Cambridge: Cambridge University Press, 1923).

Walpole, Horace, *The castle of Otranto, Three gothic novels*, ed. Mario Praz (Harmondsworth: Penguin, 1981).

*(b) Theatre history*

Booth, Michael, *English melodrama* (London: Herbert Jenkins, 1965).

Booth, Michael, *Victorian spectacular theatre 1850-1910* (London, Routledge & Kegan Paul, 1981).

Donohue, Joseph, *Theatre in the age of Kean* (Oxford: Basil Blackwell, 1975).

Richards, Kenneth and Peter Thomson, eds., *Essays on nineteenth century British theatre* (London: Methuen, 1971).

Rowell, George, *The Victorian theatre, 1792-1914* (Cambridge: Cambridge University Press, 1978).

Smith, James, *Melodrama* (London: Methuen, 1973).

Stokes, John, *Resistible theatres: enterprise and experiment in the late nineteenth century* (London: Paul Elek Books, 1972).

Trewin, J. C. *The Edwardian theatre* (Oxford: Basil Blackwell, 1976).

*(c) Genre art*

Maas, Jeremy, *Victorian painters* (London: Barrie and Jenkins, 1967).

Strong, Roy, *And when did you last see your father?* (London: Thames and Hudson, 1978).

Tomory, Peter, *The life and art of Henry Fuseli* (London: Thames and Hudson, 1972).

(d) British film
Banham, Martin, 'BBC television's dull Shakespeares', *Critical quarterly*, Vol 22. No.1 (1980).
Chanan, Michael, *The dream that kicks: the prehistory and early years of cinema in Britain* (London: Routledge and Kegan Paul, 1980).
Curran, James and Vincent Porter, eds., *British cinema history* (London: Weidenfeld & Nicolson, 1983).
Manvell, Roger and Rachael Low, *The history of British film 1896-1906* (London: George Allen & Unwin, 1948).
Low, Rachael, *The history of British film 1906-1914* (London: George Allen & Unwin, 1949).

# Shakespeare film and 'the theatre of light'

(a) The theatre of light
Appia, Adolphe, *Music and the art of the theatre*, trans. Robert Corrigan and Mary Dirks (Florida: University of Miami Press, 1962).
Joll, James, *Europe since 1870: an international history* (Harmondsworth: Penguin Books, 1976).
MacGowan, Kenneth, *The theatre of tomorrow* (New York: Boni & Liverwright, 1921).
Senelick, Lawrence, *Gordon Craig's Moscow Hamlet* (London: Greenwood Press, 1982).
(b) Expressionist Shakespeare film
Bessy, Maurice, *Orson Welles: an investigation into his films and philosophy* (New York: Crown Publishers, 1971).
France, Richard, *The theatre of Orson Welles* (Louisburg: Bucknell University Press, 1977).
Jarman, Derek, *Dancing ledge*, ed. Shaun Allen (London: Quartet, 1984).
Roddick, Nick, *A new deal in entertainment: Warner Brothers in the 1930s* (London: British Film Institute, 1983).

# Russian Shakespeare and the films of Grigori Kozintsev

(a) Shakespeare and the Russian intellectual
Kochan, Lionel and Richard Abraham, *The making of modern Russia*, second edition (Harmondsworth: Penguin Books, 1983).
Bakhtin, Mikhail, *Rabelais and his world*, trans. Helen Iswozsky (Cambridge, Mass.: M.I.T., 1968).
Braun, Edward, *The theatre of Meyerhold: revolution on the modern stage* (London: Methuen, 1986).
Carr, E. H., *The Bolshevik revolution*, part 1 (Harmondsworth: Penguin Books, 1979).
Leskov, Nikolai, 'Lady Macbeth of Mtsensk', *Lady Macbeth of Mtsensk and other stories*, trans. David McDuff (London: Penguin Books, 1987).
Turgenev, Ivan, 'A Prince Hamlet of the Schigrov district', *The hunting sketches*, trans. Bernard Guerney (Geneva: Edito Service, 1969).
(b) Hamlet and Korol Ler
Eisenstein, Sergei, *The film sense*, J. Leyda, trans. (London: Faber, 1977).
Kozinstev, Grigori, *Shakespeare: time and conscience*, trans. Joyce Vining (London: Dennis Dobson, 1967).
Kozinstev, Grigori, *King Lear: the space of tragedy* (Berkely: University of California Press, 1977).
Leaming, Barbara, *Grigori Kozintsev* (Boston: Twayne Publishers, 1980).

# Japan and the films of Akira Kurosawa

(a) Japanese history

Buruma, Ian, A Japanese mirror: heroes and villains in Japanese culture (London: Jonathan Cape, 1984).

Keene, Donald, The Japanese discovery of Europe 1720-1830 (Stanford, Ca.: Stanford University Press, 1969).

Morris, Ivan, The nobility of failure: tragic heroes in the history of Japan (Tokyo: Charles Tuttle Co., 1982).

Pyle, Kenneth, The new generation in Meiji Japan: problems of cultural identity 1885-1895 (California: Stanford University Press, 1969).

Reischauer, Edwin, Japan: the story of a nation (Tokyo: Charles Tuttle Co, 1984).

(b) Japanese culture

Brandon, J., ed., trans., Kabuki: five classic plays (London: Harvard University Press, 1975).

Keene, Donald, ed., Anthology of Japanese literature to the nineteenth century (Harmondsworth: Penguin Books, 1978).

Keene, Donald, ed., Modern Japanese literature from 1868 to the present day (Tokyo: Charles Tuttle Co., 1960).

Komparu, Kunio, The Noh theatre: principles and perspectives, trans. Jane Corddry and Stephen Comee (Tokyo: Weatherhill and Tankosha, 1982).

Tsuda, Noritake, Handbook of Japanese art (Tokyo: Charles Tuttle Co., 1976).

Ueda, Makoto, Literary and art theories in Japan (Cleveland, Ohio: Western Reserve University Press, 1967).

Waley, Arthur, ed., The Noh plays of Japan (Tokyo: Charles Tuttle Co., 1981).

(c) Shakespeare in Japan

Toyoda, Minoru, Shakespeare in Japan: an historical survey (Tokyo: Iwanami Shoten Press, 1940).

Niki, Hisae, Shakespeare in translation in Japanese culture (Tokyo: Kenseisha Ltd, 1984).

(d) Films

Anderson, Joseph and Donald Richie, The Japanese film: art and industry (Tokyo: Charles Tuttle Co., 1959).

Blumenthal, J., 'Macbeth into Throne of Blood', Sight and Sound, Autumn 1985.

Burch, Noel, To the distant observer: form and meaning in the Japanese cinema (London: Scolar Press, 1979).

Kurosawa, Akira, The seven samurai, trans. Donald Richie (London: Lorrimer Publishing, 1970).

Kurosawa, Akira, Something like an autobiography, trans. Audie Bock (New York: Alfred Knopf, 1982).

Richie, Donald, Focus on Rashomon (New Jersey: Prentice Hall Inc, 1972).

Richie, Donald & Joan Mellen, The films of Kurosawa, second edition (Berkely: University of California Press, 1984).

Zambrano, Ana Laura, 'Throne of blood: Kurosawa's Macbeth' Literature/film quarterly 2, 1974.

n Mayer, 83
evolod, 87, 114-15, 118, 119,
125, 127, 130, 140, 144, 147,
ummer night's dream, 114; Mystery

ro, 174, 180
omon, 146-7
verett, 27, 135
an, 1, 53, 56
r, 165
shitsune, 153, 171, 176
up, 155
60, 165
vel, 112, 134
les, 7
185
anty, 194
hail, 125-6, 132-3
152
m, 67
er, 17
and Literature Society, 114
Theatre, 70, 72, 114, 118, 134,
t, 70-2; Othello, 114
 Theatre, 112
versity, 125

ami, 168; Atsumori, 184
rd, 118
 Hugo, 7

uya, 184, 186
oshio, 158
ko, 180
Gance), 83

, 5, 188, 189, 194

ft', 63, 70, 77, 78, 92 see 'theatre

143, 144-5, 146, 147, 148, 152
-81, 184-5, 190

ence, 2, 33, 47, 57, 63, 89, 134,
138,, 141
Sir William, 27
, 160
ly, 27
isa, 169
agraph), 40
elles), 62, 63, 79, 93-8, 102, 106,

Pasternak, Boris, 5
Patent Laws, 14, 15, 18, 20, 23
Paul, R. W., 39, 75, 76
Perry, Matthew, C., 154
'Peter', 171, 185
Piranesi, Gián Battista, 21, 138
Polanski, Roman, 2
Polevoy, Nikolai, 112
Pop art, 99-101, 106
Porter, Edwin, 45
Prince of Wales Theatre, 29
Prince Yamato, 153
Proletcult Theatre, 119, 120
Propp, Vladimir, 123, 147
Punk Rock, 99, 106
Pushkin, Alexander, 111,112,125,134,141

Radischev, Alexander, 110
**Ran** ('Chaos', Kurosawa), 1, 150, 162, 171,
181-7
**Rashomon** (Kurosawa), 171-3, 174, 175,
180
Reinhardt, Max, 80, 81, 83, 87, 88, 90, 92,
105, 106
**Rescued by Rover** (Hepworth), 45
Revolutionary Association of Proletarian
Writers, 122
RFSR Theatre No. 1, 119
Richards, I. A., 3, 188
Richie, Donald, 5
Robinson, Edward G., 91
Roddick, Nick, 82, 86
romanticism, 14, 20, 22, 31, 61, 67, 78, 85,
88, 92, 98, 111, 113, 123, 125, 127, 128,
131, 134, 137, 144, 147, 148, 150, 189,
192-3, 194
**Romeo and Juliet** (BBC), 54
**Romeo and Juliet** (Gaumont), 40-41
**Romeo and Juliet** (Vitagraph), 40, 46
Rooney, Mickey, 91-2
Rousseau, Jean-Jacques, 26, 61, 155
Royal Circus, 14
royal patents, 13
rumpen mono, 171
Russell, Ken, 101
Ryunosuke, Akutugawa, 171

'Sadanji', 160
Sadlers Wells Theater, 37
Saikiku, Jono, 158
'saragaku', 166, 168
Schepkin, Mikhail, 134
Schlegel, Friedrich, 63, 66

# Index

Film titles are shown in bold print

Abraham, Richard, 110, 117
**A gag in three acts: the electrification of
Gogol** (FEKS), 130-1
agit trains, 129, 140
Akimov, Nikolai, 134
**Alexander Nevsky** (Eisenstein), 72, 95
*All for money*, 158
All Union Party Conference on Cinema
(1928), 132
Alma-Tadema, Laurence, 29, 88, 89
Althusser, Louis, 6
**A midsummer night's dream** (Coron-
ado), 74, 103, 105
**A midsummer night's dream** (Warner),
62, 63, 78, 79, 80-1, 83, 84, 85, 86, 87-93,
95, 99, 103, 192
*A mirror of Roman vicissitudes*, 157
**Angels with dirty faces** (Warner), 87, 91
animation, 85-6
**Antony and Cleopatra** (Vitagraph), 40
Appia, Adolphe, 51, 61, 64-7, 73, 76, 78, 81,
84, 87, 102, 105, 120, 121, 137, 150
Asano, Wasaburo, 159-60, 161

Bakhtin, Mikhail, 113, 120, 123-4, 126, 127,
129, 133, 140, 141, 143, 147, 148
Ball, Robert Hamilton, 2, 3, 37, 40, 188
Banham, Martin, 52
Barker, William, 41-2, 46, 47, 56, 62, 87, 192
Barthes, Roland, 190
Bayreuth, 64, 66
Bazin, André, 7
BBC, 33, 52-7, 150, 192, 195
Belinsky, Vissarion, 112, 134
Belsey, Catherine, 3, 4, 8
**Ben Hur** (Kalem), 40
*benshi*, 169
Benson, F. R., 42, 43, 47, 56
Bergman, Andrew, 85
Berkely, Busby, 83, 84, 91, 191
Bernhardt, Sarah, 69-70
*Biography of Universal History*, 158
Bioscope, 41

**Birth of a nation** (Griffith), 46
Blake, William, 25, 67
bolshevik movement, 116, 194
Bouchier, Arthur, 28
Bower, Dallas, 49
Boydell, Josiah, 24, 193
Brecht, Bertolt, 56, 61
*bricolage*, 34, 35
British Board of Film Censors, 46
Brook, Peter, 2, 62, 150-1
Brown, Joe E., 89
Bunraku, 169
Buñuel, Luis, 76, 101
Burch, Noel, 6, 8, 9, 43, 73, 170, 177, 190

Cagney, James, 87, 89, 91
Cantor, Eddie, 89
Capra, Frank, 85
carnivalesque, 113, 115, 123-4, 140, 147, 148
Chanan, Michael, 8, 9, 34-5, 39, 73, 75, 77,
190
Chaplin, Charles, 131
Chekhov, Anton, 130, 157, 159
Cherkassov, Nikolai, 143
'Chikuyo sanjin', 158
**Chimes at midnight** (Welles), 97
**Chushingura** (Shozo), 170
cinematographe, 169
Cinematographic Act, 39
**Citizen Kane** (Welles), 96
Cocteau, Jean, 101-2
Coleman the younger, George, 15
Coleridge, Samuel Taylor, 19, 22, 24, 193
Columbia, 85
constructivism, 97, 108, 118, 121, 125, 126,
127, 129, 130, 132, 133, 134, 137, 140, 143,
147
Co-op Cinematographic Company, 42, 46
Coppola, Francis Ford, 183
Coronado, Celestino, 74, 103, 105
Covent Garden, 13, 14, 17, 38
Cox, W. D., 158
Craig, Gordon, 51, 61, 68, 70-3, 76, 77, 78,

84, 87, 95, 97, 105, 120, 121, 132, 134, 135, 138, 146, 160
cubism, 118, 119, 127, 137

Dada, 130
Dadd, Richard, 26, 67
Dal, Oleg, 146
Dalí Salvador, 76
David, Jacques, 25
Davies, Anthony, 53, 103
**Dead end** (Warner), 87
Decadents, 61, 67, 78 see symbolism
Del Guidice, Fillipo, 49
DeMille, Cecil B., 88
'dengaku', 166
Dent, Alan, 49
Dersu Uzala (Kurosawa), 183, 187
Dickens, Charles, 74, 75
Dieterle, William, 80, 83
Disney, Walt, 85
**Dodesukaden** (Kurosawa), 183
Donohue, Joseph, 16
**Don Quixote** (Kozintsev), 124, 131
Dostoyevsky, Fyodor, 113-14, 127, 133, 137, 141, 183
Dreyer, Carl, 71, 76
Drury Lane, 13, 14, 16, 17, 46
Duma, 115-16

Eckert, Charles, 2, 4
Edison, Thomas, 82, 169
Edwards, Hilton, 96
Eisenstein, Sergei, 49, 72, 95, 97, 118, 119-22, 127, 130, 137, 141-3, 144, 145
Elam, Kier, 190
**Empire** (Warhol), 101
'Enoken' 171
existentialism, 173
expressionism, 61, 62, 63, 78, 80, 105, 120, 121, 135, 138, 146

Factory of the Eccentric Actor (FEKS), 118-19, 124, 130-2, 133, 134, 140, 141, 146, 147
**Fantasia** (Disney), 85, 89, 92
Fields, W. C., 84
First National, 82
Flynn, Errol, 83
Forbes-Robertson, John, 46 see Gaumont
formalism, 125
**42nd Street** (Warner), 84
Freud, Sigmund, 61, 73, 86, 98, 105
Fuseli, Henry, 19, 24, 25-6, 61
futurism, 118, 119, 121, 127, 130, 132, 147

Gance, Abel, 83
Gaumont, 40, 46
*ge koku jo*, 152
*gendai geki*, 170, 171
*gesamtkunstwerk*, 65, 67, 68, 69, 81, 93, 97, 105, 119
*giri nin jo*, 176
Gogol, Nikolai, 13
**Gold diggers of 1933** (Warner), 84
Gorky, Maxim, 132, 160
gothicism, 15, 16, 21-2, 137, 138, 144, 192-3
Gounod, C. F., 69
Gramsci, Antonio, 6
Granville-Barker, Harley, 53
Graphic Cinematographic Company, 38
Gray, Thomas, 155
Griffith, D. W., 45, 46, 88
grotesque, 75, 93, 95, 98, 105, 123, 127, 133, 139-40, 144
Guillere, René. 119

**Hamlet** (Gaumont), 46
**Hamlet** (Kozintsev), 72, 79, 108, 124, 126, 129, 131, 133, 134-41, 145
**Hamlet** (Melies), 76-7, 78
**Hamlet** (Olivier), 51, 63
Harman, Hugh, 86
Hays Office, 83
**Henry V** (Olivier), 2, 47-51, 57, 63, 89
**Henry VI** (BBC), 56
**Henry VIII** (Barker), 41-2. 47, 56, 62, 192
Hepworth & Company, 40, 45
Herkomer film company, 69
Herkomer, Hubert von, 68-9, 76, 78, 105
Herkomer, Seigfried, 69
Her Majesty's Theatre, 31, 35
Hitchcock, Alfred, 53
*hoganbiiki*, 153
Hogg, James, 22, 137
Holderness, Graham, 7, 8, 52
Hollywood, 7, 45, 80, 81, 90, 92, 101, 103, 106, 151, 170
Hollywood Bowl, 87
'Hollywood codes of editing', 7, 43, 47, 82
**Hollywood revue of 1927,** (MGM), 83-4
Houghton, William, 158
Howell, Jane, 53, 56
Huskisson, Robert, 26, 27
Huysmans, Joris-Karl, 62

Ibsen, Henrik, 157, 159, 160
Ichimonji, Hidetora, 181, 184
**Ikimono no kiroku** ('Record of a living being', Kurosawa), 174, 175, 177, 181, 183, 185

**Ikiru** ('Living', Kurosawa), 169, 173, 187
'I novels', 156, 159
**In the kingdom of the fairies** (Melies), 76
**In the shadow of the sun** (Jarman), 101
**Intolerance** (Griffith), 47, 88, 89
Irving, Henry, 13, 18, 19, 29
**Ivan the terrible** (Eisenstein), 121, 122, 137, 139, 141-3

Jarman, Derek, 62, 63, 72, 79, 98-105, 106
*jidai geki*, 170, 171
Jones, Henry Arthur, 28
Jorgens, Jack, 2, 3, 5, 7, 45, 80, 150, 188
**Jubilee** (Jarman), 102
**Julius Caesar** (BBC), 54
**Julius Caesar** (Co-op), 42
Jung, C., 73

Kabuki theatre, 121, 139, 143-4, 145, 159, 160, 170, 171, 174, 190
Kachalov, Vassily, 72
Kafka, Franz, 74, 75, 91, 95, 96, 97, 98
**Kagemusha** ('The shadow warrior', Kurosawa), 173, 183, 185, 186
Kalem film company, 40, 46
Kanagaki, Robun, 158
*Kanjincho*, 171
Kawakami, Otojiro, 159, 165
Kean, Edmund, 18, 29
*Keiko eiga*, 170, 171
Kemble, John, 17, 18
Kemp, Lindsay, 74, 103
Kimura, Takekeiro, 158-9
*Kinematograph and lantern weekly*, 46
kinetoscope, 169
**King John** (Tree), 35-8, 39, 76
**King Lear** (BBC), 56
**King Lear** (Brook), 2, 62
**King Richard III** (Co-op), 42-6, 56
**King Richard III** (Olivier), 51
**King Richard III** (Vitagraph), 40
Klimt Gustav, 118
Kochan, Lionel, 110, 117
*Kokoro no nazo toketo iroito* ('A tangled love story with a happy ending'), 153
Korda, Alexander, 47
**Korol Ler** (Kozintsev), 56, 72, 79, 108, 124, 126, 129, 131, 135, 141-7
Kott, Jan, 22
Kozintsev, Grigori, 2, 5, 56, 72, 79, 108, 114, 115, 118, 119, 121, 122, 124, 126, 127, 128-48, 194
**Kumonosu jo** ('The castle of the spider's

web', Kurosaw[
81, 183, 184, 18[
Kurosawa, Akira, 1[
165, 166-87, 19[
*kyogen*, 167

Lamb, Charles, 3[
165, 189, 192,[
Lamb, Mary, 23[
**La mort de Jule[**
Lang, Fritz, 76
Learning, Barba[
Leavis, F. R., 3,[
Le duel d'[
Théâtre), 6[
Lem, Stanislav[
Lenin, V. I., 1[
Leskov, Nikol[
Lévi-Strauss, [
Lichtenstein,[
Limbourg, P[
Literary an[
Tsubouc[
145;[
Literary an[
Tsubou[
'Little theat[
**Lonesom[**
sey), 1[
Low, Rach[
Lucas, Ge[
Lumiére[
Lyceum[

MacArtl[
**Macbet[**
**Macbe[**
**Macbe[**
Macgo[
Maclia[
Macre[
Malon[
Mam[
Man[
Mart[
Mar[
Mat[
Mat[
Me[
Me[
Me[
m[
M[
M[

Me[
Mey[

Mifu[
Mikl[
Milla[
Mille[
Milw[
Minai[
Minyu[
mode[
Molad[
Monac[
*mono n[*
Morga[
Moroz[
Morris[
Morris,[
Morton[
Moscov[
Moscov[
145;[
Moscow[
Moscow[
Mosfilm[
Motokiy[
Munch,[
Munster[

Nakadai,[
Nakamur[
Naniwa, [
**Napoleo[**
naturalism[
New Critic[
New Deal,[
'new stage[
of light[
Noh theat[
166-8, 1[

Olivier, Lau[
135, 137[
Orchardson[
Osani, Kaon[
Osborn, Em[
Oshima, Na[
**Othello** (Vi[
**Othello** (W[
128[

'screwball comedy', 84-5
sentimentalism, 14, 22, 23
Shakespeare, William, 109, 131, 153, 158; *A midsummer night's dream*, 26; *Coriolanus*, 29; *Cymbeline*, 29; *Hamlet*, 1, 15, 16, 22, 46, 109, 112, 131, 134, 138, 146, 153, 155, 158, 159, 160-1; *2 Henry IV*, 155; *Henry VIII*, 29, 41, 155; *Julius Caesar*, 29, 157, 159, 160-1, 176; *King John*, 31, 35-8, 39; *King Lear*, 1, 9, 126, 131, 155, 158, 160, 181, 187; *Macbeth*, 5, 9, 14, 15, 143, 151, 160, 161, 175, 176, 177, 178, 181, 186, 187; *Othello*, 1, 14, 17, 126, 160; *Romeo and Juliet*, 103, 153; *The merchant of Venice*, 29, 155, 158; *The merry wives of Windsor*, 109; *The tempest*, 26, 30, 35
Shibukawa, Rokuzo, 153
**Shichinin no samurai** ('The seven samurai', Kurosawa), 173, 174, 175, 177, 183
'Shimpa', 159
*Shintai ka*, 155
*Shintai shisho*, 155
Shostakovich, D., 124-5
Shozo, Makino, 170
**Simple people** (Kozintsev, Trauberg), 132
Sinfield, Alan, 4
Smith, G. A., 75
Smith, James, 17
**Snow White** (Disney), 85
social realism, 122, 127, 132, 141, 148
**Solaris** (Tarkovsky), 140-1
Sontag, Susan, 7
Soviet Central Committee, 122
Special Attack Forces, 153
Stalin, J., 121, 122, 123, 124, 126, 127, 129, 131, 132, 134, 138, 143, 144, 147, 194
Stanislavsky, Konstantin, 70, 71, 114, 118, 121, 134, 145
State Higher Theatre Workshop, 119
State Jewish Theatre, 146
Stokes, John, 18
**Strike** (Eisenstein), 121, 137
Sumarakov, Alexander, 109-10
Summers, James, 158
supreme commander of the allied powers (SCAP), 163-4
surrealism, 76
symbolism, 31, 61, 63, 67, 73, 79, 85, 88, 92, 93, 98, 102, 105, 106, 118, 120, 121, 123, 127, 130, 131, 137, 160 see Decadents

tableaux vivants, 16, 28, 30, 36, 46, 69
*Taisei meigen*, 153

Tarkovsky, Andrei, 140-1
Taylor, Neil, 56
taylorism, 119
Tearle, Godfrey, 40, see Gaumont
**Testament d'Orphée** (Cocteau), 102
theatre acts: (1737), 13, 16, 18, 27; (1751), 13; (1755), 13; (1843), 16, 18,; (1878), 18, 19, 30
'theatre of light', 51, 81, 83, 92, 93, 97, 102, 106, 128, 125, 146 see 'new stagecraft'
**The adventures of Octyabrina** (FEKS), 132
**The adventures of Robin Hood** (Warner), 82
**The art of mirrors** (Jarman), 101
**The blue Danube** (Warner), 85
**The cabinet of Dr Caligari** (Weine), 90
**The devils** (Russell), 101
**The dish ran away with the spoon** (Warner), 86
**The great train robbery** (Porter), 45
**The jazz singer** (Warner), 82, 83
**The magic sword** (Paul), 76
**The merchant of Venice** (Vitagraph), 40
**The old mill pond** (MGM), 86
**The old water mill** (Disney), 86
**The passion of Joan of Arc** (Dreyer), 71
**The private life of Henry VIII** (Korda), 47
**The ride of the Valkyrie** (Graphic), 38
**The roaring twenties** (Warner), 91
**The shipwreck scene from The tempest** (Urban), 35, 37-8, 39, 41
*The strange affair of the flesh of the bosom*, 155
**The taming of the shrew** (Co-op), 42
**The tempest** (Jarman), 62, 63, 79, 98-105, 106
**The trial** (Welles), 96
**The witch** (Melies), 76
**Throne of blood** (Kurosawa), see Kumonosu jo
Time/Life, 33, 62, 192, 194
Toho films, 174
**Toro no o o fumu otokotachi** ('They who step on the tiger's tail', Kurosawa), 171
**Tora, tora, tora!** (Twentieth Century Fox), 183
Tozana, Masayasu, 159-60, 161
Trauberg, Leonard, 129, 130, 132
Tree, Herbert Beerbohm, 13, 19, 28, 29-31, 33, 35-8, 39, 41, 47, 53, 62, 76, 77
Tsar Alexander, I, 111
Tsar Alexander, II, 112, 138
Tsar Alexander, III, 114, 127

Tsar Ivan the Terrible, 108, 111, 141
Tsar Nicholas I, 110-11
Tsar Nicholas II, 115
Tsar Peter the Great, 108-9, 110, 127
Tsarina Catharine the Great, 109
Tsubouchi, Yuzo, 157-8, 159, 161, 165, 176;
    Shizaru Kidan: jiyu no tachi nago no kireaji
    ('Emperor Caesar: the sword of liberty
    displays its sharp blade'), 157; Hamlet,
    160
Turgenev, Ivan, 112, 114, 127, 133, 134
Twentieth Century Fox, 183
Two Cities, 49, 50

underground cinema, 101
Urban, Charles, 37-8, 39, 41
USSR Theatrical Society (VTO), 126, 132

Vakhtanyov Theatre, 134
**Vampyr** (Dreyer), 97
Vitagraph, 40, 46, 82
Vitascope, 169

Wagner, Richard, 51, 64, 68, 73, 81, 93, 121,
    150; Parsifal, 64-5, 66; The ring, 66
Wallace, Lew, 40
Walpole, Horace, 21, 22, 138, 192
Warhol, Andy, 99, 101
Warner brothers, 62, 63, 72, 78, 80-1, 82-7,
    89, 92, 93, 95, 103, 105, 106, 192
Welles, Orson, 50, 62, 63, 71, 72, 79, 93-8,
    105, 128, 133; theatre productions, 93
Welsh, Elizabeth, 103
**White heat** (Warner), 91
Williams, Raymond, 20, 34
WPA Negro Theatre project, 93

Yamada, Isuzu, 180
Yamamoto, Kajiro, 170
Yarvet, Yuri, 146
Yuktevich, Sergei, 130
**Yume** ('Dreams', Kurosawa), 183, 187

Zambrano, Ana Laura, 5

# Index

Film titles are shown in bold print

Abraham, Richard, 110, 117
**A gag in three acts: the electrification of Gogol** (FEKS), 130-1
agit trains, 129, 140
Akimov, Nikolai, 134
**Alexander Nevsky** (Eisenstein), 72, 95
*All for money*, 158
All Union Party Conference on Cinema (1928), 132
Alma-Tadema, Laurence, 29, 88, 89
Althusser, Louis, 6
**A midsummer night's dream** (Coronado), 74, 103, 105
**A midsummer night's dream** (Warner), 62, 63, 78, 79, 80-1, 83, 84, 85, 86, 87-93, 95, 99, 103, 192
*A mirror of Roman vicissitudes*, 157
**Angels with dirty faces** (Warner), 87, 91
animation, 85-6
**Antony and Cleopatra** (Vitagraph), 40
Appia, Adolphe, 51, 61, 64-7, 73, 76, 78, 81, 84, 87, 102, 105, 120, 121, 137, 150
Asano, Wasaburo, 159-60, 161

Bakhtin, Mikhail, 113, 120, 123-4, 126, 127, 129, 133, 140, 141, 143, 147, 148
Ball, Robert Hamilton, 2, 3, 37, 40, 188
Banham, Martin, 52
Barker, William, 41-2, 46, 47, 56, 62, 87, 192
Barthes, Roland, 190
Bayreuth, 64, 66
Bazin, André, 7
BBC, 33, 52-7, 150, 192, 195
Belinsky, Vissarion, 112, 134
Belsey, Catherine, 3, 4, 8
**Ben Hur** (Kalem), 40
*benshi*, 169
Benson, F. R., 42, 43, 47, 56
Bergman, Andrew, 85
Berkely, Busby, 83, 84, 91, 191
Bernhardt, Sarah, 69-70
*Biography of Universal History*, 158
Bioscope, 41

**Birth of a nation** (Griffith), 46
Blake, William, 25, 67
bolshevik movement, 116, 194
Bouchier, Arthur, 28
Bower, Dallas, 49
Boydell, Josiah, 24, 193
Brecht, Bertolt, 56, 61
*bricolage*, 34, 35
British Board of Film Censors, 46
Brook, Peter, 2, 62, 150-1
Brown, Joe E., 89
Bunraku, 169
Buñuel, Luis, 76, 101
Burch, Noel, 6, 8, 9, 43, 73, 170, 177, 190

Cagney, James, 87, 89, 91
Cantor, Eddie, 89
Capra, Frank, 85
carnivalesque, 113, 115, 123-4, 140, 147, 148
Chanan, Michael, 8, 9, 34-5, 39, 73, 75, 77, 190
Chaplin, Charles, 131
Chekhov, Anton, 130, 157, 159
Cherkassov, Nikolai, 143
'Chikuyo sanjin', 158
**Chimes at midnight** (Welles), 97
**Chushingura** (Shozo), 170
cinematographe, 169
Cinematographic Act, 39
**Citizen Kane** (Welles), 96
Cocteau, Jean, 101-2
Coleman the younger, George, 15
Coleridge, Samuel Taylor, 19, 22, 24, 193
Columbia, 85
constructivism, 97, 108, 118, 121, 125, 126, 127, 129, 130, 132, 133, 134, 137, 140, 143, 147
Co-op Cinematographic Company, 42, 46
Coppola, Francis Ford, 183
Coronado, Celestino, 74, 103, 105
Covent Garden, 13, 14, 17, 38
Cox, W. D., 158
Craig, Gordon, 51, 61, 68, 70-3, 76, 77, 78,

84, 87, 95, 97, 105, 120, 121, 132, 134,
   135, 138, 146, 160
cubism, 118, 119, 127, 137

Dada, 130
Dadd, Richard, 26, 67
Dal, Oleg, 146
Dalí Salvador, 76
David, Jacques, 25
Davies, Anthony, 53, 103
**Dead end** (Warner), 87
Decadents, 61, 67, 78 *see* symbolism
Del Guidice, Fillipo, 49
DeMille, Cecil B., 88
'dengaku', 166
Dent, Alan, 49
Dersu Uzala (Kurosawa), 183, 187
Dickens, Charles, 74, 75
Dieterle, William, 80, 83
Disney, Walt, 85
**Dodesukaden** (Kurosawa), 183
Donohue, Joseph, 16
**Don Quixote** (Kozintsev), 124, 131
Dostoyevsky, Fyodor, 113-14, 127, 133, 137,
   141, 183
Dreyer, Carl, 71, 76
Drury Lane, 13, 14, 16, 17, 46
Duma, 115-16

Eckert, Charles, 2, 4
Edison, Thomas, 82, 169
Edwards, Hilton, 96
Eisenstein, Sergei, 49, 72, 95, 97, 118, 119-22,
   127, 130, 137, 141-3, 144, 145
Elam, Kier, 190
**Empire** (Warhol), 101
'Enoken' 171
existentialism, 173
expressionism, 61, 62, 63, 78, 80, 105, 120,
   121, 135, 138, 146

Factory of the Eccentric Actor (FEKS), 118-
   19, 124, 130-2, 133, 134, 140, 141, 146, 147
**Fantasia** (Disney), 85, 89, 92
Fields, W. C., 84
First National, 82
Flynn, Errol, 83
Forbes-Robertson, John, 46 *see* Gaumont
formalism, 125
**42nd Street** (Warner), 84
Freud, Sigmund, 61, 73, 86, 98, 105
Fuseli, Henry, 19, 24, 25-6, 61
futurism, 118, 119, 121, 127, 130, 132, 147

Gance, Abel, 83
Gaumont, 40, 46
*ge koku jo*, 152
*gendai geki*, 170, 171
*gesamtkunstwerk*, 65, 67, 68, 69, 81, 93, 97, 105,
   119
*giri nin jo*, 176
Gogol, Nikolai, 13
**Gold diggers of 1933** (Warner), 84
Gorky, Maxim, 132, 160
gothicism, 15, 16, 21-2, 137, 138, 144, 192-3
Gounod, C. F., 69
Gramsci, Antonio, 6
Granville-Barker, Harley, 53
Graphic Cinematographic Company, 38
Gray, Thomas, 155
Griffith, D. W., 45, 46, 88
grotesque, 75, 93, 95, 98, 105, 123, 127, 133,
   139-40, 144
Guillere, René. 119

**Hamlet** (Gaumont), 46
**Hamlet** (Kozintsev), 72, 79, 108, 124, 126,
   129, 131, 133, 134-41, 145
**Hamlet** (Melies), 76-7, 78
**Hamlet** (Olivier), 51, 63
Harman, Hugh, 86
Hays Office, 83
**Henry V** (Olivier), 2, 47-51, 57, 63, 89
**Henry VI** (BBC), 56
**Henry VIII** (Barker), 41-2. 47, 56, 62, 192
Hepworth & Company, 40, 45
Herkomer film company, 69
Herkomer, Hubert von, 68-9, 76, 78, 105
Herkomer, Seigfried, 69
Her Majesty's Theatre, 31, 35
Hitchcock, Alfred, 53
*hoganbiiki*, 153
Hogg, James, 22, 137
Holderness, Graham, 7, 8, 52
Hollywood, 7, 45, 80, 81, 90, 92, 101, 103,
   106, 151, 170
Hollywood Bowl, 87
'Hollywood codes of editing', 7, 43, 47, 82
**Hollywood revue of 1927,** (MGM), 83-4
Houghton, William, 158
Howell, Jane, 53, 56
Huskisson, Robert, 26, 27
Huysmans, Joris-Karl, 62

Ibsen, Henrik, 157, 159, 160
Ichimonji, Hidetora, 181, 184
**Ikimono no kiroku** ('Record of a living
   being', Kurosawa), 174, 175, 177, 181,
   183, 185

**Ikiru** ('Living', Kurosawa), 169, 173, 187
'I novels', 156, 159
**In the kingdom of the fairies** (Melies), 76
**In the shadow of the sun** (Jarman), 101
**Intolerance** (Griffith), 47, 88, 89
Irving, Henry, 13, 18, 19, 29
**Ivan the terrible** (Eisenstein), 121, 122, 137, 139, 141-3

Jarman, Derek, 62, 63, 72, 79, 98-105, 106
*jidai geki*, 170, 171
Jones, Henry Arthur, 28
Jorgens, Jack, 2, 3, 5, 7, 45, 80, 150, 188
**Jubilee** (Jarman), 102
**Julius Caesar** (BBC), 54
**Julius Caesar** (Co-op), 42
Jung, C., 73

Kabuki theatre, 121, 139, 143-4, 145, 159, 160, 170, 171, 174, 190
Kachalov, Vassily, 72
Kafka, Franz, 74, 75, 91, 95, 96, 97, 98
**Kagemusha** ('The shadow warrior', Kurosawa), 173, 183, 185, 186
Kalem film company, 40, 46
Kanagaki, Robun, 158
*Kanjincho*, 171
Kawakami, Otojiro, 159, 165
Kean, Edmund, 18, 29
*Keiko eiga*, 170, 171
Kemble, John, 17, 18
Kemp, Lindsay, 74, 103
Kimura, Takekeiro, 158-9
*Kinematograph and lantern weekly*, 46
kinetoscope, 169
**King John** (Tree), 35-8, 39, 76
**King Lear** (BBC), 56
**King Lear** (Brook), 2, 62
**King Richard III** (Co-op), 42-6, 56
**King Richard III** (Olivier), 51
**King Richard III** (Vitagraph), 40
Klimt Gustav, 118
Kochan, Lionel, 110, 117
*Kokoro no nazo toketo iroito* ('A tangled love story with a happy ending'), 153
Korda, Alexander, 47
**Korol Ler** (Kozintsev), 56, 72, 79, 108, 124, 126, 129, 131, 135, 141-7
Kott, Jan, 22
Kozintsev, Grigori, 2, 5, 56, 72, 79, 108, 114, 115, 118, 119, 121, 122, 124, 126, 127, 128-48, 194
**Kumonosu jo** ('The castle of the spider's

web', Kurosawa), 5, 144, 150, 162, 174-81, 183, 184, 186-7
Kurosawa, Akira, 1, 2, 5, 9, 143, 150-1, 161-2, 165, 166-87, 194
*kyogen*, 167

Lamb, Charles, 3, 7, 23, 27, 30, 53, 155, 157, 165, 189, 192, 193
Lamb, Mary, 23
**La mort de Jules César** (Melies), 76, 77, 78
Lang, Fritz, 76
Leaming, Barbara, 131
Leavis, F. R., 3, 188
**Le duel d'Hamlet** (Phono Cinema Théâtre), 69-70
Lem, Stanislaw, 140
Lenin, V. I., 116, 117, 147
Leskov, Nikolai, 114, 124, 125, 127, 129, 133
Lévi-Strauss, Claude, 8, 34
Lichtenstein, Roy, 99, 101
Limbourg, Pol de, 49
Literary and Art Association, 160, see Tsubouchi, Yuzo
Literary and Dramatic Society, 160, see Tsubouchi, Yuzo
'Little theatre in the Haymarket', 13, 30
**Lonesome cowboys** (Warhol and Morissey), 101
Low, Rachel, 42-3, 45
Lucas, George, 183
Lumiére brothers, 75, 169
Lyceum theatre, 40

MacArthur, Douglas, 163, 172
**Macbeth** (Co-op), 42
**Macbeth** (Polanski), 2
**Macbeth** (Vitagraph), 40
Macgowan, Kenneth, 60, 87
Macliammoir, Michael, 96
Macready, William, 17
Malory, Thomas, 67
Mamei ka, 160
Manvell, Roger, 2, 3, 5, 80, 188
Martin, John, 88, 89
Marx, Karl, 116
Mattelart, Armand, 54
Maturin, Charles, 22, 137
Melies, Gaston, 76
Melies, George, 72, 73-9, 85
Mellen, Joan, 183
melodrama, 13, 15-17, 28
Mercury Theatre, 97
Messina, Cedric, 53, 54

Metro-Goldwin Mayer, 83
Meyerhold, Vsevolod, 87, 114-15, 118, 119, 121-2, 124, 125, 127, 130, 140, 144, 147, 194; *A midsummer night's dream*, 114; *Mystery bouffé*, 119
Mifune, Toshiro, 174, 180
Mikhoels, Solomon, 146-7
Millais, John Everett, 27, 135
Miller, Jonathan, 1, 53, 56
Milward, Peter, 165
Minamato, Yoshitsune, 153, 171, 176
Minyusha group, 155
modernism, 160, 165
Molachov, Pavel, 112, 134
Monaco, Charles, 7
*mono no aware*, 185
Morgan, Guaranty, 194
Morozov, Mikhail, 125-6, 132-3
Morris, Ivan, 152
Morris, William, 67
Morton, Turner, 17
Moscow Art and Literature Society, 114
Moscow Art Theatre, 70, 72, 114, 118, 134, 145; *Hamlet*, 70-2; *Othello*, 114
Moscow Maly Theatre, 112
Moscow University, 125
Mosfilm, 183
Motokiyo, Zeami, 168; *Atsumori*, 184
Munch, Edvard, 118
Munsterburg, Hugo, 7

Nakadai, Tatsuya, 184, 186
Nakamura, Yoshio, 158
Naniwa, Chieko, 180
**Napoleon** (Gance), 83
naturalism, 61
New Critics, 3, 5, 188, 189, 194
New Deal, 84
'new stagecraft', 63, 70, 77, 78, 92 *see* 'theatre of light'
Noh theatre, 143, 144-5, 146, 147, 148, 152 166-8, 178-81, 184-5, 190

Olivier, Laurence, 2, 33, 47, 57, 63, 89, 134, 135, 137, 138,, 141
Orchardson, Sir William, 27
Osani, Kaoru, 160
Osborn, Emily, 27
Oshima, Nagisa, 169
**Othello** (Vitagraph), 40
**Othello** (Welles), 62, 63, 79, 93-8, 102, 106, 128

Pasternak, Boris, 5
Patent Laws, 14, 15, 18, 20, 23
Paul, R. W., 39, 75, 76
Perry, Matthew, C., 154
'Peter', 171, 185
Piranesi, Gián Battista, 21, 138
Polanski, Roman, 2
Polevoy, Nikolai, 112
Pop art, 99-101, 106
Porter, Edwin, 45
Prince of Wales Theatre, 29
Prince Yamato, 153
Proletcult Theatre, 119, 120
Propp, Vladimir, 123, 147
Punk Rock, 99, 106
Pushkin, Alexander, 111, 112, 125, 134, 141

Radischev, Alexander, 110
**Ran** ('Chaos', Kurosawa), 1, 150, 162, 171, 181-7
**Rashomon** (Kurosawa), 171-3, 174, 175, 180
Reinhardt, Max, 80, 81, 83, 87, 88, 90, 92, 105, 106
**Rescued by Rover** (Hepworth), 45
Revolutionary Association of Proletarian Writers, 122
RFSR Theatre No. 1, 119
Richards, I. A., 3, 188
Richie, Donald, 5
Robinson, Edward G., 91
Roddick, Nick, 82, 86
romanticism, 14, 20, 22, 31, 61, 67, 78, 85, 88, 92, 98, 111, 113, 123, 125, 127, 128, 131, 134, 137, 144, 147, 148, 150, 189, 192-3, 194
**Romeo and Juliet** (BBC), 54
**Romeo and Juliet** (Gaumont), 40-41
**Romeo and Juliet** (Vitagraph), 40, 46
Rooney, Mickey, 91-2
Rousseau, Jean-Jacques, 26, 61, 155
Royal Circus, 14
royal patents, 13
*rumpen mono*, 171
Russell, Ken, 101
Ryunosuke, Akutugawa, 171

'Sadanji', 160
Sadlers Wells Theater, 37
Saikiku, Jono, 158
'saragaku', 166, 168
Schepkin, Mikhail, 134
Schlegel, Friedrich, 63, 66